Praise for
God Gave Me Diarrhea

"Wow! What a story of superheroes and a God who is always there. These heroes do not wear capes. Instead, the heroes are parents, friends, and total strangers whose super powers are unconditional love and faith in a God whose love never ends. A perfect read for anyone looking for hope and encouragement."

—Chris A. Kersting, children's book author of The Shepherds Went with Haste and more

"What a beautiful story of sacrifice, love, and growth. Well conceived and carefully written, at times shocking and raw, and with characters to really care about, the book was hard to put down. Thank you, Rachel, for making your own sacrifices to bring this inspiring story to the world."

—Mary Calvez, professional editor and book reviewer

"In the face of overwhelming challenges, can faith truly sustain us? In God Gave Me Diarrhea, Rachel Young presents a powerful, true story of love, resilience, and the transformative power of faith. When Ann's adopted son Damian suffers a life-altering brain injury, she and her husband Lincoln face the unimaginable task of caring for him, all while grappling with their own doubts, fears, and questions about God's plan. But this is not just a story of struggle—it's a story of hope. As Ann learns to see God's hand in the most unexpected places, her faith is not only restored but strengthened in ways she never imagined. Through heartwarming and often humorous moments, Ann, her family, and those around them discover the beauty of unconditional love, the power of forgiveness, and the peace that comes from trusting in God's purpose.

Join Ann on her journey from despair to hope, and witness the extraordinary impact of a life lived with faith, compassion, and an unwavering belief in God's goodness.

Rachel Young's deeply personal and inspirational account will leave you reflecting on your own faith journey and the surprising ways in which God can work through even the most challenging circumstances."

—Rev. Dr. Garrett J. Andrew, author of Peace Be With You

"This is a powerful book about hope. Through difficult life events a family struggles to find healing, redemption and reconciliation. Readers will love walking alongside this family and clinging to hope in their own story."

—Dave McIntire, Professor Emeritus, Azusa Pacific University

GOD
GAVE ME
DIARRHEA

A true story of God's Redemption
through Adoption and Brain Injury

RACHEL YOUNG

THE PROVIDENTIAL PRESS
COLLINS LAKE

For more information, visit rachelyoungauthor.com

ISBN: 979-8-89316-8-310 (paperback)
ISBN: 979-8-89316-8-327 (hardcover)
ISBN: 979-8-89316-8-303 (ebook)

Library of Congress Control Number: 2024916011

Author photograph by Bria Rose

Published in Browns Valley, California in the United States of America

*For Ann and Lincoln, the most self-sacrificing, gentle,
abundantly generous, loving, smell-like-Jesus people I know*

Contents

Author's Note

Warning: This book is not funny. The title is meant quite literally, as in my main character, Ann, truly believes God rescued her via the tool of diarrhea. It is not meant to be taken as a joke or self-deprecating humor. I do hope it makes you laugh. In fact, Ann said, when faced with a traumatic event, you can cry or laugh, so she chose to laugh. I do hope you laugh and cry and experience every emotion in this book, but especially that you are inspired to believe God can use absolutely anything, even something as outrageous as diarrhea, to catch your attention and show you that He sees you and has been holding you in His palms all along. I believe our God cares very much about small intricate details and wants to use them to surprise you with how deep and unfathomable His love is for you.

I must begin by saying I did not want to write an acknowledgments page or other note. I find beginning acknowledgments a long list of boring information that is preventing me from getting to the good part of the story. So here is your permission slip granting you access to skip the rest of this bit and get to the story that begins in the prologue (definitely don't skip that part; it's my favorite, if I'm allowed to have a favorite.)

Secondly, this is the only part of the book where you will hear me in my own voice. I am writing on behalf of Ann, my mother-in-law—or, as I like to call her—my mother-in-love. Most "true stories" are written in first person and typically written by the main character. Ann asked me several years ago to write her story with Damian because she didn't know where to start. Over a decade later—with many breaks in between—we have accomplished this book together.

I have a journalism background, so I wrote this more as a creative or narrative nonfiction rather than a typical memoir. It reads much more like a novel than nonfiction and could be considered a novel, as I have had to imagine many of the conversations and inner workings of the characters involved.

Since I am not the person who experienced the scenarios, I have done extensive research and interviews to remain as close to the truth as possible; however, I did not write it to relay the hard facts but as a story to be enjoyed. I chose to write their story as a narrative because I believe stories have a powerful way of illuminating truth. I did take creative liberties to create a story rather than a fact-by-fact retelling— therefore, although all the scenes are true events, they are sometimes told out of factual order or connected in a way that makes it a readable story. I tried to capture the essence of the truth as it was told to me. Where possible, I used their own remembered words as the dialogue but also added in responses to complete all their thoughts. Again, I was not in the room when these conversations happened; therefore, it cannot be an exact retelling. I have also opted to change all the minor characters' names to protect their identities.

As I went on the journey of writing this book, I discovered it was not simply Ann's story or Damian's story, but an interweaving of stories, and most importantly a God story. Upon that discovery, I have taken time to interview all of the characters, and they have also read the story. We have worked to make the events as true to life as possible; some exceptions to that are due to the loss of memory over time. The "true story" continues to evolve as new events transpire and the old events are seen through that lens. There is also the bit about the "truth" where it is all according to whose perspective is telling it. Therefore, when the various characters' versions varied on what was "true" according to their memory, I opted to go with Ann's version since she is the reason I wrote this book. To be human is to be fallible, and I admit I cannot have gotten it all right. And yet I know without a shadow of a doubt God can use it anyway. He has a habit of using disheveled messes, screw-ups, and those willing to admit their weakness. I hope that the bigger Truth will be told within this story, a truth about a God who is in control. I also hope that you will find truths for your own story.

I am compelled to write this story because too many "true stories" are about crime or tragic trauma. Not enough truth is told about seeing the good in the mire.

Ultimately, I completed this large writing project over several years because God continued to convict my heart repeatedly that it was a story worth sharing, despite all my doubt. I pray that reading about how the beauty of answered prayers comes in unusual forms, and that our God is intricately interested in the details, will encourage and uplift you.

Prologue

FALL 1987

SHEILA HAD ONE WEEK TO DECIDE. SHE LOVED THE three boys in her home as if they were her own. In fact, they had filled the void in her life so well she had begun to settle into the idea of being a single mom of three forever. She'd stopped dreaming of finding the perfect man.

But that's when it happened.

It had been a fluke, really; Pete had stopped to help her with a flat tire on the side of the road. He'd asked for her number, and they went to dinner for the first time three weeks ago. And now he wanted to marry her. With one condition.

"I don't want the boys," he said.

Sheila reeled back in disbelief. "But they're my life! They've been with me for over a year now. We're a family."

"Well, it's up to you," Pete said. "I want to get married on Friday in Reno, so you have until then to decide."

With that, he slammed the door and left her alone with her thoughts. Her mind raced. How could she choose between the fulfillment she found as a foster mom and her newfound love?

That was almost a week ago, and she was still torn in her heart. She had told the truth—the boys were her life. But then again, she loved the way Pete held her in his arms. Her whole life she had waited for someone to appreciate her like he did. The cost was high, but the boys would find a new foster home. She had to do what was best for her.

Unable to handle seeing the tears in their eyes, Sheila decided it would be best to not tell them at all. She dropped LB off at preschool, and Damian and Milo at the elementary, and called their social worker.

LB'S EYES WIDENED WHEN HE SAW THE BIG WHITE VAN waiting for him. Where was his mama Sheila? Why was Emily Elliot here to pick him up?

"I go home," the four-year-old stammered through his tears.

"You get to go to a new home today," Emily said, trying to sound cheerful. This would be his eighth new home in two years. "Your new family is very nice. And you get a baby sister. Won't that be fun?"

"Sister?" LB's curiosity heightened. "Where my Damian?"

"You'll get to see him soon," Emily said, hoping it was true. With only a few hours' notice, the best she had been able to do was separate the three boys into three homes for emergency placements. She sent up a quick prayer, asking God for a family to become available soon that would be able to take all three boys.

Ann and Lincoln had surprised her with their tenacity as foster parents. Almost a year ago, they had called up her agency, saying they had extra love to give and wanted to open their home to children in need. They said they would take anyone, so she had given them their hardest case. He was an impossible seven-year-old boy. But they had committed to him for a year, and so far she hadn't received a single complaint from them.

The van squeaked to a stop in front of a white two-story home with a well-groomed lawn in a Sacramento suburb. Emily thought LB was fortunate to go to Ann and Lincoln's home, even if it was only for a month or less. Their love for their own daughter was obvious.

"LB, let's go meet your new family," Emily said, removing his sparse belongings from the seat next to him.

LB clutched her leg as the doorbell rang.

"Come on, LB, I'm sure you'll like it here," Emily coaxed, trying to gently ease him off of her.

"No, no, NO," LB cried, clinging tighter.

After prying him from her leg, he fell to the ground crying. Emily offered to stay to give him a tour of the house before she left. Trembling, he nodded.

A short, ordinary blonde woman wearing green shorts and a blue T-shirt opened the white door with bronze inlay and welcomed the two inside. Her blush cheeks and merry eyes brightened her round face. "Hi, LB. We're so glad to meet you. Would you like one of these peanut butter brownies I just made?" Ann extended her arm to offer the treats stacked on a white plate.

LB's shoulders bobbed up and down as his crying subsided and turned to sniffles. He kept his eyes on the ground.

"Why don't we go look around, first?" Emily suggested. "Would you like to see your new room?"

LB nodded his head without looking up.

"Come this way," Ann said, setting down the brownies to lead him up the stairs.

LB eyed his new bed with a sideways glance, not fully lifting his head. It was a simple room, a single bed in the corner fitted with a dark-blue comforter and a wooden dresser next to it. A painting of a ship in the ocean filled one wall, and a bold painting of a lion stared at LB on the other. Ann talked with ease about where he could find the bathroom and keep his belongings.

When they came back down the steps, Ann introduced LB to the rest of the family, who emerged from the kitchen, their dinner interrupted.

"LB, this is Lincoln, my husband. And this is Nicole—she just took her first steps last week," Ann said as the one-year-old tottered toward them. "And this is Landon."

Landon was their first foster child. Ann looked from Landon back to LB, biting her lower lip. Two boys at once. Ann enjoyed fostering and loved getting the opportunity to be a light in a child's life, for however long or short they needed until they could be reunited with their parents. But they had hoped to have only *one* child at a time, so they could give that child their full attention and love. Ann wondered if they could split their attention and still love each boy well. For one month, at least, she figured they could try.

"What's that?" LB pointed outside the back window.

"Let's go take a look," Emily said.

LB skipped across the lawn toward the above-ground Doughboy pool, with Lincoln following closely behind. The large pool boasted a deck all the way around it. LB climbed the steps up to the deck with Lincoln trailing him. His eyes lit up at the thought of having a pool at his home.

"LB, wait!" Lincoln called.

Excitement welling up within him, LB took a hasty step onto the blue cover on top of the pool, thinking the cover was hard. He then fell onto the soft bubble cover, tangling his legs into the meshing and slowly sinking the cover and himself into the water.

Lincoln swiftly scooped LB up into his arms and untangled him from the pool surface coverings. He set LB down next to the pool and stooped down to LB's level so he could see directly into his eyes. "Are you okay, LB?" Lincoln asked in a gentle tone.

LB nodded his head up and down.

Ann scrambled to the scene, arms flailing and frantic worry rushing out of her. "We don't do that. You could drown."

Emily stood back, observing the scene, allowing the family to sort out the small crisis.

LB looked down, away from them, embarrassed that he had made a scene in the first few moments at their home.

Lincoln held on to LB, patting him on the back. "We're so glad to have you in our home, LB. But there are just a few rules, and the pool is the most important one. We have to ask before we use the pool and always have an adult there. Can you do that for us?"

LB kept his eyes glued to the ground without answering. Ann bent down to give him a hug.

Emily looked at her watch as Lincoln walked toward the house to grab a towel. "Okay, LB, I think you're going to settle in nicely here as long as you don't go walking on top of the pool. You're going to be just fine. I'll see you in a few days, okay?"

LB ran after her to grab on to her leg again. He was still sopping wet. "No go, no go," he said.

She untangled LB for the second time and gave him a little hug before walking into the house, followed by LB and Ann. As she crossed the house to the door and opened it, she turned to see LB running away from her toward the kitchen. She shrugged and promised Ann, "It's only going to be for a month."

Ann closed the door and turned to follow LB. He was so small and vulnerable, she couldn't imagine what kind of person would leave a four-year-old so abruptly. "LB, where are you?" she called out.

Silence met her call.

"LB?" Ann searched each room, panic rising within her as she remembered LB's encounter with the pool moments ago. Her heartbeat steadied when she glimpsed a small shoe under the table. "What are you doing under the table? Do you want to come out and dry off?" Ann asked.

LB backed up farther under the table, shaking his head.

Ann stood a few moments, unsure of what to do next. Then, surprising herself, she bent down and crawled under the table, plopping down next to him.

"Are you feeling sad?" Ann asked, to no response. "I want to be your friend. I know it's probably scary coming to a new person's house. I don't mind sitting under the table with you if this is where you want to be. Do you want me to stay under the table with you?"

LB nodded his head.

"Do you want to tell me about what you're feeling?"

"Www-what happened to Gwandma?" LB asked through tears. His big blue eyes met hers for the first time.

"I don't know who Grandma is."

LB rummaged through his pocket and pulled out a crumpled paper. He held it out for Ann to see. It was a picture of a woman with gray hair, spectacles, and tight-fitting clothes. She looked too old to match Emily's description of the woman LB had lived with for the past year.

"Is this your grandma?"

"Don't let huh get me."

"She can't find you here."

Ann stayed with him under the table until he cried himself to sleep in her lap. Then she gathered him up in her arms, scooted out from under the table, and walked up the stairs to the bedroom she had prepared for him. There, she expertly changed him into dry clothes. As Ann laid him down, she couldn't help staring at his sweet, sleeping face, memorizing all the features. He was an angel, and she was falling in love.

ONE

Home Sweet Home

JUNE 1991

. . . .

"Sometimes you will never know the value of
a moment until it becomes a memory."

—Dr. Seuss

. . . .

ANN HEARD CROAKING IN THE BATHROOM. WHEN SHE opened the door, a little creature hopped right into her kitchen before LB could catch it.

"LB! THROW THAT FROG OUTSIDE NOW!"

"Are you scared of it, Ann?" Seven-year-old LB snickered at her, catching the frog and bringing it even closer to her face. The frog lurched forward in his hand.

"No, but it's disgusting. Get it away from me," Ann said, feeling a wave of nausea come over her.

Ann shuddered as LB scuffled toward the door carrying that nasty speckled toad with bumps covering its brown, putrid body. She was reminded of yesterday when Damian captured a rattlesnake, holding it up like a prized possession around the neck, the tail dangling down to his feet with the rattle shaking. Her blood pulsed just imagining it again.

Interrupting her thoughts, Jacob, her sweet four-week-old baby, kicked his foot and grabbed her finger. Gratitude rushed through her body; she was home at last. That is if she could consider this new house "home" yet. They timed their move to the country so they could be settled before the baby's arrival. LB and Damian seemed to adjust to country living much faster than she could. It was hard to believe the two brothers had lived with them for three-and-a-half years now. It was even harder to believe that Nicole would be five in a few months.

But she was grateful to have Jacob in her arms away from the hospital, and she couldn't help admiring him. Ann could stare at his face all day long just taking in the incredible masterpiece God had given her. After several weeks in the NICU, the doctors said his stridor would eventually resolve on its own. No noise came out when he cried, so she had to pay extra attention when his face got red and he squeaked, showing his discomfort.

She knew this was her last newborn. Her first pregnancy with Nicole had sucked the life from her, draining her with endless vomiting. Her second pregnancy with Jacob had been even worse. Happy tears welled in her eyes as she counted and recounted all his tiny toes, memorizing every line on his face, pulling at tufts of hair. "One, two, three . . ."

"Ann, what are you doing?" LB asked innocently, returning to her side from his frog adventures.

"I love to count his toes. Do you want to count with me?" Ann asked. She gestured for him to sit next to her on the couch.

"Wemembo when God answo-ed my prayers and gave me a baby bwotha?" LB whispered. LB was seven, but he still had a hard time with his r's. Ann found his speech impediment endearing.

2

"Of course, I remember calling you from the hospital to tell you the news. You wanted another brother so badly. I could hear your jumps for joy through the phone," Ann said. "God delights to give us the desires of our hearts."

She had believed in God since she was five years old when she had tangibly felt His presence. She had been at an Easter Sunrise Service watching the sun come up. As the sun rose over the horizon, a shadow blocked her view. She happened to be standing in the shadow of the cross. She felt His powerful presence surrounding her as the bright sunlight shone all around the darkened cross, and from that moment, she had never questioned if God was real. She had even fought people who thought otherwise. His love for her inspired her to love people—currently, that included only the people in her home, until she found more out about her new community.

While her faith hadn't wavered, lately it had been difficult to know if God was truly listening to her. She sent up prayers, but they often went unanswered, as far as she could tell. Nonetheless, she mustered up more faith and showed her children how to love God through her own actions. She lived her faith out through the generous giving of her time and money to church ministry. She wasn't entirely confident that God took any notice, but she never let her feelings stop her from finding creative avenues to love and serve people. Faith must be exercised, and she had no reason to doubt God's goodness.

"Can I hold him?" LB asked, reaching his arms out with expectancy.

"Yes, sit right here next to me," Ann said as she cuddled the baby in closer before adjusting the couch pillow around LB. She gently placed the baby into LB's waiting arms. LB looked into his baby brother's eyes and smiled his big toothy grin. "Hold his head up," Ann reminded. "That's it, gentle."

"Wemembo when I thought you were gonna die?" LB asked.

"Yes. It must have been hard for you to see me so sick," Ann said as she pulled him in close for a side squeeze.

She had been sick all nine months of her pregnancy, not even able to smell a pot of boiling water, vomiting five times a day or more. Remembering those terrible days, she wondered, how did she keep all these kids alive? She had spent most of the days in bed. When her second pregnancy was worse than the first, her doctor said her body was adverse to the pregnancy hormone. Getting pregnant again could endanger her life. "You were sweet to bring me water and stay by me so often. You would sit on my bed and rub my face. I appreciated how helpful you were, my own personal attendant."

"I'm glad you didn't die," LB said as he grabbed Jacob's little toe.

"Me too." She chuckled and kissed the top of LB's head. Her love for him had grown immensely in the last three years since meeting him. Since she couldn't have more children of her own, she was thankful to have the two boys in her home, even though some days could be difficult. "Do you like living here in the country?"

"Yeah." LB shrugged his shoulders up to his ears. "I miss the pool. And I wish we could get a dog."

"Now we have a lake you can run down to at any time. When our new home is built, you'll have so much outside space to run around, and we can talk about getting an animal then too," Ann said. The phone rang, interrupting her time with LB. Ann grabbed the baby and told LB to run along and play.

"It's Larry. I want to talk to the boys," the gruff voice of the boys' birth father said into the receiver.

"Larry, you know you can't talk to them unless you clear it with their social worker." Ann swayed the baby back and forth mindlessly and bit her lip as she paced around the house.

"Put them on," Larry demanded.

"We don't have a social worker here," Ann said.

"Then set up a meeting for me."

4

Ann could hear the impatience in his voice growing. It was typically this way when she communicated with Damian and LB's birth parents, Connie and Larry. The times they chose to care about the boys were sporadic at best. "Larry, I've been there three times this week. You haven't shown up to a single visit. I refuse to come back again just to disappoint the boys because you don't show up," Ann said, standing her ground.

"It will be different this time. I bought them a gift. I bought a truck for Damian and LB. Can you tell them?" Larry pleaded through the phone.

"What are the gifts for?" Ann asked, her suspicion rising.

"We've disappointed the boys a lot, so we wanted to get them something special," Larry answered.

"I'm going to call the social worker and ask her if she wants to meet with you. It's her decision. If she sets it up, we will meet you at the park," Ann said reluctantly.

"I'm going to be there. Make sure the boys know," Larry said.

"Please don't disappoint them again," Ann said.

"I won't. I promise I'll be there," Larry replied.

Ann hung up the phone and called Emily to make the arrangements. Unbelievable. It was just like Larry. He didn't show up time and time again, then just when everyone was about to give up on him, he resurfaced. She didn't trust it, but in her heart Ann wanted the boys to have a relationship with their parents. She kept showing up, trusting, believing, and hoping they might come to one of the visits. Everything in her screamed, *"Don't go, don't go, don't go."* But she loaded the four kids up into the car anyway.

Ann prayed as she started the hour-and-a-half drive to Sacramento. *Please, Jesus, for the boys' sake, let him show up this time. We all can't bear another disappointment.*

The drive was much farther for visitation since moving to the lake to run the family business a few months ago. Lincoln gave up his job working for Granite Construction, one of the more well-respected engineering companies in California. He was quickly working his way up in the company with monetary doors opening up to them, but money ranked as a low priority to her husband, especially when it came to family. He chose to continue the campground his father built up when no one else wanted the job.

Ann, on the other hand, liked the comforts that came with a high-paying job. As she drove the routine route, Ann's mind drifted to the things they had given up by moving to the cabin at the lake. She thought of the vacations she had planned and the annual fancy dinners. She remembered that life-changing conversation with one of the wives at the Granite Construction staff Christmas party almost five years ago. The elegant scene played in her mind, all the ladies in long ball gowns. She wore a sapphire silky dress. The woman admired them as parents with their sweet baby girl, Nicole, and thought they would make great foster parents. That conversation started a whole series of unexpected events.

Lincoln felt confident about the decision to move to the lake, but it was a harder pill for Ann to swallow. She loved their home in Elk Grove. Country life was not what she signed up for when she married Lincoln. She had always lived in cities growing up. Her dad worked in shoe stores all over the country, from South Carolina to Las Vegas. Las Vegas was her favorite, with all the bustling people. She loved being in the high school marching band for its sense of community and fun. She taught herself four different instruments, but french horn was her favorite. And now the closest grocery store was thirty minutes away.

The worst part was that everywhere she went in her new hillside community she was "Lincoln's wife," or "MJ's daughter-in-law," or "Bart's brother's wife."

"I just want to be Ann," she accidentally exclaimed under her breath.

"What, Mom?" Damian asked from the back seat.

"Oh nothing. Did I say that out loud?" Ann gasped, surveying her children through the rearview mirror.

Regardless of where her "home" was, Ann loved Damian and LB living in it. Milo, the third brother, stayed with them for a short while, but a better placement for him emerged shortly after he ran LB's head over on his bicycle. Ann giggled aloud, remembering LB screaming, "I don't want 'tiches. I don't want 'tiches." After several attention-getting incidents with his brothers, they realized Milo had liked the sole attention he received when he was an only child for that short period of time, so his social worker placed him in a home by himself. Ann tried to set up visits for the four brothers as often as she could, LB, Damian, Milo, and Mario, the oldest brother who lived with an aunt in the Bay Area.

And she suspected Connie, the mother of the four boys, might be pregnant yet again. At the last visit Connie and Larry made an appearance—over a month ago—Connie was high and stayed in the car most of the visit. Larry said Connie had been feeling ill lately, which reminded Ann of how ill she felt during her pregnancy. It only raised her suspicions when she saw Connie open the car door to vomit. In that quick glimpse, Ann thought she saw a growing belly. Larry slurred his words as though he had been drinking, but managed to talk to the boys in his rough way. The boys didn't notice; they hung on every slurred word and clamored around him, begging him to push them on the swings and play. He remained on the bench.

God, if it's within your will, please let Larry show up for these boys today.

Ann's heart felt restless.

The light turned red, and she slowed the car to a stop. Four-year-old Nicole noticed a man on the side of the road.

"Mommy, why is that man standing there with a sign?" Nicole asked.

"He is asking for money," Ann said, noticing the man's ragged clothes and weather-beaten skin. "But what he really needs is a job."

Ann had compassion for many people, but not for the homeless population. This man looked fully capable of joining the workforce. His time would be better spent at a job center than on the side of the road with a sign.

"Why does he need a job, Mommy?"

"So he doesn't have to beg for money."

"Can we give him some?"

"Maybe another time."

Ann averted her eyes from the pitiful sight, willing the light to turn green. She noticed a floral shop across the street and was reminded of her beloved time working with flowers.

After high school, she had to pay her own life expenses. College didn't interest her at all, so she found work at a floral shop and learned the intricacies of working with the delicate beauty of nature. She had loved that job dearly and was sad to give it up when she married Lincoln at age twenty-one and moved to Davis, where he was taking engineering courses. She found a few other odd jobs. And then child-rearing became her full-time endeavor, which she was thankful they could afford. She didn't mind that both Lincoln's former and current occupation kept him too busy to help much on the childrearing front; she was used to doing things on her own.

"Do you think he will show up today, Mom?" Damian asked with a quiver in his voice, pulling Ann from her thoughts.

"Who? Larry? He said so on the phone, and the social worker said she was convinced. So that's something," Ann said.

"Why do they keep having so many babies?" Damian asked.

"That's a great question. One I've asked myself many times. I wish I had an answer for you," she answered.

"I just wish they loved us like you do," Damian said, gazing out the window in the back row of the suburban.

"They do love you. It's just hard for them to show it," Ann said. She didn't understand it herself, so how could she explain their parents' actions to them?

"They don't love us," LB chimed in from the back seat.

"Why do you say that, LB?" Ann asked.

"We wouldn't be with you in the first place if they loved us," LB said.

Ann heard a yelp and glanced back to see Damian punching LB in the side. "Don't say that, LB," Damian said. He rarely showed anger, but apparently, that crossed his line.

With a sigh of relief, Ann pointed out the window. "Look, boys, here's the park now. Let's head over to Emily."

"Hi, Ann," Emily called out from a picnic table across the stretching green lawn. "Hi, Damian. Hi, LB, and Nicole, and who's this new little person?"

"He's my new bwotha. I asked God for him," LB told her, standing up taller with a big, goofy grin on his face.

"What's his name?" Emily asked.

"Jacob," LB answered.

"Come and join me over here. LB, tell me about your favorite subject in school right now. Is it still PE?" Emily said as LB nodded excitedly.

"I lost my two fwont teeth," LB told her, showing off his toothless smile.

"Now you can ask for your teeth for Christmas, just like the song," Emily said in a jovial tone. "How about you, Damian? What are you interested in lately?"

"I like playing chess. And I want to start riding horses," ten-year-old Damian said. He pretended to gallop up and down while holding on to reins.

Ann whirled around. "Really? This is the first I've heard of that."

Emily laughed easily. "Well, it sounds like we'll have to look into that for you, Damian."

Twenty minutes past the hour, Damian stood up, abruptly interrupting the conversation. "He's not coming. It's just like every other time."

Checking her watch, Emily said, "Let's give him just a few more minutes. Maybe he lost track of time. He sounded like he wanted to be here. Why don't you all go to the playground while I talk to Ann for a few minutes?"

As the two boys and Nicole sprinted toward the swings, Emily took her compact mirror out of her purse and reapplied her red lipstick. Then she asked Ann, "Have you ever considered adoption?"

"To be honest, no. We didn't think it was an option," Ann said in surprise, picking up fussy Jacob out of the infant carrier to feed him a bottle.

"Usually the judge rules in favor of reuniting birth families. But in my experience, if the birth parents have had this many kids taken straight to the system, the judge is more open to terminating rights. If she gets pregnant one more time, that will likely be the tipping point," Emily explained. "The boys can stay in the foster system until they age out, but it might be better for your family if you consider adopting them. If you are able to adopt them, you will have more freedom with them. You won't have to do visitations or court dates or home inspections, and you can travel freely with them, which I know your family likes to do."

Emily paused and scanned the playground before beginning again. "Of course, you would lose the fostering stipend, and I believe the adoption process will have some fees that come along with it. Damian's health journey may also have costs to it. You know he had a brain shunt placed at birth to remove excess fluid and pressure from his brain. The shunt was replaced just before he came to your home, and may very well have to be replaced in the future."

"I'll have to talk to Lincoln about it. The money wouldn't be a problem. It would be nice for the boys to actually be a part of our family. They have been with us so long now. Do you think we would get approved?" Ann asked, rocking her baby gently as she fed him.

"I've been with these boys since the first day they were pulled from their home. I see how well you love them and do your best to make them a part of your family. I know LB still refuses to call you Mom and Dad. I think he may have long-term attachment issues because of being moved around so much at such a young age. Providing them the stability of a loving home is what these boys need, and I know you can give it to them," Emily said.

"We are trying our best. It is challenging to split my attention between them all with a newborn. Right now, I'm concerned about how Damian will handle another disappointment," Ann said, looking around the park again for any sign of Larry. "Do you think he's coming?"

"I had hoped so," Emily said with a sigh and a longing look toward the street. She got up from the table to go use the pay phone on the corner to try calling Larry. Then she walked back with a long face.

An hour past the agreed-upon meeting time, it was obvious Larry had forgotten. Again.

"I'm so sorry, boys. It looks like he's not coming," Emily said, giving each of them a hug. "I'll follow up with you all soon," she added, and walked back to her car.

Damian's face fell. He had been so hopeful, and now he looked crushed. Ann's heart broke. These two little people so desperately wanted their father to show up for them, and he kept blowing it.

"But what about the twuck?" LB asked.

Ann couldn't hold back the floodgates. She let out a sob, and tears flowed down her cheeks. How could he do this to his children again? How could she and Emily have believed him? She had wanted to give him another chance but realized ten million chances wouldn't be enough. Sweet little Nicole sat on her lap and gave her a big hug.

"It's okay, Ann," LB comforted, sitting on her right and rubbing her arm. "I don't need a twuck. You don't have to cwy."

"Thanks, LB," Ann said, hugging him. "Damian, do you want to talk? Tell us about how you're feeling." Ann dabbed her eyes with a Kleenex she pulled from her purse.

Damian sat at the edge of the picnic table, facing away, staring off into the distance.

"I'm fine," was all he offered.

"It's okay if you're not. I believed him too, that it would be different this time, just like you did. But he is out of chances. We have to let go of the past and make our future together," Ann said, hearing the birds chirping overhead.

"What do you mean?" LB asked.

"Emily and I were talking. We're done getting your hopes up for visits. She said she won't set up any more unless something changes. We are going to focus on *our* family," Ann said. "Now. Let's go to the store." She picked up the baby carrier and marched to the car with the three kids following behind her like ducklings.

Ann reached into the depths of her heart to somehow create joy on this hard and sad day. She stopped first at the Disney store because Disney captivated her imagination and helped her feel childlike joy. She let Nicole and the boys dash around the store looking for anything they wanted. LB brought a monster truck over.

"Of course, I'll buy you a truck. Damian, do you want one too?" When he didn't reply, she decided to buy the same truck in every color. Then she found a giant Dumbo, a Tigger, and a Minnie Mouse stuffy, thrusting one into each of their arms. They walked out to the car with quite a load and mostly smiles.

"Let's go buy some new clothes too," Ann said. So they went to the mall, and she let the boys pick out a whole new outfit from Levi's. She bought a new dress for Nicole too.

Ann was hungry after the shopping escapades, so she said, "Let's go get ice cream." She pulled into their favorite ice cream shop. *Surely, Damian can't resist a smile while licking an ice cream cone,* Ann thought. She got her favorite—mint chip—and savored each lick, trying to erase the hardship of the day. While they were finishing their ice cream, Ann leaned in, as if to tell them a secret.

In a low voice, she whispered, "Did you know it's illegal to shout, 'Fire,' in a public place?" All the kids leaned in, listening intently, and shook their heads no. "It's illegal because it can create pandemonium with everyone running out the door. So, I've always wanted to create our own kind of pandemonium. Do you think we should try it?" Nicole vigorously shook her head no. She was a rule follower. Damian's and LB's eyes grew wide as they nodded yes.

"Okay, so as soon as we finish our ice cream, I'm going to shout the opposite. I don't want to go to jail today, after all. So instead of shouting fire, I'm going to shout, 'It's raining, and I didn't close my car windows!' Then, everybody, run."

Damian and LB started giggling and shifting their bodies uncomfortably. Everyone except for Nicole scarfed their ice cream down. She sat licking her cone, one lick at a time until the bitter end. When Ann saw the last bite enter Nicole's mouth, she stood up in the ice cream parlor and shouted as loud as she could. "Oh, no! It's raining outside! Quick! I left my windows open!"

Just like she had coaxed them to, they all stood up and sprinted outside as quickly as they could. When they got to the car, they all bent over in laughter, holding on to their sides.

"That's more like it," Ann said when she could take a breath. "All right, let's head home."

A while later, Ann turned off the highway toward their home. "Let's stop by the store to get Dad, then check on our new house." Damian hadn't said a word since the park. Maybe Lincoln could say something to him.

Up at the construction site, the backhoe was digging huge holes. The boys darted out of the car to get a closer look at the big machinery in action. They waved and pointed and pretended to drive their own big heavy machinery.

Ann scanned the hillside that looked completely different; piles of red dirt replaced all the shrubs, dead grass, and trees. It was hard for Ann to imagine what the house would look like, but the view was incredible. Atop the hill, she could see for miles and miles down into the valley.

"Show me again where the house will go," Ann prompted, letting Lincoln guide her around the construction site. "It looks like such a tiny part of the land for our house to sit on. I want it to have plenty of space. Are you sure it will be big enough?"

Chuckling, Lincoln said, "Yes, I'm positive. It looks small, but when all the walls go up, it will be a spacious five-bedroom house. I've gone over the plans endlessly, and I know you'll love it." Lincoln walked over to another part of the plot, motioning for Ann to follow. "I've asked them to leave as many trees as they can. I imagine this oak over here will be the perfect spot for a swing for Jacob."

"I can't wait for it to be done. This whole process has me so excited," Ann told him. "How much longer will it take?"

"Right now, they're leveling the ground. After they begin construction, it will take up to a year, depending on how many road bumps they hit along the way," he said.

"That feels way too long," Ann said, wondering if she could last that long in the log cabin. Then she caught sight of the boys. "I wanted to see if you could talk to Damian. Larry didn't show up again."

Lincoln called Damian over. Ann watched in admiration as her husband strolled away with Damian through the trees. He always had the right words for moments like these.

THE SUBURBAN PULLED INTO THE DRIVEWAY AT DUSK with all four children. LB darted out of the car and into the house. Before Ann unbuckled the two littles, LB ran back toward her.

"Ann, I caught the bat," he said, holding something black in a fishing net and swinging it closer to her. "It was in the house again!"

"Get that thing away from me!" Ann said, swatting him away. "I'm not kidding. Get away from me with that bat or I'll smack you." Ann ducked back inside the car, hiding from the bat.

LB keeled over roaring with laughter. "I got you. I got you so good." He held up a black wallet, showing Ann it was not a bat.

"LB, I've had it with you. March yourself inside this minute," Ann said, flustered and on edge. She trailed behind LB and Nicole with Jacob's car seat hooked on her right arm and parcels of purchases filling her left arm.

As she walked in the door, a whirling black dot whizzed past Ann's head. "THERE IS A BAT! A REAL BAT, IN THE HOUSE," Ann screamed at full capacity, dropping the packages and ducking down behind the couch with the baby beside her. "Someone help!"

Ann crouched, paralyzed. Why did the bats have to make their home right outside hers? The eaves of the house had a tiny gap between the roof and the side of the house, perfect for a bat cave—and now, they were even moving in! She couldn't wait to get her family out of here. Why did construction have to take so long? Country living was too much.

"Anybody?"

LB appeared in the doorway. "Hurry, grab the net," Ann pleaded from behind the couch.

"Oh, Ann, you don't have to be so afwraid," LB said, snickering, as he grabbed the net. He expertly snuck up on the bat, tiptoeing and using the net like a big rifle, as if he were on a safari. "I'll get you," LB said to the bat.

Then Nicole came running. "Hurry, Nicole, open the door wide," Ann said.

Nicole dashed back to the door and flung it open with a bang. LB scampered up onto the step stool and took a good swat at the bat. The bat dodged his swing, then swarmed around in a circle twice before darting again near the couch Ann was hiding behind.

"Nicole, get the lights," LB ordered.

Diligently, Nicole ran around the room flicking lights off and on to get the bat to scurry toward the door.

Ann yelped. "Help, get that thing out of here. Don't let it bite me."

Armed with a broom and a net, Nicole and LB then attempted to corner the bat. Nicole stood blocking the hallway with her broom, and LB snuck up behind it to catch it in his net. Nicole smacked the wall hard right next to where the bat was. At last, the bat flew into LB's net, and LB triumphantly paraded the bat outside.

Ann sighed in relief and fell over onto the couch. "I don't like bats. Your cousin Simon told me they could fly into my hair. They terrify me."

"It's okay, Mom," Nicole comforted her and gave her a big hug. They all sat down on the couch to recover from the episode.

"Where's Damian?" Nicole asked. "He's usually the best at getting the bat out of the house."

"Hey, *I'm* the best bat hunter," LB said with disdain.

"You're all wonderfully helpful," Ann said. "LB, go check in his room."

He was back in a jiffy, with no sign of Damian in any of the rooms. Maybe he never came in from the car? Where would he go? Everyone scrambled back outside to go look for him with darkness closing in. Ann sent LB to the office to see if Damian went down to talk to Lincoln again.

She took Nicole and Jacob up to the shop to look around there. The ten-year-old boy loved watching the outside staff do their work at the shop right above their house. Maybe he had gone to see Bart, Lincoln's brother, welding the boats, or up to the workout room where some of the guys hung out. As Ann searched his normal hideouts without success, she felt panic gripping her. She stumbled on a rock but balanced without dropping the baby. Damian never ran off without telling her first. He was so upset from the events of the day. Where could he be? She worried about him being alone.

She called out Damian's name, getting louder and more desperate with each call. When they didn't find him, they met LB back at the house. "Lincoln said to check at Bob's house."

With her heartbeat quickening, she walked over to the house next door that belonged to her in-laws, Bob and MJ. Bob had recently retired, which was why Lincoln had returned to the lake. Bob built the two log cabins right next to each other when he first opened the business.

Ann knocked on the door, peering in the glass while she waited for them to answer. She drew in a deep breath of relief when she saw Damian sitting there at the table with Bob playing chess.

"Damian!" she cried when they opened the door. "We've been searching everywhere for you." Damian looked up at her and then back at the chess game, unaffected by her concern.

"He's been telling me a little bit about your day," Bob said. Then he lowered his voice. "He's extremely upset. I'll send him home when we finish our game."

"Okay, thanks," Ann said, turning around and walking the twenty feet back to her house. Although she had panicked just a moment ago, she couldn't be mad at Damian after such a difficult day. The corners of her mouth curved up, knowing that Damian had a place he felt safe, even if it wasn't with her.

Ann and the kids were eating dinner when Damian marched in the door enraged. "Why don't they ever show up for us? Why is it the same every time?" He picked up the closest chair and threw it across the room, then bolted into his bedroom.

She had never seen him this upset. Ann followed him to his bed and wrapped him in her arms. Damian started weeping.

"I'm so sorry." Ann held him closer and smoothed his hair. "I can't imagine how hard this must be for you. I know you love your parents. You have every right to be upset. We want to do whatever we can for you to make this feel like home. We love you no matter what happens."

Damian wept uncontrollably in her arms until the tears faded away. Then he looked up at Ann with wet, shining eyes. "Ann, I love you too. I'm glad you found us." Then he cuddled up into her arms as she stroked his back lovingly until he drifted to sleep with a smile of contentment on his face.

Ann's heart felt sick knowing she could not mend the broken hearts of these two precious boys she loved so deeply. She sent up desperate prayers.

Was Emily right? Was adoption—becoming a real family—the answer? And if they adopted these boys, would they ever accept her fully as their mother?

Damian playing chess with Grandpa Bob

Damian and Nicole
ready for school at
the log cabin house

Damian, LB, and Milo

LB and Damian after
swimming in the Doughboy
pool at Sacramento house

Family photo at Donner Lake: Ann, Nicole (5),
Damian (11), Jacob (infant), Lincoln, LB (8)

TWO

A New Name

MAY 1992

. . . .

Even before he made the world, God loved us and chose us
in Christ to be holy and without fault in his eyes. God decided
in advance to adopt us into his own family. . . . He is so rich
in kindness and grace that he purchased our freedom with
the blood of his Son and forgave our sins. He has showered
his kindness on us, along with all wisdom and understanding.
Furthermore, because we are united with Christ, we have
received an inheritance from God, for he chose us in advance,
and he makes everything work out according to his plan.

—Ephesians 1:4–5a, 7–11

And you will be given a new name
by the LORD's own mouth.

—Isaiah 62:2b

. . . .

DAMIAN SQUIRMED IN HIS SEAT UNCOMFORTABLY,
pulling at the tie Ann forced him to wear. His clothes felt itchy and
suffocating.

Everyone in the small courtroom sat silently waiting. Damian
tried to count on his fingers how many times he had sat in this exact

same seat, waiting. Damian watched the judge look up from his desk, scanning the audience. Absent, again. Damian had long clung to the hope that his parents would change and want to take him home. Historically, his parents remained absent until the last opportunity. Almost a year had passed since Ann and Lincoln first talked about adopting them. He had lived in their home for four years, which meant six years away from his parents. *Would the judge delay again today?*

As an eleven-year-old, it was difficult to wrap his mind around the whole court process, but he had gathered that today was the day his parents needed to prove they had interest in getting him and his brother back or else they would lose their parental rights. In his calculations, they had already been to court six times without his parents showing up.

Damian felt the familiar anger bubble up inside but pushed it back down like he always did. He knew better than to expect them to be here. Why had he thought this time would be any different? Ann told him Connie was having another baby. Would his parents love that baby more than they loved him? Would they ever realize how much he loved them and longed to live with them? Would they move on and forget about their older children and start only caring about the new baby?

He longed to know what it felt like to be wanted, to be somebody's son, someone who wouldn't disappoint him, who might even—*dare he hope?*—love him. Lincoln and Ann often said they loved him like their own son, but it was difficult to believe. He replayed Lincoln's words in his mind as he sat waiting, trying to understand them all: "Son, we love you and your brother. We want you to be in our family forever. That means we will treat you just like our own; we will give you anything we would give to Nicole and Jacob. That's why we want to adopt you. We want to give you the freedom to become a part of us, to have a firm foundation beneath you. We have so many wonderful plans. We want you to be abundantly free."

But what did it mean to be abundantly free?

The knock of the judge's gavel interrupted his thoughts.

"We have waited long enough," the judge declared, glancing down at the papers in front of him and checking the clock once more before proceeding. "This case has already dragged on too long in my watch. The birth parents, stated here as Connie and Larry, have run out of time for actionable change. The report in front of me tells me last month they brought a sixth child into the world on methamphetamine. This child has also been placed into foster care." The judge looked at Damian. "Son, your parents' rights are terminated. I am ruling in absentia. You are eligible for adoption. Case closed."

Deep sadness overcame Damian first, as the finality of the moment set in. The wait was over. Why didn't they show up? Why didn't his parents want him? Didn't they know it was their last chance? Flashbacks of years of disappointing moments whizzed through his eleven-year-old mind. He recalled the time he was suddenly yanked from their home six years ago. He remembered the countless visits he had waited for them with great anticipation, only to be let down.

Then a new emotion welled up within him. Damian looked down the row he sat in, filled with his new family. Unlike his birth parents, Ann and Lincoln stuck to their word. If they said something, they did it. They never missed his soccer games. They said they loved him and wanted to adopt him. The judge said he could be adopted now. The thought of their active choice to adopt him brought a fleeting smile to his face.

Was this . . . joy?

But he was afraid to believe that this joy—and their love—would last. After all, it didn't make any sense to him. Why would they want

23

two troublesome boys? Would they change their minds if he messed up?

He allowed the anger in his heart toward his birth parents to grow. *I'm moving on. I won't let them hurt me anymore. I won't let anyone hurt me.*

He resolved to be good, no matter what. He would play by the rules and say the right things. He couldn't risk the heartache of losing Ann's and Lincoln's love and trust. He wanted this family, and he would do whatever it took to keep it.

The family filed out of the courtroom, dazed by the final verdict. When they reached the more spacious hall outside, Ann and Lincoln enveloped the family in a group hug.

"I'm sorry your parents didn't show up again," Lincoln said, noticing the long faces of LB and Damian. "But now we can officially get the adoption process started. This calls for a celebration. A *big* celebration. First, I think we should go fill our bellies. Where do you want to go?"

"Red Robin," Damian and LB said simultaneously, grins widening.

"Red Robin it is. And second, we have to plan how we're going to celebrate adoption day."

"What does that mean?" LB asked.

"It all still has to become official, but now that your parents' rights are terminated, it opens you up to be adopted by us. We just have to get all the paperwork filed. It could take a few months. But this is no small deal; you are officially becoming a part of our family. It means you will take on our name."

Damian looked up in surprise about that, he hadn't considered his name would change. He didn't know how to feel. It felt equal parts nerve-wracking and exciting. But could he live up to the Young family name? Would he stop feeling like a Navarro? Would changing his name help him feel more loved?

"And it means *freedom*," Lincoln continued. "If you get adopted, we could go anywhere, and we don't have to call and get permission. We could just do it. So the big question is, if we could go anywhere, where would you want to go?"

"Like anywhere, anywhere?" Damian said, afraid to hope. Damian remembered how Lincoln and Ann had taken Nicole on vacation to Canada before Jacob was born, leaving him and LB behind, since they couldn't cross state lines. Damian wondered if it was true, at the time, or if it was just an excuse to leave him and his brother behind. They had to stay at an awful temporary placement while the family was away for what felt like forever.

"Absolutely anywhere, and especially out of California," Lincoln added. "I have some thoughts . . . but my best one is Disney World."

"What? We could go to Disney World?" LB exclaimed, jumping up and down now.

"Yes, none of us have ever been. It would be a big grand adventure," Lincoln said.

"Really? You mean it? One of my friends at school just came back from Disney World. He said it was *sooo* cool. And it's super far away. Can we really go there?" Damian asked. He realized he had been wrong; it was true that they couldn't bring him and LB before. Maybe these people really did love him.

"Yes, we really could. We can put you on an airplane and fly you to a whole different place. Should we do it?" Lincoln asked.

Now all the kids, including Nicole, were jumping up and down, with a chorus of, "Yes, yes, yes."

After the excitement settled, the family walked down the courthouse steps. LB lingered behind, his head hung low. Ann slowed down to walk beside him. Damian walked slow enough to hear their conversation.

"LB, do you want us to be the ones to adopt you? You know this could be your opportunity to go to another home if you really want to," Ann said.

"No, Ann. I like it with you," LB replied and grabbed her hand, holding it the rest of the way to the car.

Damian wondered why Ann didn't ask him the same question, but he knew his answer was the same. He would like to never have to go to another home unless it was back with his parents. Of all the other homes he had experienced, Ann and Lincoln's was by far the best.

A FEW WEEKS LATER, LB'S BUS PULLED ONTO COLLINS Lake Road, about a mile from their home. "Looks like we're walking home again today," eight-year-old LB said to his older brother Damian, giving him a shove down the last step of the bus. Sometimes Ann picked them up, but most days they walked.

"Watch where you're going, man," Damian said, shoving LB back.

"I'll race you," LB taunted. Damian was older by three years, but LB was faster.

"I don't want to race you. Not after what you did today," Damian called after him.

"What do you mean?" LB asked, pausing just long enough for Damian to catch up to him.

"You know what I'm talking about. Everyone at school was talking about it," Damian said. "Don't you want to be adopted? Don't you want them to like us? Why did you steal all those things anyway?"

"I didn't think I would get caught," LB admitted, running ahead again. He couldn't resist the first candy bar he spotted in his counselor's office; it was his favorite, and Ann never bought him candy. He didn't think anyone would miss it, and it tasted so good. When he got away with it the first time, he saw how easy it was, then it became like a game of stealth: how much could he take without getting caught? Over the last several months, he had filled his backpack with stolen goods from his teacher and classmates: pencils, the fancy markers, things from the treasure box, and Milk Duds.

"But you did. And now they might not want us. We have to be careful, LB. It's not too late for them to change their minds," Damian called after him.

LB turned around with his hands on his hips, challenging his brother defiantly. "So what?"

"So what? You don't even care that we might be separated again? Sent to ten different families again?" Damian said, panting as he trotted to catch up to LB. "You need to be better, LB. I'm not going to let you put our home at risk."

"You know they don't love us as much as they love their own kids," LB said back. "We're different, and we will always be different. Remember when they left us behind to take a vacation with *their* kids?"

"You know they couldn't take us with them."

"Yeah, but they could have stayed in California so we could go with them. And you know how awful that week at that other home was."

"Which is exactly why we shouldn't mess it up here. We don't know where we could get placed if the adoption doesn't work out. It could be even worse than that place."

"Nicole gets to go anywhere and do anything—she gets to go to friends' houses. And she gets exactly what she wants for her birthday."

"You didn't even tell them you wanted a BMX bike for your birthday."

"They wouldn't have gotten it anyway. They don't like to get the brand name. But I bet they will get brand-name stuff for Jacob when he wants it. And maybe even you."

"Well . . ." Damian faltered.

LB flashed his toothy, cunning smile at Damian.

"Well . . . what? They obviously love Nicole and Jacob more. Ann sits there counting Jacob's toes and holds him all the time. She looks at him with those big loving eyes and then just asks us to do chores." LB arrived at the store in a final sprint. "I'm going in to ask Lincoln for a ride."

"You honestly think he will give us a ride after what you did today?"

LB swung open the door and entered the store without answering.

Damian hesitated a moment at the door before opening it slowly and following his brother.

LINCOLN SAT AT HIS DESK FILLING OUT THE LAST OF the adoption paperwork to get finalized by the end of the month. He saw LB sprint through the doors, then pause to catch his breath, followed shortly by Damian. LB strode toward his office with a smirk on his face.

"Hey, boys. I'm so glad you stopped by the office. I have some great news. Our Disney World trip is booked for the day after your adoption becomes legal," Lincoln said, rubbing his hands together with excitement.

LB glanced at his brother. "Have you talked to Ann yet?"

"Not since this morning. Why?"

Damian blurted out, "He doesn't want you to find out that he was caught stealing today at school. He stole from his teacher and the kids in his class and the counselor's office. They found candy and school supplies in his backpack."

"Really, LB? I'm surprised. Why?" Lincoln asked.

"I didn't do it. Someone put all that stuff in my backpack," LB said without blinking.

Lincoln paused to survey the two boys, then melted into an understanding smile.

"LB, you don't have to steal things to get our attention. We love you, and we will always love you, no matter what you do. I told you this before—it's our choice to adopt you, and we're not going to change our minds. We're not going to ship you off if you mess up. You're stuck with us for life, if you'll have us." Lincoln's eyes twinkled with merriment. Then his tone became stern. "However, telling the truth is something I highly value, and stealing is absolutely not okay. But I still love you; you are family. We can discuss the consequences later as a family."

Lincoln glanced at Damian, who had started to cry. LB's smirk never changed. It surely wasn't the first time LB had lied to him without batting an eye. Stealing and lying were things that would have to be curbed. But far stronger than Lincoln's disappointment in LB's actions was his heartbreak knowing that his soon-to-be son was rattling the cage of their love by acting out at school.

Lincoln could tell they were each responding to the adoption in their own way. He knew they had been dealt some bad cards and no matter how much he and Ann loved them, it wouldn't make up for what the boys had experienced prior to coming to their home. Nevertheless, he wished he could erase it all for them and help them to see how loved they were. He hoped the adoption could show them that the footing underneath them was as solid as concrete and wouldn't change.

"I have some other good news for you both," Lincoln continued. "I was filling out your adoption paperwork and discovered you can completely change your name. Of course, you will be taking on the Young family name. Well, I assumed you would want to, but do you?"

Damian quickly jabbed LB in the gut and beat him to the answer. "Yes, we want our name to be Young."

"And you, LB?" Lincoln leaned forward in his chair with his full attention on LB.

"Yeah, I guess."

"Good, that settles that. But you can also change your first and middle name if you want to. Which is especially good news for you, LB."

Lincoln knew that LB hated his name. Word had gotten around to him that his parents were expecting a girl, so they had chosen the name Laura Bonita. When he entered the world as a boy, they simply changed the ending of the name to make it a boy's name: Lauro Benito.

On the first day of school—or anytime a teacher or someone else didn't know his name yet and read it off the roster—all the classmates would snicker and call him "Laura." He had been sent to the office more than once for causing a scene, adamantly saying, "I'm a boy. I'm not a girl. My name is not Laura. And I'll fight anyone who calls me anything except LB!"

"Do I get to pick?" LB inquired, a look of sheer delight and awe coming over his face.

Before Lincoln answered, he thought to himself, *How much power do we want to give an eight-year-old?* But he settled in his mind that the boys needed some empowerment in this adoption process to feel a part of it.

"Yes, you can choose," Lincoln said. "As long as you come up with something Ann and I agree with. You could be Dylan, or Zach, or Pete. You know, God gives us a new name when he adopts us as his sons. He calls us beloved, cherished truth-tellers."

"What about . . ." LB trailed off with his face contorted as though he were putting his full effort into thinking.

Lincoln's face lit up. "Hey, I just realized I'm an LB too, Lincoln Berryhill. You could take my name. New family, new name, it could work. What do you think?"

LB scrunched up his face, saying, "No way. I could never see myself with your name."

"You can take your time. You could even make your official name on your birth certificate 'LB.' That's your name; that's what you've always been called. Then when anyone asks what it stands for, you say it doesn't stand for anything; it's just LB."

In the end, LB settled on LB Navarro Young, keeping part of his old identity with him and taking his birth name as his middle name. Damian chose to Americanize his name, taking on a new identity from Damiano Pasqual Navarro to Damian Paul Young.

As the boys left his office, Lincoln watched LB stoop to grab something quickly. LB glanced around to the left and right, then stuffed a Slim Jim down his pocket. Lincoln sighed deeply, throwing up a prayer to heaven for guidance.

Lincoln's faith ran deep, with God's truths implanted in him by his parents. Getting into the family business, Lincoln was reminded daily that he had to trust in God for His provision. He knew from watching his dad go through several droughts that the lake campground business was largely dependent on rain to fill the lake and good weather for the campers, all things in God's hands. Lincoln leaned heavily into God's promises and found his faith unwavering even through difficult circumstances.

Lincoln yearned to impart God's truth to these two boys; he hoped they would catch on to his actions and see how everything he did was done through the scope of pleasing God. He trusted fully in God's provision, from the way he did business, to how he interacted with the people who meant the most to him. He loved the boys through the lens of how his heavenly father loved them.

He was about to trust God in a whole new way as he plunged into loving LB and Damian for life. When they signed up to be foster parents, he had always viewed it as a temporary season, loving kids through a specific time in their life until they could return to their parents. But adoption would be a lifelong commitment to these boys, an opportunity to love them through all of life's trials. He desperately wanted LB to grasp his own love for him as well as God's love, but this stealing behavior was something he did not understand.

When Lincoln arrived home from work, Ann stood at the stove stirring a pot, talking to LB, who sat on the counter. LB shot a quick glance toward Lincoln, then hopped off the counter and ran to his room.

Lincoln walked over to give his wife a kiss, dancing her around the kitchen as she clutched a wooden spoon in her hand. She laughed and kissed his nose.

"I'll be right back," he told her, smiling and spinning her back to the stove. "I have to talk to LB."

Lincoln walked to LB's room and entered, shutting the door behind him.

"LB, I saw what you did at the store. You took something that wasn't yours. I'm going to need you to return it."

"I don't know what you're talking about." LB squirmed, keeping his eyes on the ground.

"Don't play games with me, young man. I saw you take the Slim Jim."

"I don't have it."

"LB, you need to return what's not yours."

"I ate it."

"In that case, you're going to have to work to pay for it."

"What do you mean?"

"You can come scoop ice at the store every day after school for the next week. That should pay for it. But don't let me catch you stealing from my store again. This is a family business, and you're part of the family. Don't heap ruin upon yourself."

Lincoln spotted LB's backpack on the bed next to him. "Empty the backpack and show me what's inside."

LB unzipped his backpack and tipped it upside down, shaking out the contents onto his bed. Lincoln watched as countless empty candy wrappers and school supplies fell out.

"Why did you take all these things?"

"Because I wanted them."

"You know you could ask us if you have a need."

"You wouldn't buy them for me."

"You don't know until you ask. LB, we love you. If you have a need, we will surely fill it. But seeing that you took all these things disappoints me. I want better for you, LB. People won't trust you if you steal from them. You need to return everything you stole."

"But I ate all the candy bars."

"Looks like you'll be working more hours to earn them back then."

With that, Lincoln turned around and walked out of the room, praying he could find a way into LB's heart. He rejoined Ann, who was plating dinner for their family of six.

"Did you hear about what happened at school today?"

"Yes, they called," Ann said, "and I'm still having a hard time believing it. Not my sweet little LB. He couldn't have stolen all those things. It could just be a misunderstanding."

"I don't think it's a misunderstanding. I caught him stealing on his way out of the store after I had a talk with him. He's just acting out to see if it's really true, if we really will love him no matter what he does," Lincoln said. "But I have been thinking we should be more intentional with how we introduce ourselves to new people. We have been saying, 'This is our son and daughter and our foster sons,' but instead of saying, 'This is our adopted son,' I think we should just say son with no explanation. I want to remove any reason for the two of them to feel disconnected from us."

"What consequence should we give him for stealing?" Ann asked.

"I talked with him, and we are sorting it out. He is going to come bag ice at the store. I don't want to overreact and push him further away. This is the first time that we have been made aware of the situation. I want him to feel safe telling us the truth. I know right now that's not the case for him."

That night Ann lay awake thinking. *What have we gotten ourselves into?* He was always so sweet. LB was her favorite little second grader. Could he really have stolen those things? Why did he keep denying it? She would love to see into the way his little mind worked. What were they signing up for by adopting a boy who could so easily lie to her? She settled on the only thing she could do: show him her love. She hoped it would be enough.

BEFORE DAMIAN KNEW IT, ADOPTION DAY ARRIVED. Their flight to Disney World was scheduled to leave the day after their official swear-in ceremony in the judge's chambers. They wanted to celebrate their newfound freedom the first moment they could.

The adoption finalization hearing lasted only about twenty minutes. Each member of the family, including Nicole, was sworn in, followed by Emily Elliot and the representing lawyer. The judge asked Damian and LB to introduce themselves and their new family. He then addressed Ann and Lincoln, "Do you promise to give Damian and LB a loving home? Do you understand that this process will make these two boys a permanent member of your family and they will become your sole responsibility, the same as your biological children?"

"Yes, we are ready to give them a permanent loving home," Ann declared.

"And what about you, Nicole? Do you want these two brothers for the rest of your life?"

Nicole smiled and nodded sheepishly, keeping her eyes on the ground.

Lincoln interjected, "We have all been waiting for this moment for a good long time."

With that, the judge signed the decree of adoption and invited the new family up to take a photo to celebrate the uniting moment. Damian smiled but couldn't ignore that twinge of sadness that came with the finality of the moment, the closure of his old identity and final break with his birth family. He couldn't deny that he still loved Connie and Larry even if they had constantly disappointed him. But it felt right to be here in the moment with his new family. He was now officially a part of them.

The morning of the trip, Ann woke Damian and LB up with a wrapped present. Damian ripped into the glossy paper and then held the contents in awe. He grasped the red clock, tracing the gold engraving with his finger that boldly stated his new adopted name, Damian Paul Young, and today's date, August 7th, 1992, the date of his adoption. A ray of sunshine streamed through the skylight above him, causing the words to glimmer in declaration of this moment in time when his life forever changed.

Damian bounded out of bed and squeezed Ann tight, then bounced off to get dressed and bring his neatly packed suitcase down the stairs. He quivered with happiness; nothing could burst the joy he felt as he repeated his new name to himself over and over in between bites of Lucky Charms. The sadness that usually twinged his happiness had completely dissipated like the morning mist. He couldn't remember ever feeling happier in his life than in that moment, anticipating a whole week in Disney World. He might float up to the ceiling knowing that Ann and Lincoln chose him. They chose *him,* as in *Damian Paul Young,* to be their son. No one ever chose him. But they did. And he would be theirs forever.

He felt a shifting in his identity. No longer was he an unwanted Navarro. He was a desired Young, part of a family who gave him more abundance than he could imagine. He hoped to live up to the family name and make them proud. Or at least not tarnish the name entirely.

When they arrived at the airport, Damian felt butterflies in his tummy. This would be his first-ever plane ride. Every minute brought new and exciting experiences. Tiny bathrooms, free soda, and a little snack. They landed in Florida on a balmy August afternoon. On their ride from the airport to their hotel, the blue sky turned to a thunderstorm.

"Is it going to rain like this the whole time we're here?" Ann asked Lincoln.

"I did hear from someone that rain storms move in almost every afternoon here in this season. But we won't let it stop us," Lincoln replied.

And they didn't. They spent four days in the theme parks and one day at Universal Studios. They went to the beach and a water park. But the best memories were made inside Disney World when the afternoon showers came down. They bought Mickey Mouse ponchos and kept on exploring when most others left the park.

Damian and LB, with their ponchos on, jumped straight into a large puddle of water. They started whooping and hollering as they stomped in all the puddles they could find.

Ann said, "Hey, you're going to get all wet." Then she laughed at herself. "Oh, we're all wet. Keep on jumping in those puddles."

They went romping through Disney World, soaked and having the best time, letting the rain pour on them. It felt refreshing, anyway, in the tropical, humid air.

They went home with wonderful memories and headed straight back to school. At the end of the week, Damian wasn't sure he felt entirely different, having a new name, but he did like the new benefits that seemed to come along with the name.

LB and Nicole

LB swimming in Doughboy pool
outside Sacramento home

Lincoln with LB

Lincoln reading to LB and Nicole

Nicole, LB, Lincoln and Damian in ponchos at Walt Disney
World for adoption celebration

THREE

Muddy Waters

SPRING 1996

. . . .

"That's the real trouble with the world,
too many people grow up."

—Walt Disney

. . . .

AS HER FOUR CHILDREN GREW, ANN VOLUNTEERED
to be with her kids in every possible capacity. As the president of the
PTA, she planned rallies and brought popcorn and popsicles every
Friday. She instigated extravagant outings with all the extended family
who lived at the lake. She attended every single sporting event and
performance. She coached softball teams and ran the snack shack at
the ballfield. She hosted parties, made buttercreams, and fed masses
of people, pouring out her vibrant energy to everyone around her. She
also worked as the secretary and worship director at the local church.

Even with all this, Ann felt she had more love to give, so she
assessed the needs in her community. One day, she was having a
conversation with her friend as the elementary school bus pulled into
one of its stops at the local market across from her church.

"Look at that." Ann gaped. "It's a busload of untapped potential. I don't recognize any of those kids from church, but they stop here, right across the street, every day."

"Where are you going with this?" her friend asked quizzically.

"Can't you see? We could do a program for them. Almost like a youth group, but for elementary kids," Ann said, her vision growing every minute. "They could come over right from their bus stop."

Her friend's face lit up like a light bulb. She stood up straighter, realizations dawning in her eyes. "I like where you're going with this. Imagine all the families we could reach who may have never been to church but start coming because their son or daughter hears about Jesus. Imagine the fun we could have."

"Exactly!" Ann felt she might be a balloon about to launch into the air. With her imagination at work, the possibilities were endless.

And that was exactly how it started. Ann and three of her closest friends launched a ministry they later coined "TGIT" or Thank God It's Tuesday, named by one of the kids who loved the ministry. It started with twenty kids and within weeks grew to over one hundred. With her connections at the local elementary school, she convinced the principal to bus anyone who was interested to the church (with signed permission slips from home, of course). Word among the kids spread like wildfire, and soon two busloads of kids were dropped off weekly on Tuesdays. They had to recruit more help quickly.

Ann let her creativity soar as she planned witty skits, engaging games, inventive snacks, and simplistic Bible lessons that let Jesus shine—like a weekly Vacation Bible School. Many of the kids had never been to church before and asked questions like, "What's prayer?" and "What's God?" Eventually, they organized into classes and had a curriculum, but they always made it fun.

Ann simply loved being around kids. In her opinion, adults were starchy and stale, always talking people to death. She was drawn to kids because of their pure, unadulterated joy. When they had joy, it was over-the-top joy, shown expressively through their whole bodies. Of course, sadness and anger were the same full-body experience, but those moments of raw joy made those more challenging moments worth it, as they brought life to her soul.

She created moments of joy by tapping into her own childlike wonder, especially through the power of the bubble. The mesmerizing, perfectly round, iridescent spheres made anyone and everyone smile. Ann became a bubble connoisseur, mastering the recipe and getting bubble gadgets of all shapes and sizes. If any kid ever looked uncertain or afraid, she spent one-on-one bubble time with them until she cracked open a twinkling of a grin.

Kids also expressed their opinions without any filters. She had never laughed so hard as when one of the kids at TGIT asked her, "Miss Ann. Why is you so fluffy?" She loved that kids simply said it like it is, without holding back or worrying about others' opinions.

A FEW WEEKS AFTER STARTING TGIT, ANN ARRIVED IN the school line to pick up LB from junior high, with Damian already in the back seat. As she pulled up in the line of cars, she saw a swarm of junior high girls huddled around LB. When LB spotted her car, one of the girls ran ahead of him toward her car. As she saw the girl approaching, Ann rolled down her passenger-side window.

"Hi, Miss Ann," the girl with bobbing blonde curls said. She held on to the car window, looked back at her friends, and then resolutely turned to Ann. "What is LB's real name?"

LB walked up behind the girl to get into the car. Ann looked at LB with a smile and then said, "His name is LB. It's just LB. It doesn't stand for anything."

The girl looked flustered. She put her hand on her hip and looked at LB, then back at Ann. "But it has to stand for something. Nobody names their kid two initials. You have to tell us. We can't get it out of him."

LB opened the car door and got into the back seat. He looked at Ann with big puppy-dog eyes, waiting to see what she would say.

"There is nothing to tell. His official name is LB. That's it," Ann said.

The girl gave one more glance back at LB with both hands on her hips, and then ran back to the other girls. They stood with their heads together in a circle. Suddenly, it appeared they reached a decision when a brunette with pigtails ran toward the car.

"Hi, Miss Ann. Are you sure it's just LB? We know it stands for something," the brunette with freckles across her nose and cheeks prodded. She put her hand next to her cheek and leaned in closer to whisper, "We think it stands for Lunch Box." She giggled into her hands.

"That is too silly. I told your friend over there. It's just LB. There's nothing to tell. Go and tell everyone that his name is LB, that's it," Ann said, waving her hand to the girls and pushing the gas pedal to pull away from the school.

As she pulled away, LB sat smiling in the back seat. "Thanks, Ann. They never leave me alone." From the smile pasted on his face, it appeared he enjoyed the added attention and mystique of his name.

Ann smiled at him in the rearview mirror. "Of course, LB. Your secret is safe with me." Then she eyed Damian, who was laughing at his brother's name game. "Hey, Damian, I could use your help at TGIT tomorrow. This week we're learning about Moses and the Egyptians. I wanted your help leading the song 'Pharaoh, Pharaoh.' Do you think you could dress up like Pharaoh for me?" Ann asked.

"If you really need me, I could do it," Damian replied. "Swim practice is canceled tomorrow anyway. Hey, are you going to be able to make it to my swim meet on Saturday? It's a big one."

"Of course I'll be there. I wouldn't miss it," Ann told him.

ALMOST EXACTLY TWENTY-FOUR HOURS LATER, Damian stood in the broom closet at the church, waiting for his entrance cue. He wore a large piece of white cotton draped over his body with a black-and-white-striped rope tied around his waist to secure it. On his head, he wore an Egyptian headpiece, striped with black and gold, boasting a gold snake at the tip of his forehead. A gold beard attachment completed his ensemble. He thought he must look ridiculous but enjoyed the opportunity to embody another person.

At last, he heard his musical cue. He flung the door of the closet open and walked out with his head held high. As he walked toward the front of the eighty kids seated on the floor, he felt himself becoming Pharaoh. He strutted back and forth in front of the kids, lording over them with his fiercest facial expression. The kids roared with laughter and then quieted down when he pointed at a stalky fifth-grader sitting in the back with his arm and finger outstretched and the rest of his body still, following the end of his finger with a pointed stare. When the boy acknowledged that he had been chosen, he motioned with one swing of his hand for the boy to come forward.

Everyone sat breathlessly, waiting to see what would happen. When the boy stood next to him, Damian stood up taller and then clapped twice for the new song to begin. He motioned for the kids to stand up by bringing his open palms up from his waist to above his head. He whispered to the boy to follow his lead.

As the music started, he felt himself bobbing back and forth, naturally jiving to the beat. He allowed the contemptuous Pharaoh personality to melt into his goofy self, animated with movements for the song. He started marching in place, with his helper following along. He went over the top with all his movements, fully immersing himself into the motions. "Pharaoh, Pharaoh. Oh baby, let my people go." He did the "Walk Like An Egyptian" move, bobbing his head in the direction of his upper hand. Then he put his hands above his head for the "Oh" and motioned with his arms as if he rocked a baby. All eighty kids followed along, imitating his enthusiasm for each motion.

At the end of the song, the kids shouted, "Do it again." After the second rendition, Ann came to the front and said the kids could ask Pharaoh any question they had. A brave girl raised her hand.

"Why did you keep all of God's people for so long?" she inquired.

Damian crossed his arms and stood frozen in time like an Egyptian statue, holding his head up high. "It was all part of my pyramid scheme," he said. The adult volunteers in the room chuckled.

"What plague was the worst?" another child asked.

Enjoying himself, Damian again paced back and forth, bringing a finger to the side of his face and staring above their heads thoughtfully as though he were thinking hard. He let the suspense build as he waited to answer. "I liked them all equally." He paused as the kids laughed at the unexpected answer. "I learned to 'B-positive' when the Nile turned to blood. The frogs exponentially expanded our green space."

"Why did you chase after them after you said they could go?"

"That's easy. I wanted to go *down* in history. And you see, you're still talking about my wonderful mistakes today."

"That's all the questions for today, kids. You're dismissed to your classes," Ann told the audience. The kids all rose up to get in their lines behind their teachers. Ann turned to Damian and gave him a big hug. "Thank you. I knew you could do it. You're a natural."

"Glad to be here for you, Mom."

"Do you want to help with our special surprise at the end?"

"What is it?"

"We're doing a water slide."

"That sounds awesome."

Damian walked outside to see the inflatable waterslide. Without anyone around, he climbed up to the top and slid down headfirst into the water. He was an all-in kind of guy. When the kids streamed out, the timid ones stayed on the side gaping at the large attraction. But the older, rowdy boys climbed right up and met Damian, who was waiting at the top. Damian challenged the boys to a slide race. They raced down the slide over and over again until they shivered with cold.

After all the kids left, Damian stood shivering in the sunlight, pining for a hot shower. But he felt on top of the world, totally alive and energized.

BACK AT HOME, DAMIAN'S CONFIDENCE LEAKED OUT of his smug smile. He crossed the hallway to LB's room with his new guitar in hand and started strumming away, trying to get a feel for it with LB as an audience. Five-year-old Jacob barged in, hearing the music. He swayed his body back and forth and then jumped up on the bed.

After a while, Ann called for everyone to come down for dinner. LB whispered in Damian's ear. Damian hesitated as he looked at Jacob and then broke into a wide grin, chuckling and winking at LB. Damian said, "Hey, Jacob, do you want to go down to dinner in style?"

"What do you mean?"

"You should slide down the banisters. It will be so much fun. Just hop up like this and slide down," Damian said, showing him what to do. LB covered his mouth to hide his laughter.

Jacob hopped up on the oak banister and rode it all the way to the bottom. The brothers bent over in laughter from the top, knowing it was forbidden. Ann caught a glimpse of movement and saw Jacob as he slid down the end of the banister and landed on his feet.

"Jacob Young," Ann scolded. "Do not do that again. That's dangerous. You could fall. You cannot slide down the banisters."

Jacob looked up sheepishly. "They told me to." He pointed to LB and Damian.

Nicole stood at the bottom of the stairs squealing with laughter.

"Boys." Ann pointed her finger at them. "If I hear of you coaxing Jacob into trouble again, I'm going to punish you both, especially you, LB. Now get in here for dinner."

"Hey, Damian's the one who told him to do it," LB said, his belly laughter turning to a sour face. Why was everything always his fault? She believed Jacob and said nothing to Nicole, who was laughing harder than he was. She always believed Jacob without question, but that was never the case for him. Why did she single him out as the culprit?

Before Ann could reach the table, the phone rang. LB watched her bustle over to answer it.

"Yes, hello?" Ann said, with one hand on her hip and the other pointed toward the table motioning for her children to sit down. LB skulked around the corner, just out of eyesight, but within eavesdropping range.

"It's Peter Barry's dad, Phil. What the hell kind of parents are you letting your son bring a gun to school? This is your courtesy call to let you know I'll be calling the police," the voice on the other line raged.

"What are you talking about?" Ann asked.

LB's ears perked up, and he hid deeper in the corner as he watched Lincoln walk in the back door and remove his jacket. He saw Ann waving her arms frantically for Lincoln to come over. He couldn't quite make out what Phil's reply was.

"I still don't know what you're talking about," Ann said. "LB doesn't own a gun. That's not even possible. Just a minute. My husband's right here." Ann tossed the phone at Lincoln, and threw her hands up in the air. "Phil's on the phone saying LB brought a gun to school and Peter came home with it. He's calling the police."

Lincoln juggled the phone up to his ear, keeping a calm look on his face. LB inched toward the front door. He had seen and heard enough. He had to get out of there. *That little twit couldn't keep his blabber shut.* As LB opened the door, he heard Lincoln repeat the words, "A .357 revolver? Are you sure?"

LB shivered as the night air sucker punched him with its chilly bite. He should have grabbed a jacket, but there was no time. He couldn't bear to be there when the shit hit the fan. He just had to get away from there and fast. But where could he go? That was the problem with being stuck on this God-forsaken hill. There was nowhere to go. That's why he was in this pickle to begin with. If he lived in town or at least close to one friend his age, he wouldn't be so bored. It was at least a mile's walk to the closest relative. That was it. Maybe he could hide out at his cousin Simon's house while this all blew over. Then he could go on pretending like it never happened.

LB ran down the hill, down and down the big gravel hill that seemed to mock him as he whipped past, reminding him of the countless grueling walks up it. When he passed the top of the road that turned to Bob and MJ's house he slowed to catch his breath.

He had been so gleeful with his newly stolen item walking up that road three weeks ago. He was on his long walk home from school when he got the brilliant idea. His life would be so much better with a gun. All his friends at school always talked about how cool their guns were. He knew his parents would never buy him a gun, so he didn't even ask. But then he remembered the .357 Magnum revolver he had seen at his grandpa's house. Bob probably never used it anymore. He wouldn't even notice if it was gone. The work was easy. Bob and MJ were away at church like usual. LB quickly unlocked the gun safe like he had seen Bob do when he showed him the gun and stole away out the back door. He marched triumphantly up the hill—he lived for the thrill of a good steal—and found a secluded place to try it out.

In a grove of trees, LB loaded the gun and scanned his surroundings for something to shoot at. His eye caught sight of a dirty rusted can. He stood it up on the ground and braced himself to pull the trigger. He had not expected the ear-deafening boom. *Oh no,* he thought, *I can't keep this. I'll get caught in an instant. It's way too loud. I'll never be able to shoot it right.* He didn't want to risk getting caught by breaking back in, so he found a place to bury the gun behind the garage. A few weeks later, he overheard Peter bragging about how many guns he had at home. If this kid had too many guns at home to count, surely his dad wouldn't notice if another showed up.

That's when the new brilliant idea hatched. He could trade the gun to Peter and be rid of the blasted thing for good. No one would ever be able to trace the gun back to him.

They had worked out a deal. LB would trade Peter the gun for his brand-name baseball bat. LB thought it was a great deal, a bat he could actually use. He had played baseball for eight years and dreamed of owning a TPX.

LB brought the gun to school that morning in his backpack, and they swapped during lunchtime behind a tree. He was in the clear.

But somehow that little snitch had ratted him out. How was he going to get out of this one? Lincoln would likely call Bob immediately and find out the gun was missing from the safe. Maybe if he could hide out for the night it would all blow over in the morning.

He saw the light on in Simon's room from a distance. He inched through the darkened night, with just a few glittering stars above him. It wasn't too cold. Maybe he could just hide out in the garden shed. It looked big enough to spend the night in. He swung open the door and tucked himself into a corner to wait until his 6:30 a.m. bus.

Sometime in the night, he heard faint sounds of knocking coming from the house and voices that he couldn't make out. He crouched down lower in his hiding spot in case they came searching.

The night passed slowly and uncomfortably, but finally he saw streaks of sunlight through the cracks and walked out to the bus.

AT 10:30 A.M., LB'S TEACHER HANDED HIM A NOTE saying his mom was waiting for him in the office. *Uh-oh.* He traipsed to the office, feeling a pit of dread in his stomach and a bit lightheaded, as if he were living someone else's reality. He saw Ann standing there—obviously livid by the way she arched her back and pursed her lips.

"LB Young," Ann said in a scary, quiet tone. "We're leaving now."

She didn't say another word until they got to the car. LB plodded behind her.

When they reached the car, he slumped into the front seat, still waiting for her to speak. She sat in the driver's seat, started the engine, and then pointed to the back seat without a word.

LB's eyes bulged out of his head.

Sprawled in the back seat of the car, his entire collection he had stashed under his mattress for years lay exposed. The stolen goods included baseball cards, a black leather wallet, candy bars, a handsome stack of one- and five-dollar bills, a few knives, and a machete.

"We're returning all of it to its rightful owner." She reached for the wallet. "Whose is this?"

"Where did you find all this stuff?" he demanded.

"Under your mattress, with the police. They came last night. They searched everywhere for you but couldn't find you. They searched your entire room for other stolen goods. I wouldn't have believed it myself if I didn't see them pull the mattress up."

"It isn't yours."

"Well, it isn't yours either."

LB seethed under his skin. This was all Peter's fault. He couldn't wait to get a hold of him and duke it out. He was in such a mess because Peter snitched on him. LB tried to play it cool with Ann and not be affected by it.

"I didn't take them. I found them."

"Found them where?"

"Around."

"Uh-huh. So where are we going first?"

"Auntie's."

They pulled up to the house he had slept outside of. Ann handed him the wallet. He trudged to the door with his head hung down, barely holding the wallet, as if it were a bad omen. Ann knocked on the door three times before Auntie answered.

With excitement on her face, she said, "Do come in. I'm so glad to see you both—I love having visitors. What do I owe the honor today? Would you like some tea?" She chattered without noticing the article in LB's hand.

LB held up the wallet without crossing the threshold. He didn't want this to last any longer than necessary.

"You found my wallet! Thank you, thank you, child. I've been missing it for months now. Couldn't imagine where it had gotten off to."

"He didn't find it. He stole it," Ann said slowly, enunciating each word.

LB continued to stare at the ground.

"Well, now, he brought it back, so it's good as new to me, like it never happened. Thank you, LB. I see you don't want to come in, but I do appreciate your visit."

LB turned around without saying anything and got back into the passenger seat. Ann stood whispering a few words to Auntie before following him.

"You didn't even say sorry," Ann hissed at him in the car.

LB didn't reply. He stared out the window.

"Are you even sorry that you stole a gun from your grandpa? Do you have any remorse at all? Do you realize how much trouble you're in? The law is getting involved. I'm scared, LB. I don't want to lose you. But you have to let me in. Denying it will not help your case. I want to help you, LB." Ann started out angry but broke into tears by the end of her speech.

"I don't know what the big deal was. I wasn't going to use it."

The rest of the car ride passed in cold, eerie silence that seemed to drum all around LB in deafening tones. He felt a shiver travel down his spine.

One by one, they went to friends' and relatives' homes until the pile in the back seat dwindled. LB squirmed in his skin, dreading each stop more than the last. Then Ann held up the machete.

That had been one of his proudest mastermind moments. While Ann was shopping, he caught a glimpse of shiny metal. He stalked back to that aisle while she was looking for her perfect paper towels. That was a whole process that would give him plenty of time to accomplish his mission. He snuck away while she was lining paper towel packages up and down the aisle, emptying the cardboard bin until she found either shells or a plain white paper towel design with a border. He looked all around to make sure no one was watching and then stuffed the entire packaging down his pant leg.

Making a quick excuse to Ann why he needed to head to the car while she was still distracted by her paper towels, he grabbed her keys and walked confidently toward the exit. It was too easy.

"We'll have to go all the way to town for that one."

"I have all day," Ann said with an icy snap. She sat back in her seat. Her body looked relaxed, but she gripped the steering wheel with an iron fist.

LB reached over to turn on the radio. Ann quickly turned it back off.

The twenty-five-minute car ride seemed to last an eternity. Ann parked in her usual spot on the side of the building and came around to his side to open the door. She pulled him out by the ear.

She marched LB to the head of security, still not saying a word to him.

Ann spoke to the security guard. "My son stole a machete from your store. I am returning it to you, and I need you to scare him, like really scare him. He's going to juvie if he doesn't change his act quickly."

The menacing six-foot, broad-shouldered man stood up. "Oh, I'll scare him. Don't you worry. He will never want to steal anything again."

"Don't be easy on him," Ann said, pointing her finger up at him with her other hand on her hip.

He motioned for LB to follow him inside his office.

LB smiled once he was inside, away from Ann's gaze. He told the security guard a joke. He apologized for taking the machete.

The security guard chuckled a bit and then said LB was good to go.

He motioned for Ann to come back over. "Ma'am, I wouldn't worry too much about him. He's a good kid. He'll straighten out."

"But this is a big deal. Did you lay into him?" Ann asked.

"He's a nice kid. I scared him just enough. We worked it out," he answered. Then he winked at LB.

LB winked back at him before staring at the ground again, avoiding Ann's gaze.

When they got into the car, he glanced over at Ann with that twinkle in his eye.

"Are you smirking at me, young man? How do you charm everyone so easily? You're not getting away with this, you know. He let you off way too easy. I don't even think he scared you."

He hadn't.

When they finally reached home, LB found his mattress had been moved to the garage.

"You're going to spend a few nights sleeping here," Ann said. "We can't trust you right now. And I need to search your room to see if you have any other weapons stashed. It's not over. The police said the judge will not take a gun at school lightly. We don't know what's coming. I want you to do some serious thinking about where you're going to end up if you can't stop stealing. And you won't be going anywhere except school for a while."

LB threw himself on the mattress, defeated for now. It had all been a fun game. If only he hadn't traded the gun to Peter, he would still have all his treasures. He had always known his parents treated him differently. He was sure Jacob or Nicole would never have to stay in the garage. Even Damian always got off easier than he did, which was why he had Damian pull the banister prank. This was more proof.

LB lay on his bed pondering his new situation when Papa, Ann's dad, thundered into the garage.

"Who do you think you are, young man? Do you think you are exempt from consequences? Do you even think about your actions before you do them?" Papa seemed to roar at him.

LB cowered on the bed, not wanting to face Papa after all the bad things he had done. He loved Papa.

"Why on God's good earth are you behaving this way, sonny? Do you realize what it's doing to your parents? They have the biggest heartache over you."

"I don't know. It just happens," LB said, still not meeting Papa's gaze.

"Well, you've got to stop it from just happening. I want to keep you around a long time, you hear?"

LB broke into a smile at those last words and looked up. He rose and gave Papa a hug. "Why do I have to stay in the garage?"

"I'm not entirely sure, son, but they must have a good reason for it. You've got to knock it off, you hear. I don't want to hear about this happening again."

LB nodded. They sat and talked a long while until Papa decided to return to the main house. LB felt loved, grateful that Papa came to visit him, even if he did ask a lot of nosy questions.

Above: Damian before going to prom

Right: LB

Damian with cousins at annual camping trip to Donner lake

FOUR

Chronic Pain

. . . .

"Not only so, but we also glory in our
sufferings, because we know that suffering
produces perseverance; perseverance,
character; and character, hope."

—Romans 5:3-4 (NIV)

. . . .

ON SATURDAY, DAMIAN FELT HIS HEART THUMPING
faster and faster, as though it might thump right out of his chest. He
stood in line behind the starting block, waiting for his turn in the
one-hundred-meter fly. The racers in front of him neared the finish
line. Cheers from the spectators echoed off the water as his friend
came in first for that heat. He felt the pressure of the competition,
as their team was behind by three. If he and his friend took first and
second, it would boost their score by four.

The shrill whistle sounded. Damian took position on the block,
setting his feet for maximum pushing propulsion as his hands grasped
the edge. He readjusted his goggles once more, stretched his neck
side to side, then shifted back into place. The starting gunshot rang
in his ears, and he thrust his body into the water. He easily found
his rhythm, bobbing up and down, his arms flying through the air
and into the water in unison. He felt the euphoria of allowing his
body to do what he had practiced thousands of times, trusting the

process and giving his thinking mind a break. As he pushed off for the second and final length of the pool, he concentrated all his effort on gliding through the water with perfect form. He took no notice of the swimmers to his left or right until he reached for the wall at the finish line.

Looking around him as his head popped out of the water, he realized he had won by several strokes. The next swimmer barely pushed into the finish. Damian checked the time on the clock and pumped his fist out of the water above his head, ecstatic that he had bested his own personal record. He whooped and hollered as his best friend, Connor, came to high-five him and help pull him out of the water. Connor congratulated Damian, giving him a quick hug and patting him on the back. Then Damian squared up toward him and they bumped their chests together in celebration.

As Damian walked to look at the wall of scores and swim lineups, he felt the familiar churning in his stomach. *Not now,* Damian thought, *I still have two more races.* He tried to ignore the rising pain and concentrate on the list of names in front of him. He traced the line that had his name in the first-place slot of the fifty-meter free race with a smile on his face. Suddenly, his body keeled over as he experienced a sharp pain stabbing his gut. He could no longer ignore it. Damian had to find a bathroom immediately.

Searching frantically for the locker rooms, Damian darted through the crowded area, squeezing his thighs together to hold it in. This scene was all too familiar. His stomach pain often interfered in his life, especially lately. He sighed with relief as he pushed through the door to relieve himself.

But then the pain continued, too unbearable to go back out to finish the meet. Damian lay down on the bench in the locker room, unable to stand any longer. He heard his name being called on the megaphone. His next race was about to begin. He willed himself to get up and go out there, but his body held him to the bench. His team needed him, but the gut pain increased in intensity.

After an hour, he finally felt he could stand again. His teammates clamored into the locker room with raucous shouts and exuberant smiles. They won the swim meet by one point. Connor rushed to his side. "We were looking everywhere for you, man. We needed you out there. Where have you been?"

"I didn't feel good. I had to lie down." Damian held on to his stomach, which still had sharp, shooting pains.

"Your mom's out there looking for you. Here, let me help walk you out to her." Connor put his arm around Damian and guided him to his family waiting outside.

"Congratulations on the win, Damian! You got first place in two heats!" Ann exclaimed as she rushed to give her son a hug. "What happened to you? You never came back out for your last two swims. We've all been worried about you."

Damian was released from the strong embrace of his mother. His hands clutched his stomach. "I'm having those stomach pains again. It's really bad."

Lines of concern etched Ann's forehead. "It must be bad for you to miss your swims. I'm calling your doctor about this." Then she brought him in for another hug. "I'm proud of you. You raced so well today. Let's get going, so you can get some rest. I'll schedule the first appointment they have when we get home."

DAMIAN SAT BITING HIS NAILS IN THE WAITING ROOM at the doctor's office two weeks later. He hoped he would get some answers for the seemingly constant gut pain. Four years ago, when he went to see a doctor for his stomachache for the first time, they had given him a few medications to try. It seemed to help for a while, but recently nothing he tried eased the pain or diarrhea. That's why he was getting a colonoscopy. He hoped he had followed all the doctor's instructions correctly, rubbing his empty stomach that gnawed with hunger pains. The last twenty-four hours had been spent mostly in the bathroom, emptying his colon of all food after taking the laxative medication.

"Damian," the woman in scrubs called from the doorway.

He and Ann followed the nurse in sync down the long hallway of the gastrointestinal specialist's office. She sat them in a room and instructed them to wait for the doctor. One loud knock on the door announced his presence.

"We're doing a colonoscopy today to see if we can find the issue. We need to pinpoint the area of inflammation. We will put you under, then use our tiny camera to look over your entire gastrointestinal tract. I assume you followed all our preparation instructions. Do you have any questions?" The doctor spoke quickly.

Damian's eyes had glazed over hearing all the big words the doctor said. He tried to concentrate and think of a question, but nothing came. He looked over at Ann, who simply nodded.

When neither of them replied, the doctor said, "Good. If you have no questions, then we will begin the procedure. Ma'am, I'll ask you to come to the family waiting area to preserve his privacy during the colonoscopy."

Ann followed the doctor, leaving Damian alone. He shivered on the bed, knowing what was coming. Going under anesthesia made him nervous, and how would it feel to have something up his rear?

The doctor returned promptly, suited up for the procedure. Damian overheard the doctor ask the nurse to give Damian a sedative. The nurse hooked him up to an IV, and he shortly felt overcome by drowsiness.

Damian felt like he was still in a dream world when he overheard his mother's voice asking pointed questions. He blinked his eyes open in confusion.

"Why did you even try the operation if you knew the machine was too big?" Ann questioned the doctor in a shrill voice.

"I'm sorry, ma'am. I thought the machine would work, but it's meant for adults. He needs to have the procedure repeated with a pediatrician specialist in Sacramento. I'll escort you to the front, and they can help you set up an appointment for next week to repeat the colonoscopy," the doctor said.

In the car, Ann asked Damian how he felt after the procedure.

"I just feel extremely tired, and my stomach hurts," Damian answered as he pushed his seat back to the lying position.

"I think that's normal. They said you might feel a little gassy even. If the pain worsens or gets unbearable, they said to take you back in."

"I think it's going to be okay. I'll just rest."

"Are you hungry?"

"I thought I would be starving, but my stomach just hurts too bad."

That evening as he was going to bed, Damian had piercing gut pain, even worse than he had experienced before. He sought out Ann. "Mom, I think we need to go into the emergency room. It hurts really bad."

Ann called their trusted doctor friend to ask for advice. He advised them to go straight down to UC Davis and bypass the local emergency room. By that point, Damian looked pale and ashy. They needed to act quickly.

At UC Davis Medical Center, the doctor team had Damian drink oral contrast before x-raying him to illuminate any gastrointestinal issues.

"He has a perforated bowel," the doctor told them. "We have to operate immediately. The bowel is perforated close to where his brain shunt leaks fluid. If we don't fix this immediately, it could leak toxins to his brain."

Damian looked at Ann's worried face as he was rolled away into surgery. He gave her a weak smile and a wave.

HOURS LATER, AFTER A SUCCESSFUL SURGERY, DAMIAN came to. After a few disoriented moments alone, the doctor came in to check up on him.

"We were right," the doctor said. "The colonoscopy machine perforated your bowels. We were able to fix you up, but there's more we discovered along the way."

"Oh, my," Ann said from where she sat in the corner. "Good news or bad news?"

"A bit of both. The good news is we believe we discovered the source of your stomach pains," the doctor said. "The not-so-good news is I believe you have Crohn's disease. You are on the younger side for it to develop, which is probably why no one has mentioned it before as an option. Crohn's disease means that your bowels will have chronic inflammation. It's a painful, often lifelong disease that irritates your intestines and can cause severe diarrhea and stomach cramps. Flare-ups can come and go. There are several ways to treat it—I'm going to start you on medication, and I will have the dietician follow up with you on how a healthy diet can help ease your symptoms. But I also want to do a second surgery to remove a piece of your colon to help settle your current Crohn's inflammation."

"Wow, that's a lot," Ann said. "We want to do what it takes to help him, so it's a relief to have the start of this problem answered. When do you want to do the surgery?"

"We will let him rest and recover overnight, and we'll do that surgery tomorrow," the doctor replied.

The next day was Damian's sixteenth birthday. It wasn't the way he had hoped to spend his birthday, but he was thankful to be solving his pain issues. He would have just had an easy kickback with a few guys if he was home, but he could do that when he got out of there.

ANN LEFT TO GO HOME WITH THE OTHER KIDS WHILE Lincoln stayed overnight with Damian in the hospital. The next afternoon, the door to Damian's hospital room swung open. Ten kids walked through the door with balloons and a giant stuffed panda. Damian sat up, a wide, goofy grin on his face. He had never been happier to see all his siblings and cousins.

"Happy birthday to you!" they sang in unison as they gathered around Damian's bed.

Ann passed out popsicles to everyone. It was the only thing Damian could eat at the moment because of his colon issues and surgeries. Nicole came over to give Damian a popsicle "cheers!" and plant a big wet kiss on his cheek.

Damian called everyone over. "Hey, look, I will finally have more scars than Alex." He lifted his shirt to show off the large incisions in his abdomen.

"Ewww," a few of the girls screamed, while some others got closer and said, "Oooh, so interesting."

Then Damian showed them how he could use the controls to shift around the hospital bed. He sandwiched himself and folded himself in half. The kids all laughed.

LB stood by Damian's bed. "Happy birthday, brother. We miss you at home. Looks like you're living the high life in here."

"It's the absolute worst," Damian said, sadness peeking through his smile. "I can't stand being in the hospital. All they will give me is popsicles. I'm starving. And the little beeping noises never stop. But

I'll do anything to get rid of this pain, so in the end, it's worth it." Damian lowered his voice to a whisper. "Hey, how did you get off with all the stolen goods? Is everything back to normal?"

"Normal enough." LB shrugged. "I have court in a few weeks."

"Dude, that sounds serious."

"Not as serious as you being in here."

"Are you gonna lie low for a while? I'm worried about you, brother. I don't want you to get sent away. Please tell me you're going to stop stealing," Damian pleaded.

"Don't worry about me. You just get better and get home," LB said with his classic cool smile that suggested he had everything under control.

Damian watched LB's hand rest on a stethoscope hanging on the wall. LB quickly jerked it down and stuck it into his pocket. LB then busied himself reminiscing with a cousin about their last family camping trip—catching crabs and wallowing in the shin-deep mud pit.

"I hope it's even better this year," LB said.

Damian lit up remembering it all. "Yeah, we were covered from head to toe in mud." The three cousins laughed together.

"Time to get back to the lake everyone," Ann announced to the room and everyone filed out after her, leaving Damian alone again until she returned later.

AFTER THE SURGERY TO REMOVE A PORTION OF Damian's colon, the doctor suggested removing his brain shunt. A shunt had been placed in Damian's brain at birth to remove pressure from his brain and allow for a place for extra fluid to drip out. It appeared during the colon surgery that the shunt was no longer needed, so he suggested a third surgery to remove it.

Quickly after removing the shunt, Damian's brain started pressurizing. A fourth and fifth surgery was done to replace the shunt, and to move the exit of the shunt tube so it wasn't next to his colon.

Three weeks later, Damian was finally ready to leave the hospital. Ann thanked the doctor for helping them finally get an answer for the constant stomach pain.

Before the doctor left the room, Damian asked, "If I'm leaving tomorrow, can I finish my swim season?"

"No, son," the doctor said with compassionate eyes. "Unfortunately, your healing from your surgeries will require you to limit strenuous activity for up to a month."

Damian looked downcast, then asked one more question. "Can I at least go cheer for my teammates?"

"I like your tenacity, son," the doctor said. He smiled and touched Damian's shoulder. "Yes, I'm sure that will be just fine."

As he recovered, Damian returned to school, determined to put the hospital behind him and get back to normal life. He attended every swim meet and became his friends' unwavering cheerleader for the remainder of the season.

Family vacation to Hawaii: (top) Lincoln, Damian and Jacob;
(middle) Damian and Jacob; (bottom) Nikki, Nicole and Damian

FIVE

Growing Pains

SUMMER 1999

. . . .

"Love like there's no tomorrow, and if
tomorrow comes, love again."

—Max Lucado, *Great Day Every Day*

. . . .

LB SAT IN HIS BEST FRIEND'S LIVING ROOM, PLAYING
their favorite racing game.

"You took that turn so fast!" Matt exclaimed. "I can't believe you
beat me again."

"Hey, you have a real car. Let's go try out our killer driving skills."

"Let's do it. My dad and I just got the engine working again."

LB and Matt dropped their video game controllers in the middle
of the living room and ran out to the old blue Toyota truck. LB loved
coming over to Matt's house after school—no parents and no rules.
He was finally rid of that program that had stolen the fun out of his
life with rules for two and half years.

Matt and his dad had been working on the truck for two years now, getting it ready for when he turned sixteen in February. Their birthdays were only five days apart. LB couldn't wait for that day.

Freedom.

The wind whipped through his hair, and he could feel freedom calling, beckoning him to hop in the car and drive.

"I'm the better driver. I'll go first," LB said as he hopped in the driver's seat, started the engine, and waved for his friend to join him in the front seat.

Matt told LB earlier he had been dying to get behind the wheel since they finished it, but his dad was too busy lately.

LB revved the engine three times before putting it into drive. "Let's go." He started slowly down the precarious driveway perched at the top of a steep hill. It was a dirt road, just like the racing game they had been playing minutes ago. LB powerslid around the first corner and gained confidence.

"That was totally awesome, just like the game," Matt said, encouraging his friend.

"I think I can do better. Watch this," LB boasted, getting braver every minute. He drifted around another two corners and slammed the accelerator pedal to the floor. "This is fun."

Matt started to look a little uncomfortable. "Slow down, man. You're going fifty around the corners. I don't want you to crash."

"Hey, I'm a good driver," LB retorted, taking his eyes off the road for a minute to give Matt a good shove. He had slowed just enough to make the wide curve, but they got to it faster than he anticipated. As he looked back to the road, he couldn't act fast enough.

It all happened in slow motion. The truck skidded off the road, he lost control of the wheel, and he heard a giant CRUNCH.

LB had closed his eyes for a minute. As he opened them, everything seemed a bit blurry. Slowly, he focused and saw Matt pinned to his seat by an airbag. They were alive, thank God.

The truck didn't make it. It had bounced off an oak tree, smashing in the whole bed of the truck. But the tree had saved them from falling down the edge of the cliff.

How was he going to get out of this mess?

They both managed to get out of the car and walk to the neighbor's house. LB called Lincoln, who quickly came to their rescue. Back at the house, Lincoln talked to LB about the incident.

"Son, you'll have to replace your friend's car. It's the right thing to do, to take care of your friend," Lincoln explained.

"I'm not doing that." LB spat on the ground in defiance. "He doesn't even care. He told me it was no big deal. It was just an accident."

"It doesn't matter. It was your fault in the end. You were the one driving. You owe the money back that your friend put into that truck. You already have that in savings. I won't let you buy your own car until you make it right with your friend," Lincoln told him. "Before you spend money on yourself, you need to take care of your friend."

ONE YEAR LATER, ANN GRIPPED A LITTLE HARDER ON to the steering wheel she had been white-knuckling for two hours as a semi-truck passed her. Her best friend, Kate, sat in the passenger seat, encouraging her as she drove home from their four-night camping trip at Spirit West Coast.

"You're doing great, Ann. I can't believe this is your first time pulling a trailer. Just keep your eyes on the white line as you go over this bridge, and we're going to be fine," Kate said, a quiver in her voice as though she might be bluffing but wanted to keep them all alive.

Ann took a deep breath to try to relax. "Thanks, Kate. I never would have made it this far without all your encouragement. I'll never forget you standing up for me when we got there and David tried to take over backing in the trailer. I mean, it took me eighteen times back and forth, but you guided me in, and I felt so accomplished afterward. Now I know we can do this every year."

"Count me in. I can't miss your hilarious antics next year. Your sunburn the first day was so bad. And then I've never seen Nicole belly laugh so hard as when you came out with the paper towel flaps over your ears tucked into your hat." Kate chuckled. "You did look outrageous."

"I wasn't doing it for the laughs!"

"But it gave us a good laugh, regardless. I do love being friends with you. I never know what to expect," Kate said. "But I can't wait for a nice hot shower at home. How do you think your boys got along without you?"

"Now that is a tricky question. I'm sure Jacob did just fine. But LB can't seem to stay out of trouble. It's a miracle I didn't get some kind of urgent message from Lincoln about him. I hope they're all fine," Ann answered. She looked in the rearview mirror to check that all the teens were completely passed out. Nicole's chest was moving slowly up and down. They were all exhausted from singing their hearts out and having so much fun together.

"LB has been a load of trouble. How are you handling everything?" Kate asked.

Ann took another deep breath before answering that loaded question. Events flashed through her mind; feelings of pain mingled with confusion. "Where do I even begin with that question? It's been a lot. I mean, I loved him the moment I met him. When he came into my house, I knew he was meant to be in our lives. But I have never been so challenged. It's not even that he gets into trouble; it's that he has no remorse. Anything I say, any consequence we come up with, it all just rolls off of him. He just keeps on doing it without ever thinking about the consequences or how it might make us feel—or anyone else, for that matter. I feel completely lost on how to parent him at this point. I thought he might come back changed from his time away, but he's right back into trouble this whole last year."

"How long was he gone?"

"He spent the better part of two years going through the Rites of Passage program. After the stolen gun incident, the judge wanted to send him to the California Youth Authority—the state's facilities for the worst juvenile offenders—but when Lincoln found this program, the judge relented. I think LB still blames us for having to leave, but it was the court that ordered it—and it was so much better than the alternative. The teens who go to CYA would have been a terrible influence on him—it's like real prison. We saved him from turning into a real hardened criminal.

"Rites of Passage seemed like a good alternative. It's a strengths-based program for juveniles that focuses on rigorous structure, calisthenics, and group counseling. He had to work his way up three levels, starting at the desert location where he had very few privileges and ending in a normal high school experience in South Lake Tahoe where he got to play football. He had to start over at least once, but he finally graduated from the program. We spent lots of hours driving to visit him, but he usually had a pretty poor attitude toward us.

"He told us how much he wanted to come home every time we visited. He said he's not like all the other kids who were there. But I know better than to believe his lies now. He has a way with words and charm. He's such a ham; everyone always falls in love with him, including myself. But I'll never forget the shock of seeing all the stolen goods under his mattress. I never would have believed it if I didn't find it myself—with the police."

"You've really got your hands full there, Ann."

"You can say that again. And now LB's in big trouble again. Seems like one thing after another. A break-in, an explosive, breaking school rules. They kicked him out of school again, and he has another court hearing in a week. I don't even fully know the extent, but something about another parent saying he's a bad influence on their kid after he got expelled. I just wish I could help get through to him. I'm worried about him. Especially after he cut out his best friend, Matt, a while back."

"What happened there?"

"He crashed his friend's car before either of them had a license. We told him that he had to pay to help his friend replace it—it wasn't that much, maybe six hundred dollars. He was angry. He didn't want to. We insisted that he pay Matt from his savings. He had been working at the pizza parlor for a while and had a good amount saved up for his own car. He didn't do it right away, but eventually he paid Matt the money, and that was the last time he ever talked to him. He just cut him out completely, his best friend."

"I wonder why. I mean, that feels so strange. It's not like his friend did anything in the situation."

"He's done it before to other friends too. I think he's afraid of what will happen if he messes up, so he cuts people out before they can do the same to him. His counselor was trying to explain to me that he has 'failure to bond' syndrome. It's caused by so many people early on in his life letting him down. He had people in and out of his life promising to be his mom and dad, just for him to be torn out of their home weeks or months later. He still has never called us Mom or Dad. He has this wall he puts up; he won't let himself get too close to anyone. But the thing I just don't get is how rebellious he is."

"Think of yourself back in your teenage years. You had a bit of a rebellious streak," Kate reminded her. "I still laugh about that hilarious story you told me about throwing up on the church steps after binge drinking with your friends all night. And you felt so bad that you went to the confessional the next day and admitted to the priest that you did it. You weren't even Catholic! And he made you scrub the steps with a toothbrush. The whole story makes me roll in laughter every time."

Ann smirked. "That's true. I was a bit of a rebel."

"You were! And did you have even one thought about how your actions might make your parents feel?"

"Well, no, I don't think so."

"All you thought about was yourself, right?"

"Not at all! Like you said, I apologized to the priest."

"Well," Kate said with a sigh, "regardless, it's a selfish time of life, being a teenager. I'm trying to drive it into my boys' heads too that life is all about choices, and every choice has a consequence, positive or negative. We can mess up, but then we still have choices to make. Every choice we make, every single minute of every single day, affects our future in unknown ways."

"That's the truth."

Nicole peeped an eye open. "Mom, can't we stop yet? I'm famished. And I have to pee."

"Yeah, I'll look for a place to pull over. You're right, Kate. I'm not going to be too hard on him. We all have hard times we have to get through to find ourselves. I just pray he doesn't kill me with stress before it's all over."

"What about Damian?" Kate asked. "You haven't mentioned him at all."

"Oh, Damian. The funny thing is, LB and Damian couldn't be any more different. Damian has always tried to please us and stayed out of trouble, but he lacks ambition and direction. When he was a senior, he waited until the month before graduation to pick out his senior project, which turned out amazing once he chose it, but we had to put some fire under his belt to get him to move on it. He welded a workout bench with his uncle."

"He's been out of high school for a year and hasn't made any effort to get a job or find his way. He's been flunking all his college classes. He sleeps in until noon every day and then just sits around the house. And then he hangs out with this good-for-nothing friend, gambling what little money we give him. I'm at my wits' end with him. I want to support him if he could choose a path, but I don't see him doing that anytime soon. He's too comfortable."

"You're being a little hard on the boy. He does have an intensive medical condition after all. But I hear you. It's hard to see your kids floundering. And even harder to know what to do about it."

"Mom! Pull over. I see an IHOP," Nicole shouted from the back.

"Okay, honey. Does everyone else like pancakes?" Ann asked.

A sleepy chorus of yeses echoed in the back of the suburban.

Ann pulled off and parked at the far edge of the parking lot, pulling through a double spot so she didn't have to back up with the trailer attached. She was relieved to be almost home with the whole ordeal finished. Driving a trailer was more than she bargained for.

The group of girls flooded the restaurant bathroom and then joined Ann and Kate around the large circle booth inside IHOP. Ann ordered a coffee to keep herself alert for the remainder of the journey home.

"Mom, can we make you a concoction like last time? I have some special ingredients I want to add," Nicole said. She exchanged a sideways glance with two of the girls, who looked suspicious, as though they had conspired in the bathroom together.

Ann's eyebrows lifted, and her eyes danced with mischief. A wide grin hovered around the corners of her mouth, and with a broad gesture, sweeping her arms across the table, she announced, "I'll drink anything you come up with." Then her voice lowered to a whisper, and her eyes darted from girl to girl. "See if you can make me gag. Make me your cra-zi-est concoction yet." She shimmied her shoulders as if to taunt the girls.

"This should be good," Kate said, leaning her back against the booth to watch the action.

Nicole started mixing ingredients from the condiment tray, insisting that Ann couldn't watch. She mixed in syrup, hot sauce, a jelly packet, lots of pepper, a squirt of mustard, a bit of Dr Pepper, a splash of milk, coffee, and orange juice. She kept adding to the concoction as food arrived. She stirred the brown goop until it mashed together into a drinkable liquid, then handed it across the table to Ann. The girls around the table giggled.

"Are you really going to drink that, Miss Ann?" one of them asked.

"It has to be disgusting," another said.

Ann took the cup and held it up as if to toast them all. She took one quick glance inside the cup and then gulped the entire contents. She kept a straight face and simply said, "Delicious," without any added expression. She sat calmly licking her lips with no sign of disgust.

"EEWWWW! She really did it! Just like you said, Nicole. Your mom is crazy. She didn't even wince. Did you like it, Miss Ann?"

"Oh yes." Ann laughed, rubbing her hands together. "Make me another."

The girls all howled with laughter. They finished their meal before getting back on the road.

In the car, Kate said, "Oh, Ann, you are too much. How did you drink that disgusting concoction with such a straight face?"

"Yeah, I don't know. That was the worst thing I've ever tasted," Ann admitted, breaking the façade.

"You hid it so well, Mom. That was hilarious." Nicole giggled again.

But the closer Ann drove to home, she felt the sense of fun drain from her and the list of duties and responsibilities cloud her mind once again.

"I'll have to get back to David about if I can lead that Bible study he asked me about," Ann said.

"Aren't you already involved in too many things?" Kate inquired.

"But how can I say no? It's a good thing."

"Well, here's your lesson for the day. Are you ready for this?"

"What?"

"No."

"What?"

"Come on, Ann. Repeat the word. You can do it. No. N-O."

"No??" Ann said quizzically.

Kate laughed at seeing Ann look so uncomfortable. "You say, 'I'm very grateful that you thought of me for this, but I'm going to have to decline.' You don't have to give a reason. You can just say no."

"I can do that??" Ann asked.

"Yes—I mean, *no.*"

"Wow, okay, I think I can do this," Ann said, starting to feel the burden lifting a bit. She imagined herself blowing into her french horn in triumph when she got home. It had been a great four days, so why get worked up about all the future to-dos just yet?

ANN ARRIVED HOME WITH THE TRAILER AND DROPPED everyone off by the late afternoon. Lincoln came out to greet her with a kiss and congratulations on her feat of driving the first time with anything hitched up. Before they went inside, he informed her LB had been caught stealing yet again.

Ann's shoulders drooped as her victory from a moment ago turned to defeat and anguish. "Again? What can we do to get through to him?"

"I haven't figured that one out yet. And not to be the ultimate bearer of bad news, but Damian's latest college grades arrived in the mail. He flunked all his classes again," Lincoln said, his eyes full of wistful sorrow.

"Wow, big news around here to arrive home to. I wish it was good news. I'm at a loss of what to do with both of them. I think it's time to give Damian an ultimatum. He needs some fire to get him motivated. I think we should give him one more month to find a job, or else he needs to move out into his own place."

"That's a little harsh, Ann." Lincoln frowned. "It's not bothering us to have him stay here. We have plenty of room. We can give him more time. I think eventually he will find his way. Maybe we can just give him less of a stipend and not pay for any more college classes, since he obviously isn't taking them seriously."

"I had to figure it out on my own after high school," Ann pointed out. "He should do it on his own too. We've helped him enough as it is. The only thing that will get through to him is a hard-and-fast boundary. I want to help our kids thrive, but I don't think staying here is going to help him."

"You do have a point. He does seem to need that extra push to get him motivated. Let's give him two months at least."

"Fine. You talk to him. He responds better to you."

Ann left Lincoln to do the work of putting the trailer away and got to work chopping vegetables for dinner to get her mind off the troubles.

Lost in thought, she hardly noticed LB jump onto the counter next to the kitchen sink. She almost jumped in fright when she saw him there.

"Why are you sitting there? I don't want to talk to you right now," Ann said to LB, who was perched where they always had their 'talks.' She knew LB loved to sit there while she cooked a meal and talk to her about problems in school or about girls, anything really. She had always enjoyed their talks too, but she was fuming over his constant theft problem right now. "Go outside."

LB just sat there on the countertop, watching her, drinking his glass of water, not saying anything.

"Are you at least sorry for what you did?" Ann asked, hoping to rile him into a response. She busied herself with cutting cucumbers from the garden.

"I don't want to go back into a group home," LB spoke at last, setting his water down on the counter.

Looking up from her slicing, thankful he had finally spoken, Ann asked him, "Is it that bad? What do the guys do there?"

"They are so much worse than me. They're real hardened criminals. They did things like grand theft auto and murder and more," LB said. "I'm just a country kid who stole a few things."

A few things? More like hundreds. Or at least it felt that way. She felt uneasy, remembering how he said something similar when they visited him at his last group home. But he told so many lies; this must just be his cunning way of pulling on her heart strings. She couldn't trust anything he said. "How can I go to sleep at night knowing you're not going to come in and shoot me?" Ann challenged.

LB sat there and grinned.

"You're grinning at me when we're talking about this. That's bad enough," Ann said. "I have to make sure Damian, Nicole, and Jacob are safe. I don't believe you would do anything to hurt them, but you say things to Damian like, 'You think you're so good. You need to come with my friends, and we'll rough you up.' We don't talk like that in our family. I don't want you to go away. But I don't know how to help you get better either. You have to be the one who wants to change."

"You always told me that you care for kids and you want to help kids," LB replied. "You don't care for kids. You just keep kids in your house. You care more about other people's kids than your own."

Ann reeled back at the insult, stunned and unable to say anything for a moment. What did he mean? She cared about him immensely.

With that, LB jumped off the counter and left.

Then Lincoln came in the door.

"I just don't know what we're going to do with him. It never stops." Ann rubbed her temples with her fingertips, exasperated.

"Well, all we can do is show up at court and answer the questions they ask. There's no stopping what's already going to happen. But it does make it difficult to advocate for him the more he continues to break our trust. I can't come up with any consequences we haven't already tried. He already has no privileges as it is."

Ann caught a glimpse of her reflection in the dining room mirror, adjacent to the kitchen. She noticed a few more wrinkles shadowing her forehead and eyes. She hardly recognized the woman staring back at her. Ann had never imagined herself as the mother of a criminal. She had many other roles, but that was not one she had braced herself for.

ONE WEEK LATER, THE CAR PULLED UP TO THE courthouse. No one had spoken the whole way there. They had left the two younger kids with Lincoln's brother, Bart. Lincoln helped Ann out of the car, then Ann hugged LB.

"You know we love you no matter what happens," she whispered in his ear. He acted as though he didn't hear her and turned away from her to walk briskly up the stairs to meet his parole officer at the top. She waved to him anyway as she turned to go into the hearing room where she and Lincoln would speak with the judge first.

Ann shuffled her feet to the front, taking the oath, to tell the truth and nothing but the truth. Happy memories started streaming through her mind, of the times she had stood in a courtroom to officially adopt the boys. She snapped back to reality quickly.

"I see cases like this all the time. You're just like all these other parents. The behavior has to do with how you raised them. This is just another case where you want the court to step in and parent for you," the judge accused. "So let me ask you this, do you have control over LB?"

"I don't understand what you mean," Ann said, raising her eyebrows in question.

"If you tell LB, 'Don't drive the car,' will he drive the car anyway?"

"Yes, he would." Ann shuffled uncomfortably.

"If you tell LB, 'Don't leave the house,' will he wait until you go to bed at night and then leave the house?"

"Yes, he's done that before too."

"So you're telling me you don't have control over him then?" the judge said, looking down at her from his high seat.

Ann glanced at Lincoln. She couldn't lie. How was she supposed to control LB? He was so secretive. He had gotten away with so many things without them knowing. "No, I can't 100 percent say we have him under control."

"Bring him in," the judge ordered.

LB came through a door on the other side of the room in handcuffs. He kept his eyes glued to the floor in front of him without looking up.

The judge spoke to LB. "We've been asking your family some vital questions about how you've been behaving at home. Your parents said they can't control you, so you can't live there."

Ann stood there, flabbergasted. That's not what she had said. "Excuse me, your honor."

"Ma'am, please remain silent."

"Can I—"

"No, you cannot speak right now."

Ann went silent, appalled. *I can't say anything? That's not at all how I said it. I want him in our home. Maybe when he's done talking he will give me a chance to say something.*

"I will honor your family's preference to avoid sending you to California Youth Authority. You are sentenced to Juvenile Hall until a group home becomes available. You are seventeen, young man. I need you to think seriously about how your actions could end you up in prison if you don't change in the next year. You won't have youth on your side much longer."

The parole officer took LB back out the door. Before LB slipped out the door, he turned around, looked at Ann, and stuck his middle finger up in the air as a final salute.

Paralyzed by shock, Ann's feet felt as though they were glued to the ground. It felt like she was living a nightmare. The judge never gave her an opportunity to explain.

Now LB was gone.

SIX

A Time to Mourn

JUNE 2003

. . . .

"He has showed you, O man, what is good. And what
does the Lord require of yor? To act justly and to
love mercy and to walk humbly with your God."

—Micah 6:8 (NIV)

. . . .

ANN SAT AT THE KITCHEN NOOK TABLE WITH HER
sister, Sue, both drinking a cup of coffee in the silence that hangs on
the air in times of grief, in those times that no words seem prudent
enough to break the meaningful silence that cloaks the sufferer in her
thoughts. Simply sitting near one another was enough companionship.
Their brother, Wayne Jr., paced around the house, inside and outside,
unable to sit. And their mother, referred to lovingly as Nana, sat alone
in her room.

Wayne Sr., Ann's father, died of a stroke without warning
yesterday. They all came to sit with their mother in her home in Elk
Grove as soon as they heard. Ann could hear Nicole in the living

room on the telephone. Nicole sounded upset, so Ann picked up the extension in the kitchen to listen.

"You can't miss Papa's funeral. You know how much he loved you. And you loved him. I won't let you miss something so important, LB. You'll regret it forever," Nicole begged her brother on the phone.

"I'm not coming," LB said in an indignant tone.

"I don't care how you feel about Mom and Dad right now. You can sit in the back. It's on Friday at 10:00 a.m. at the church. You know Papa would want you there. You used to golf with him, and you were always his favorite. And I want to see you. I know you're going to do what you want to, but I think you need to be there."

"You will always be my sister, but I can't take a chance of seeing them. I don't want to. Your parents ruined my life. I fucking hate them. I never want to see your piece-of-shit parents again. They are dead to me."

Ann had heard enough. She slammed the phone back onto the receiver and shuddered.

Hot tears stung Nicole's cheek and a catch in her throat threatened to render her unable to speak. "You're wrong, LB. You've always been wrong about them. They love you."

Nicole hung up the phone without waiting for a reply and ran into the kitchen crying. Ann flung her arms around her daughter and stroked her back lovingly.

"How can he be so hateful?" Nicole sobbed. "I couldn't bear to hear him say another word about you. He was horrible on the phone just now."

"It was noble of you to call him to let him know about Papa. I'm sure he's thankful even if he couldn't show it."

"I just wanted him to come. Papa would have wanted him there."

"You did your best." Ann felt a tear stream down her cheek. "I wanted to see him too."

ON FRIDAY MORNING, ANN SAT SHROUDED IN BLACK, her least favorite color to wear, in the brown leather reclining chair and refused to get in the car.

"Ann, we have to go. We can't be late to our dad's funeral," Sue prodded her.

"I don't want to go. I don't like funerals." Ann sat without budging.

"This isn't any funeral; it's Dad's. You have to go. You can't miss it," Sue hissed at her through her teeth.

"Come on, Mom," Nicole pleaded. "What are you doing? You have to go to Papa's funeral. Dad and Jacob are already in the car waiting for us. I know you don't like being sad, but we're all sad together. Just come."

"I just don't want to," Ann said.

At that, Nicole and Sue grabbed her arms and practically dragged her to the door. Finally, Ann stopped resisting and trudged behind them.

No one spoke as Lincoln drove the car expertly to the church. Ann's eyes grew wide when she saw how many cars were already in the parking lot.

Walking into the lobby, Ann didn't recognize any of the faces. She stood close to her mother and whispered, "Mom, do you know all these people?"

"Well, I do know a lot of them, various church people. But there are many faces I've never seen before. Maybe they're just here to help. They said they would do a lunch after the service," Nana said.

Ann held on to her mom's arm, walking her to the family room where they would wait until the beginning of the service, when they would walk down the aisle to the front row.

"How are you doing, Mom?"

"I'm fine, honey, just fine. I'm happy you are all here with me. I couldn't do this alone."

"I still feel so shocked. It was so sudden."

"Me too, honey. But God has His timing for everything. I'm going to miss him. He's been my partner in life for almost fifty years. But I have good friends here to take care of me. Don't worry about me." Nana patted Ann's hands reassuringly.

The pastor signaled it was time for the service to begin. Ann stood and helped her mom. As they walked down the aisle, she scanned the crowd, looking for any sign of Damian or LB. There was no sign of them. She thought for sure Damian would be there. He had said so. Perhaps something delayed him.

The service began like most others, with a song and a teaching from the pastor. Ann's brother, Wayne Jr., read the obituary. Then the pastor opened the floor for anyone to share about her dad.

First, a tall black man walked up to the microphone. Ann nudged her mother and hissed in her ear, "Do you know him?" Nana shook her head.

The man cleared his throat before starting, and wiped a tear from his eye. "Wayne was a man of integrity. He didn't need a pat on the back. He just helped people, because he wanted to help people. When I met Wayne, my family and I were in desperate need. We had just lost our home. He found us on the streets in the winter. He gave us a blanket and a hot meal. He invited us to the church gym to get more help. Wayne helped my family get through our hardest time, and he always had a kind word for us."

As that man walked back to his seat, Ann sat stunned. *My dad helped homeless people? What? Why have I never heard about this? Why would he care about* them?

"Did you know about that?" Ann hissed again in her mother's ear.

Nana again shook her head.

Ann had always thought of her dad as a simple man of few words. She had never heard him talk about helping anyone. She knew his faith was important. He served as a deacon at the church and liked to talk about theology to the pastor. Maybe it was a one-off event.

Next, a woman in shabby, torn clothing stood up and walked to the microphone. "My story is the same. It was just last month, Wayne bought me a nice hot meal. He invited me to church. He found me a new jacket. He was a kind and good man."

Another man stood up to tell of her father's great deeds. "I needed a ride. He picked me up in his red pickup. He talked to me about my faith and invited me to church. I've been here ever since."

Story after story came tumbling out of the strangers in the room about her father's kindness changing their lives. Ann sat, flabbergasted, learning about a whole new side of her father. As she heard story after story, she felt the floodgates tear open. She began crying, not because she was sad, but because it was so beautiful. Her dad had loved people, people she had formerly judged harshly. Her heart began to soften, each story rending open her own heart, making space for newfound compassion. It was as though God ripped the blindfold off her eyes, showing her dad's heart to her. She was too overwhelmed to speak.

As the service ended, Ann remained where she was, stunned, amazed, and thankful for the opportunity to get to know her dad. These strangers seemed to know him far better than she did. A twinge of regret knotted in her stomach. Why hadn't he ever told them?

Nicole's sudden movement jarred Ann back to reality. Nicole squeezed her way through the pew aisle and then sprinted through the crowd, dodging left and right around well-wishers. Ann squinted her eyes to see why Nicole would be exiting so fast, and that's when she saw him. The distinct figure of LB slipped out of the sanctuary. Ann's heart raced as she caught the first glimpse of her son in four years. She breathed heavily and felt the urge to follow Nicole. Without running, she moved as quickly as she could toward the doors.

Ann made it out the door in time to hear Nicole shout, "LB, Damian, come back."

She saw LB hesitate as he opened the passenger door to Damian's car. Damian turned around and waited for Nicole to run up with her arms wide open and capture him in a bear hug. She did the same to LB, hugging him tightly in her embrace.

Ann walked down the steps, hoping for her own chance to hug them, but as soon as Nicole released them, they swiftly hopped into the car and pulled away. Nicole stood waving goodbye. When Ann reached her daughter, she put her arm around her.

Nicole's eyes were glistening. In a voice barely a whisper, she said, "They came."

Ann had too much emotion pulsing through her to speak. She hugged her daughter, then they turned back toward the church to find the rest of the family inside.

The pastor met them first. "Your dad was an amazing man. You must be proud of him."

"I had no idea about any of that," Ann admitted. "He never told us. He never even mentioned any of those things he did. We learned about it today for the first time. Why would he never have told us?"

"He must have taken seriously that verse that says, 'Don't tell your right hand what your left hand is doing.' He wasn't doing it for the credit or the praise of others. He clearly loved God and loved people."

Ann's thoughts raced as the pastor walked away. Who was this man everyone was speaking about? She felt this new knowledge about him, knowing how big his heart was, might change everything inside of her.

SEVEN

Brothers

AUGUST 2005

· · · · · · · · · · · · · · · · · · ·

"Our greatest fear should not be of failure but of
succeeding at things in life that don't really matter."

—Francis Chan, Crazy Love

· · · · · · · · · · · · · · · · · · ·

LB JUMPED INTO THE FRONT SEAT OF DAMIAN'S
burgundy Toyota T-100.

"Man, am I glad to see you. I can't do anything right in that
house," twenty-two-year-old LB said.

"Girl problems again?" twenty-five-year-old Damian asked.

"Yeah, well, I've been thinking about leaving her for a while now.
That's actually why I wanted you to come up. I have an apartment for
us to check out. We've been talking about it forever, but wouldn't it
be great to actually live together again? There's so much potential for
you in Roseville."

"I would like that. It would be nice to be closer to my church.
I started leading worship at the college group. You should come
sometime," Damian said. "Which way to the apartment?"

"Head up past the McDonald's and take a left," LB directed.

Damian leaned over to turn up the radio. "Beverly Hills" by Weezer blasted from the speakers. "Listen to that sick guitar solo."

The car slowed to a stop at the red light. While Damian was jamming out on his air guitar, LB reached over and shifted the car into neutral without Damian noticing.

"I bet you could learn that song in three hours. Hey, the light's green."

As Damian pushed down on the gas, the engine started revving up, as if taunting the car next to him to a race.

"What the . . . ? Are you kidding me? I told you not to mess with my truck, you idiot," Damian said, giving LB a hard shove.

A chorus of honking started up behind him. Flustered, Damian clunked the shaft into drive and pushed the pedal again. Relief flooded him when he started moving forward, and he sped down the road.

"Don't mess with my truck, man. You always mess with me," Damian grunted at LB. He looked over at the passenger seat to see LB laughing uncontrollably.

Wiping a tear from his eye, LB said breathlessly between laughs, "Gets . . . you . . . every . . . time." He took a deep sigh to calm his laughing fit. "You're just too fun to mess with." He grinned with a look of satisfaction, nestled his head into the headrest and said to himself, "Nothing better than poking the bear."

Damian didn't talk again until they reached the apartment. He questioned if it was actually a good idea to live with LB, the constant prankster and troublemaker. He thought about all the trouble LB had gotten him into when they were kids, in the name of "fun." LB had a different idea of fun than Damian.

"Come on, man, it was just a joke," LB said as Damian parked the car. "Wow, isn't this a nice part of town?"

Damian nodded, taking in the neatly planted rows of trees and a Mercedes-Benz parked on the street. It was a few short blocks from a shopping complex with an upscale grocery store and small restaurants.

The brothers walked up the steps to meet the apartment manager. From the outside, it looked like a major upgrade to Damian's current living situation—a small apartment with two roommates in Marysville, in a less-than-nice part of town. He had been in the same place since his parents gave him the ultimatum about moving out. Always a procrastinator, he had waited until the last minute and found the only place available for the price he could pay with a few acquaintances from high school.

The inside is nice too, Damian thought. This apartment boasted a newly remodeled kitchen, large bedrooms, eleven hundred square feet total, and a balcony overlooking the pool below. It felt like a dream apartment.

Damian hadn't lived with his brother since LB left in his junior year over five years ago. It was funny, he thought to himself, LB never came back to Ann and Lincoln's, and Damian had tried to never leave. He would still be happily perched in his upstairs room if they hadn't forced him out. He preferred to be comfortable and not take too many risks—the opposite of his brother. Then again, he wasn't sure if LB ever calculated the risks or if he just acted on a whim.

"Do you think we can afford it?" Damian asked as they walked back down the steps from the apartment, both of them giddy with the possibility.

"If we split it, definitely. Have you seen the house I'm renting right now?" LB replied.

"Well, yeah, but I don't make much working at Walmart." Damian uneasily watched his brother's reaction out of the corner of his eye. Although his brother was younger, he had a way of making him feel less than. LB got the looks, the charm, the natural way with people. He exuded a confidence that Damian never experienced himself.

And there was the little problem about him hating Mom and Dad. Damian wanted to keep his relationship with Ann and Lincoln strong, and LB could threaten that.

"Well, getting more money is why you're starting college classes, right?" LB said, reaching the car before Damian. "And there's so many more job opportunities over here. Let's go to our favorite spot."

"Yeah. I'd like to see Mario more too. Have you seen him lately?" Damian shifted gears and drove toward Chili's—deemed "their spot" for years now.

"I saw him a few weeks ago," LB told him. "He kept telling me about how hard it was to get to work on the bus, and I asked him why he didn't drive. The folks he used to live with scared him—said it was way too dangerous. Well, I bought an old beat-up car for him. I told him he had to get out and live. But he can't get anywhere because he's too afraid. I don't know if he will ever touch the car I put in the garage for him, but at least he has it."

Damian studied LB for a moment, wondering at the man who sat beside him making this big, kind gesture. Where did that come from? Was LB different than how he had slated him? Or did he steal the car to give to Mario? "That was real big of you. Mario's a good guy. He needs the encouragement."

Inside Chili's, they started making plans for their new place. What furniture would look good? How soon could they move in?

When the waitress came around, LB gave her a charming smile. "I'll have a twelve-ounce steak with potatoes and a rootbeer."

"I'll have the same," Damian said, bobbing his head and body in his goofy manner.

"Good choice, Damian. When you love something, you stick to it. Steak and potatoes is all I ever need," LB said. He kissed his fingers and sat back into the booth with satisfaction on his face.

"So tell me about Brooke. Are you sure you're ready to leave her? You've been with her more than two years now," Damian said, reaching to take a sip of his rootbeer.

"Yeah, and I should be in love with her after that long, but I'm not. I love her kids. I've been trying to raise them as my own. But I think she might be cheating on me," LB told him.

Their food arrived, and LB thanked the waitress, then continued, "I wanted to make a difference in her kids' lives and give them a father figure. But now I'm just in the relationship for the kids, and it's already gone on too long like this. I mean, I can't believe I already wasted two years on her. I gotta get out. That's part of why I want to make this apartment thing work, with you."

Brooke hadn't worked since the day LB started dating her. Her kids had been five and three back then, and LB wanted her to spend her time with them to give them a good childhood. He had rented a big house with a backyard for all of them to live together—it was big of him. But working three jobs barely covered rent and food. Damian knew that LB had recently suggested Brooke get a part-time job since the kids were in school now. Damian got the feeling the suggestion hadn't been taken well.

"So how are you going to break the news to her?" Damian asked.

"I'll just tell her I'm leaving. It's over," LB said. He dug his knife into his steak and brought a juicy bite to his lips but squinted at Damian before he took his bite. "Do you think you'll be able to cover the deposit? I don't have much saved up."

Truth be told, they both knew LB needed Damian's agreement to the apartment secured because he couldn't save up enough for the first and last month's rent on top of what he was already paying to support himself, Brooke, and two kids. He needed Damian's help to get out of this situation. It was a lot to weigh on Damian's shoulders, seeing as he had been living paycheck to paycheck himself. But LB didn't know how bad Damian's own living situation was, barely scraping by to afford his meals most of the time. His embarrassment about the situation kept him silent. He would try to work something out.

"I should have enough to cover it," Damian said. "Mom and Dad would probably help out if we need it."

"Yeah, they might give *you* money. Or better yet, you could ask Nicole or Jacob to ask for it. Even if they would give me money, which I'm sure they wouldn't, I don't want help from them," LB retorted with a mouthful of red meat. He almost spat it out, obviously disgusted by the idea.

"You know they still love you," Damian said with compassion in his eyes.

"Don't lie to me," LB shot back, looking away and starting to get angry.

"They ask me about you all the time. They would love a phone call, even a letter. You could finally ask them all the questions you've been wanting to ask them—why they didn't speak up at the court hearing, why they never believed you, why they didn't try harder when they knew how stupid the reason was you were getting sent away," Damian said. "It has been five years, you know."

"What's the point? They won't have any good answers. They never loved me anyway. They just shipped me off and made me someone else's problem. They gave me away to the system, after promising they never would. They are terrible, and they'll never understand me."

Damian knew LB thought they had robbed him of his childhood by sending him from one program to the next, that they didn't fight for him when they could have. Damian saw things differently now, but LB never listened when he tried to speak up about it. As a boy, Damian had always agreed on a surface level about feeling different than Jacob and Nicole. But his relationship with Lincoln now proved to him how much they loved him. He didn't agree with LB, but he also couldn't find a voice to speak otherwise. He desperately wanted LB to give them another chance. But how would he convince him?

LB raised his voice. "Don't tell them anything about me. They don't deserve to know about my life. They're as good as dead to me. I've moved on, and they should too."

Not wanting to make a scene or disagree publicly with his brother, Damian said, "You're right. Let's get you home."

THE NEXT DAY, DAMIAN DROVE THE PLEASANTLY familiar country roads to Ann and Lincoln's for dinner. He thought about sneaking away to the oak tree that couldn't be seen from the house, which was once his place of safe refuge. Anytime he felt unsure about a life decision or felt change pulling at him, he loved to go there. He could talk to God better there, away from all the distractions.

He had been praying for all his brothers' salvation since the day God became real to him. But nothing ever seemed to get through to them. Living with LB could be the difference maker. Maybe sitting in that old tree would help things become clear.

As Damian parked at the top of the hill, he glanced at the clock and saw he had just enough time to sneak off before being noticed.

Damian grabbed his guitar, followed his feet to his favorite oak tree, and took a seat on the grassy knoll underneath. He glanced out at the horizon, an expansive view. Here, he felt he could breathe easy, under no one's scrutiny and taking in the beauty. He felt God's presence in a powerful way. His thoughts soon turned to moving in with LB. He had some reservations, but it could be the very opportunity he had been praying for. He started to strum his guitar and allow his mind to relax, to open himself up to what God might speak. Slowly, he began to feel calm and confident.

When Damian reemerged for dinner, he strode confidently toward the house, ready to tell them all the big news about moving in with LB. A flurry of energy whirled around the kitchen. Since he had moved out, Ann and Lincoln had opened their home to countless other teens and young adults who needed a landing pad to break away from their home life. It seemed everyone had chosen tonight to come for dinner. Nicole, who was home visiting from college with her friend, Nikki; Tiffany and Shannon, who had been living there; and the current upstairs resident, Garry Bradley, all sat on stools or stood around the outskirts of the kitchen. Ann's best friend, Kate, stood in the kitchen attempting to help.

Garry was loudly recounting the story of the day. "This lady is crazy," he said, pointing wildly at Ann.

"Oh, did you go to town with her?" Lincoln asked.

"Yes, the biggest regret of my life. She says she has to go to town and get this list of things. It's only maybe twenty items long, so I thought, *Sure, I'll go with you.* Big mistake. We went to the first store—Sam's Club—and got five items, then she said, 'Okay, let's go to the next place.' We drove all the way across town to another grocery store—WinCo—to get three things. I looked at her list and said, 'Why can't you get those things at this store?' 'Oh, they don't have the brand I like.' We went to Bel Air for those things. Then she said, 'Okay, let's go to Save Mart.' 'Are you crazy, lady? What do they possibly have there that all these other stores don't?' 'Paper towels.' 'Paper towels?' 'Yes, I like the pattern on their paper towels.' Then, you won't believe it. In the end, we had to go back to Sam's Club. She said, 'Well, you have to get the frozen stuff at the end.' She is insane."

Most people were laughing by now, while Lincoln said, "Yes, and this is why I love her. I love her adorable, *very* particular ways of doing things."

Kate leaned over to whisper to Ann, "So where do you get your paper towels from?"

To Kate, Ann said, "It depends on my mood." To everyone else, she declared, "Dinner's ready. Everyone grab hands, and Lincoln will say grace."

After grace, Ann said, "Damian, it's a pleasure to have you for dinner tonight. What have you been up to?"

Damian loved coming for family dinners. The food, for one, was far superior to his typical bachelor pad fare. The company was good too. The first time he had realized how much he valued his home here was when he left to work at a summer camp. It had been his first time going off on his own, and it helped him realize the great life he had been blessed with. When he had brought all his summer camp counselor friends home, they couldn't believe he lived in such a great place. And they had loved his parents. They said he was lucky to have folks like that, as theirs were not as welcoming. This made Damian realize how some time away from LB helped him disagree with his negative opinions about home more easily. They slept on the trampoline watching the stars, Damian filled with greater appreciation and love for his parents, and greater hesitation toward his brother.

Damian typically shied away from the spotlight in larger groups but took the opportunity to tell his parents his update while he had their attention. "Well, I was with LB yesterday looking at apartments."

"Oooh, yes, family drama. He's the guy we don't talk about," Garry chipped in.

"We're going to move into an apartment together in Roseville," Damian said, ignoring Garry.

"Oh, really? How soon?" Ann asked. "How is he doing?" She looked wistfully at Lincoln, as though she had much to say. Lincoln returned her meaningful glance.

"Hopefully in the next two weeks." Damian didn't pick up any hints of disapproval so he bravely continued. "I feel like I could use the change. And it will get me closer to the church I've been going to. The young adults group is great. I'm leading worship next week, if you want to come. Anyway, I want to start looking for a new job, and maybe even take some college classes. It's so hard. I feel like I work all the time and never get ahead." He ignored the question about LB, not wanting to betray his brother. He was starting to feel doubts creeping in about whether or not it would be good for his relationship with his parents if he moved in with LB.

"College, that's wonderful. What line of work are you thinking of getting into?" Lincoln's face melted into a wide grin with twinkling eyes.

Damian glanced at Ann, who seemed distracted by her own thoughts.

"Well, I think I might try the nursing route like Nicole. I'd like to work on an ambulance first, so I think I'll just start with becoming an EMT, and then see what happens," Damian said, shrugging his shoulders up and down while his body shifted left and right.

"Well, you know the offer still stands, if you find a program you want to start we are happy to pay for it. We will cover room and board too. I'm happy to support your goals." Lincoln lowered his voice and turned toward him with caring eyes. "Do you think your Crohn's can handle those long shifts?"

Damian's last job of ironworking had worn him down to a thread. Crohn's could be painfully debilitating and drained his energy. The constant cloud looming over him was being close enough to a bathroom in case he had a painful bout. He had lost several jobs already because of his Crohn's. Employers just didn't understand.

"I'm going to try," was all Damian managed.

Kate, who worked as a hospice nurse, encouraged him, "I think that's very admirable, Damian."

"Speaking of EMTs, I think our dog may be pregnant," Ann said.

Damian deflated and looked down at his plate. Ann had a habit of abruptly changing conversation topics out of nowhere, but it hurt that she didn't care to ask him more questions like Lincoln had. Even her friend had paid him a compliment. She didn't even acknowledge him wanting to take this next step.

"Really?" Nicole piped up. "We get to cuddle puppies!"

"I have no clue how you got a correlation between puppies and EMT. That was from left field. But one thing I think we can all agree on is this blackberry trifle is begging us to dig in," Kate said, bringing a crystal-fluted pedestal bowl with mounds of cake and blackberries to the table. As she served up dessert, she asked Nicole, "How is college going? Making any new friends?"

"I enjoy the girls I live with. We've been playing pranks on each other," Nicole said, starting a belly laugh before she got the story out. "After one of our roommates kept pranking us. We printed hundreds of photos of her doing ridiculous things and put them all over the house. Every time she finds one, she curses us. It's hi-lar-ious." A giggle fit came over Nicole and her friends at the table.

After dinner, Ann announced, "Let's head to the living room. I want Damian to play for us."

"I'd love that," Kate declared.

Garry retrieved his guitar too and strummed along in the background. Damian played several Red Hot Chili Peppers songs. Then a few worship songs. Then began tinkering on that new song he had heard on the radio, remembering a few of the chords. He had an uncanny knack for being able to listen to a song and pluck at the guitar until he strummed out the tune. He had never learned to read sheet music, but he had an ear for it.

"Play another," Ann encouraged. Damian knew how much his mom loved music.

The evening passed pleasantly for all. Damian smiled, seeing everyone enjoying his music. *Maybe things will finally turn around,* he thought. He played until his fingers ached.

When he was finished, Ann looked at the clock. "Hey, everyone. It's time for *House,* our favorite show. Stay and watch with us, Damian."

Everyone gathered around to watch the latest drama on their favorite medical show. Nicole periodically explained that something really did or did not happen like that in the hospital. Ann simply sat, enthralled.

After the show finished, Damian went shopping in the pantry for his favorite snacks. He found some Nutter Butters and Ruffles. They always kept it well stocked. He eyed the dusty case of Mug root beer tucked into the corner of the pantry, recognizing it instantly as LB's favorite brand. He smiled and grabbed one to take to LB later. Then he grabbed a box of macaroni and cheese and ramen.

When he turned to leave, he saw Ann watching him from the kitchen.

"Before I go, Ann," Damian stammered, "I did need to ask if you might be able to help me with the last month's rent to get this apartment. Things are a little tight right now, and I'd really like to make this move."

"It's always about the money, isn't it, Damian? Every time you come here, you ask us for money. It makes me wonder if you actually come to see us or just to get what you need. LB never comes around asking us for money. Are you planning to get a better job if you move down there until your EMT stuff works out?" Ann asked.

"That's the goal," Damian said, trying to stay upbeat and not show her he was affected, though he shifted uncomfortably under her scrutiny. He stood there a moment, wishing he could earn her love, but it seemed nothing he did was ever enough. Why couldn't she see how hard it was for him? Didn't she realize how much he suffered? "Well, I'd better get going. Bye, Mom."

When he got back to his car, he checked his cell phone. He had a missed call and voicemail from LB. *That's strange*, he thought as he pressed play.

"Hey, big brother. It's not going to work out after all for the apartment. Brooke just told me she's pregnant."

Backyard kickback 2007 with LB, Damian, Mario, and Larry

Damian with his friends from Wolf Mountain camp on
trampoline at Ann and Lincoln's

EIGHT

A Call to Fast

JANUARY 2008

. . . .

"I can see how it might be possible for a man
to look down upon the earth and be an atheist,
but I cannot conceive how a man could look up
into the heavens and say there is no God."

—Abraham Lincoln

. . . .

DAMIAN SAT DOWN IN HIS OVERSIZED, GRAY,
corduroy chair with a sigh of relief that his shift was over. Damian
had lived alone in this apartment for just over a month, and it was
still sinking in that he wouldn't see anyone walk through the door. It
took him two years to move out after the apartment fell through with
his brother.

He had just finished his shift at Walmart and walked home,
enjoying the gray of the January day. The anxiety in his gut started
rising as he sat there, unsure what to do next. Usually, he would have
picked up a McDonald's double-double and strawberry milkshake on
his way home, but this was the second day of his fast.

His pastor implored the church members to participate in a forty-day fast. At the first mention of a fast, Damian perked up, eager to participate. Just two months earlier, he completed a seven-day, water-only fast for the first time. He felt God's presence more powerfully than ever before. And a secondary bonus that he had not expected—the gut issues that had plagued him since he was a twelve-year-old boy had subsided for that week. He could not remember ever feeling better. With no food being processed by his colon, the constant rumbling and aching had stopped altogether. He had even listened to his pastor's advice to stop taking his Crohn's medications and trust God to heal him. Forty days of relief had been so motivating. But this fast seemed different. His body felt weak and achy, not quite the feeling of relief he felt before.

He picked up his guitar to play his favorite Red Hot Chili Peppers song. Maybe that would help him forget his empty stomach. Suddenly, a worship song seemed to overtake him as he strummed. Worship filled the room. He sensed God's presence as he called out to Him.

God, I know you're with me in this. Help me to overcome my hunger. I am hungry for more of you. I want to be used by you. Here I am; use me. Use my life to bring glory to you. Take my life into your hands. I want to do your will. My life doesn't look exactly how I had hoped, but I love my relationship with you. Help me find a way to reach my brothers for you and bring more people into your kingdom. Whatever it takes, I'm all in.

Damian felt a sense of peace come over him. As he sat listening for God's voice, he felt he heard, "*Trust me,*" over and over again. He got the sense his prayers would be answered, but not in any conventional way. Regardless, God would use his life somehow to reach the people he cared about most.

A sense of purpose and clarity inspired Damian to get up and do his nightly workout routine. He had a full set of weights on his patio, including a bench press he had welded with his uncle in high school as part of his senior project. On the way out to the patio, he glimpsed the photo of the summer crew he had worked with for three years at Wolf Mountain Camp. Those summers had been the happiest of his life. He lingered a minute at the frame, remembering how he felt he could truly be himself with all those people. At camp, he felt that he belonged, he had a purpose, and he was loved. Being a camp counselor was the first time in his life he had felt close to God.

After his workout, Damian hit the sack. He looked forward to meeting Lincoln early in the morning for their weekly check-in breakfast date, even though he wouldn't be eating this time.

As the sun's golden streaks broke the darkness, Damian hopped into the red 1995 Toyota his parents had given him after his last car broke down. It sputtered a few times before starting. He needed to get it to the mechanic, but he had been delaying maintenance on his car until he could finish the payments for his last stint in the hospital. Since the night after his sister's wedding in June, he had been hospitalized three times. His Crohn's disease had been flaring up more than ever. His doctor had explained that his body was telling itself to respond to an issue that didn't exist, which resulted in an overreaction that caused constant diarrhea. Except lately, his intestines had stopped up completely, not letting anything escape the colon blockage. The pain in his gut was often crippling.

During his third hospitalization, the doctor ordered colon surgery and insisted he start a higher level of medication. Remicade required him to go weekly to the hospital for an IV infusion, but it seemed to be a good solution. It had kept him out of the ER for at least three months now, but he was a little worried about the long list of side effects, including heart failure, seizures, blood disorders, and liver damage. The one thing for which he was thankful about working at Walmart was the good insurance. It paid for most of his hefty medical expenses. But the leftover expenses left him wondering if he could afford each meal, let alone car malfunctions.

HE PULLED INTO DENNY'S—THE PLACE THEY HAD been meeting weekly for the last year. It was during this time he finally realized how lucky he was to have his dad. Until recently, he had never needed his dad's wise, reassuring words or recognized how his dad's patient demeanor helped bring calm to his racing thoughts.

"Damian. Good to see you. You look a little yellow," Lincoln said as he embraced him in his strong, enveloping arms. "You look thin too."

"Dad, I have so much to tell you. I started another fast. God is teaching me so many things," Damian said, still feeling energized from his time with God last night.

"Slow down, Damian. Let's get seated, and I want to hear all about it," Lincoln said.

After ordering water for both of them, Damian began to share everything on his heart. "Remember how I did that seven-day fast back in November? I felt God's presence so tangibly, like never before. And my body felt so good too. I had so much peace. Pastor Daniel is calling the whole church to do a forty-day fast. I'm doing a water-only fast for forty days. This is my third day."

"I don't know if Pastor Daniel was necessarily talking about a water-only fast." Lincoln's eyes seemed to probe Damian. "That seems like a really long time to not eat food at all. Can you survive that long on water alone?"

"Well, Jesus fasted for forty days. Why can't I?" Damian pointed out. "I feel like a breakthrough is coming. I want to hear what God has for my life."

"I can't tell you how you need to spend your time with God. That's between you and God. A forty-day fast seems extreme, but if you're feeling called to do that, I can't argue. I would recommend, given your physical state before going into it, you might want to at least go through this fast together with a doctor so they can keep an eye on you. You've had a rough six months of health issues," Lincoln said.

Standing at six-foot-three, and built to be a lineman, Lincoln's large presence filled the entire booth. Damian noticed the look of compassion in his father's azure eyes, seeming to pierce through to the innermost parts of his soul.

"But that's just the point," Damian argued. "I feel so good when I'm fasting. It gives my body a break." He didn't want to be tracked constantly. He wanted to escape his health issues and pretend he was normal, for once. Besides, God would take care of him. He was doing this for God, wasn't he?

"You look worn out, son. More worn out than I've seen you in a while. It doesn't look to me like this fast is helping your health. And your eyes seem to have a yellow tint." Lincoln paused and took a sip of his coffee. "Last time you felt good because during a fast your system is not digesting any food. It is giving your colon and bowels a break, but it's not necessarily fixing or helping the problem. At least reach out to a doctor and tell him what you're doing. You gave us all a scare on the night of Nicole's wedding."

Damian had left the wedding looking ghastly pale to go to the hospital. Another flare-up had hit. "The wedding was beautiful," Damian reflected. "I'm glad I got to be there, even though I had to leave."

"Yes, we can always thank God for those beautiful blessings. We were glad to see LB that day too. It seemed hard for him to see us, but we loved seeing his baby boy, Raphael," Lincoln agreed.

After staying away for seven years, LB made his first appearance back with the family just to support Nicole. He told Damian over and over again that he wouldn't talk to Ann or Lincoln; he wouldn't even look at them. They had tried to approach him once, but he had just stared off into the distance. LB told Damian that having a baby had given him even more justification to stay away from them.

Damian couldn't understand how LB could view his parents so differently than he did. When they were younger, they had always felt different, being the adopted kids, but Ann and Lincoln were nowhere close to the villains LB made them out to be. Ann had her moments when she didn't treat Damian very well, especially after he moved out. But Lincoln cared enough to meet him weekly to encourage him in life and hear his dreams.

"I just wish I could get through to LB—and Mario. I want them to know God like I do. I want all my brothers to feel the peace of God's presence. I just can't ever seem to get through to them. I told God I would do whatever it takes to open their eyes to Him," Damian said. "I had a dream that God would somehow use me to be a part of their salvation."

"I love your heart for your brothers. Prayer is our most powerful tool," Lincoln told him. "But be careful what you ask for. God just might take you up on your offer."

Be careful? Damian hadn't thought it might be dangerous to follow Christ. Little did he know God's answer was coming quickly, and it would require him and everyone involved to trust God to be God.

"I'm willing to do what it takes," Damian said confidently.

"Damian, as we've been sitting here, I keep noticing that your skin and even your eyes have a yellow tint. It looks like jaundice. I think you should get checked out by your doctor. You might even need to go into the ER," Lincoln said with a little more urgency in his voice.

"I'm fine, Dad. I feel totally fine," Damian assured him as he stood up to leave, a hunger growl escaping his stomach. "Thanks for coming down to meet up. I always enjoy our time together."

A FEW DAYS LATER, DAMIAN FELT A LITTLE OFF BUT
wanted to go down to Roseville for his brother's birthday anyway.
Ignoring his father's advice, he kept telling himself that God would
take care of his body. He was doing this for God, after all.

When he got to Mario's place, he had to lie down on the couch
before he could join the celebration out back. It had become a regular
part of his life, coming down to join his brothers for a kickback
BBQ on the weekends. Although they hadn't been able to grow up
together in the same household, once they became adults, there was
a brotherly bond that drew them together and bolstered them up to
face the world. His birth parents lived in the garage, but they were
usually too high to recognize him. They kept trying to tell him they
had stopped, but he couldn't be fooled when he found needles on the
counter every time he came.

He slid the back glass door open and joined his three brothers
around the small fire pit.

"Damian, glad you could make it, man. You look yellow. Are you
feeling okay?" LB asked with concern.

"Everyone keeps saying that. I'm fine," Damian said. He sat in
the chair closest to LB and folded his arms coolly.

"You sure? You might need to go get checked out," LB said. He
stood up to get a closer look at Damian.

"Okay, okay, let me hang out a minute," Damian said, swatting at
him like a pestering fly.

"Hey, Damian. Why don't you relax. Just have a drink," Milo
said, trying to hand him a beer.

Milo's chiseled figure and bulging arm muscles protruded out
of his white ribbed tank even as he slouched in his chair. Of the
four brothers, Milo was born the biggest at a whopping ten-and-a-
half pounds, so he got the nickname the Hulk. He seemed to have
superhuman strength.

"No way, man. You know I don't drink," Damian said.

"Why?" Milo asked, making himself big, as if to scare Damian into drinking. Milo's bullying side seemed to kick in when they were drinking. He seemed to have several sides to his personality.

"I never have, so I'm not starting today. And I'm doing a forty-day fast. I've been worshiping and feeling Jesus's presence." Damian wasn't afraid of Milo, and he was running strong on conviction.

"Oh, come on, Damian," Mario scoffed, joining the conversation. "What happened to the funny Damian that was quoting *Anchorman* to me last weekend? And no, you still can't be friends with it." Mario laughed long and loud at himself.

"No, I'm serious, man. God is real. God showed me he had plans for me, and that you would one day know Him too. I just pray I'll see that day," Damian said, ignoring the jab Mario tried to use to deter him.

"That's fine for you, Damian," LB chimed in. "It's not for me."

"Yeah, I'm good on it too." Mario crossed his arms and slouched back in his chair. "My aunt killed me on religion. They forced me to go to Catholic church every week with them, but it just felt so hypocritical. My uncle would be whispering in my ear about all the people he arrested, calling them names. I couldn't stand it. It's like, you gotta walk the walk or it's all talk. I even sang in the choir because my aunt was the choir director. I mean I'm grateful for their help in my life, but they were so controlling—like do you even trust the God you say you believe in?"

"It could be for you," Damian said, desperate to break through to them. He felt a sense of urgency, like this could be his last chance to convince them. *What a strange thought.* He would likely be there next weekend too. "God welcomes everyone."

"Dude, I've asked God for so many things, and everything I ever asked God to do didn't happen," Mario argued.

"I agree with Mario. All the Christians I know are hypocrites. Look at Ann and Lincoln," LB said.

Milo butted into the conversation, "Yeah, Ann and Lincoln kicked me out when they couldn't handle me. They did the same thing to LB when he didn't fit the program anymore."

LB stood up and started pacing. "They did more than that. They preached at us all those years that we were their kids, just the same as Jacob and Nicole. But they never loved us the same as them. They forced us to go to church and do all that stupid volunteer stuff. And they never trusted us. I wasn't allowed to go to my friends' houses. I wasn't allowed to have a life or just be a kid. They kept me boxed up on the hill, and then when I acted out because I was so damn bored, they shipped me away to be someone else's problem. They didn't even try to bring me back home. They gave me away just like our own damn folks. They always helped all these other people's kids and made themselves look so perfect to all the church people, and they never even tried to understand me."

"Sure, Ann and Lincoln weren't perfect," Damian conceded. "They made, and keep making, mistakes. I used to think that all Christians were hypocrites too. But God uses broken people to do his will. The church is a place for broken people like them, and you and me. Look, it's hurting you more to hold on to all that bitterness from the past than it's hurting them. It's time to forgive them, brother. It's time to forgive yourself too. I've forgiven them, and Lincoln has gone out of his way to help me time after time. God wants you to turn to him and heal all your hurt. God loves you more than you can fathom, and he will never let you down like they did."

"Forgive them?" LB spat on the ground. "Yeah, right."

Damian pressed on. "Remember how we used to talk about how we didn't feel like we belonged anywhere when we were growing up? I've heard God whisper to me that I belong. When I worship, I get this overwhelming sense of how much he loves me. For real. You have to forgive Ann and Lincoln, forget the past, and move on—with God at your side."

"I've learned from the past that I can trust no one," LB said emphatically. "But listen. Let me drive you to the hospital. You look awful."

BLINKING INTO THE BRIGHTNESS, DAMIAN OPENED his eyes to the familiar dots on the ceiling. The beeping told him he was hooked to an IV and the machine that was reading his vitals. He glanced out the window, seeing the steeple of the Catholic church and the city below. From up here it looked like a quaint, quiet town, but he knew better than to let the beauty of the view fool him. It was the type of town no one wanted to be from. The streets were dirty, the homeless overpopulated, and the highway raced through the middle with run-down empty buildings lining it.

He hadn't expected to be in the hospital again. It felt like he had been there a week, but maybe it was just a few days. Time seemed a little fuzzy at the moment. So did everything else. No one seemed to know why his liver was flaring up.

Lincoln and Ann walked through the door of his hospital room, a welcome sight for Damian.

"Hi, thanks for coming," Damian said euphorically, almost as if he were in a trance.

IS HE HIGH? ANN THOUGHT TO HERSELF. WHY DID HE sound so funny? This was not the Damian she had seen at Christmas dinner a few weeks ago. He had talked excitedly about passing his first EMT course and had shined with a new spark of ambition for the first time in years, possibly ever. He had been a good kid growing up, but certainly lacked the go-getter spirit of her other children. He typically chose to slide down the easiest path. She was certainly tired of him asking for money every time he came home. She did have to admit she was growing tired of his lack of motivation and follow-through over the last several years. But maybe becoming an EMT would be the right path for him. It seemed fitting for him to help others out in a medical crisis, given his growing number of incidents that had landed him in the hospital lately.

"Are you taking me home? I need to eat my cat. Why is there a rabbit over there?" Damian stumbled through the words.

"What are you talking about, Damian?" Ann asked, confusion clouding her mind. "There's no rabbit in here."

The doctor strode into the room then. His large and sudden presence startled Ann.

"Hi, thanks for coming," Damian repeated in the same monotone manner.

"Why is he acting so funny?" Ann demanded of the physician. "I think he's hallucinating."

"We've pinpointed the liver as the cause of his symptoms. But next to that, the tests we have run all came back negative. The nurses said this morning a small case of delirium had begun. The toxins building up in his bloodstream are unable to be processed by his liver, so the toxins are flowing to his brain, causing his confusion. Ammonia of the brain is one of the signs of liver failure progression," the doctor explained.

"So what are you doing for him?" Ann asked.

"My team has tested him for every bacterial infection and viral infection related to the liver. None of these have produced any results," the doctor told her.

"Is it the Remicade?" Lincoln inquired.

"We are looking into his medications now to see if any of those caused this type of reaction," the doctor said. "My latest theory is autoimmune hepatitis, where your own body sets up an immune response and begins attacking the liver. There is no test to tell us that, but with all the other tests running negative, that theory could prove to be true. We will keep you informed as we have more information. For now, we have been giving him steroids to try to calm down the immune response, if that is the case."

"Did he tell you about his fast?" Lincoln brought up. "Have you gotten him nutrition? He started a water-only fast last week. I asked him to get checked out by a doctor before beginning, but I have the feeling he didn't."

"I don't think he mentioned that. They have fed him, but I will ask the nurses to get him a well-rounded meal and pump some vitamins into his IV."

"We're leaving this afternoon for an overnight stay. Do you think he will be okay until Wednesday? We hate to leave him alone," Ann said.

"We can cancel the trip. Damian is more important than anything else," Lincoln said.

"Don't bother canceling your trip. Rest assured we will let you know if anything progresses that you should be aware of," the doctor said as he bowed out of the room.

Ann turned her attention to Damian. "Damian, did you want anything extra special to eat? You look so pale. We can grab you anything you like."

"Hi, thanks for coming," Damian repeated in that far-off voice.

"Damian, I'm asking you a question." Ann sounded exasperated. "Oh, never mind. Damian, we will be back in two days."

"Ann, this is our son," Lincoln said worriedly. "I think we should consider canceling. This could be really serious."

"Won't the doctor just tell him to eat and then he will be released like all the other times he's been in the hospital?"

"I don't know. This could be different. Search your heart, Ann. Think of how Damian feels."

Ann reflected on what Damian had told her before. He hated to be in hospitals. She imagined herself in his place, being left alone, and suddenly reconsidered. She felt a twinge of guilt for wanting to leave him.

"You're right. I've been selfish," Ann admitted. "We don't have to go."

"I know how badly you want to. I know you've been looking for another way to get plugged into ministry. I'll give them my cell number to reach us if anything changes. Let's pray with him before we go." Lincoln grabbed hold of her hands. "Lord, we know you have Damian in the palm of your hands. Grant us your peace in our hearts that we might feel your reassuring presence. May your insight and wisdom be revealed to the doctors as they investigate his condition."

"WE ARE RUSHING HIM BY AMBULANCE TO SAN FRANCISCO."
Click.

Lincoln looked over at Ann, who was deep in conversation with a random fifteen-year-old at camp about God, eating a cookie dough whirly. He knew he should leave immediately to be there when the ambulance arrived, but he lingered one more minute, enjoying the serenity of the tall pine trees and the buzzing of excited teenagers. On the deck of the Sugar Barrel at Woodleaf, he could look out over the entire camp. The large stretch of immaculate green lawn hosted ultimate frisbee players, a soccer game, and a couple of girls basking in the sunshine. Pairs of people sat on benches, near the pool and under the shade.

Their friend had brought them there to visualize the ministry of Young Life—to see the teens with their leaders in action—so that they might get involved. Ann had a heart for kids, and they did have a teenage son, so it seemed to be a good fit. But God only knew how this new development with Damian would progress.

"Oh, I love working with teens!" Ann said, coming over to him. "I've been wanting to find another opportunity to work with kids since we stepped out of TGIT. I love seeing what God can do in their lives, and Young Life seems like an amazing organization. I think we should do it, like Kate said, and get involved."

"I agree," Lincoln said. "But we might have to put it on pause for now."

Lincoln told her the news, and immediately they packed up to go. As they got into the car, questions flooded Ann's head. The words, *liver failure*, kept reverberating around and around.

"Damian's health journey has always been difficult, but I never imagined liver failure. I'm scared for him, Lincoln," Ann said. "How serious do you think it is?"

"I believe it's very serious," Lincoln answered. "I have a feeling it has something to do with the Remicade medication he started. Liver failure was a possible side effect. I should have connected the dots when I saw him looking yellow—jaundice is an indicator of liver issues. I wish he would have taken my advice to get checked out by a doctor when he started fasting."

"Why are they taking him to San Francisco?" Ann asked. "I really thought it would be like all the other times he's been to the hospital recently, they get his colon working again and send him home."

"They said his case is out of their league. The hospital in San Francisco can do a liver transplant if that's what they decide is needed. We will just have to wait and see what the doctors there say," Lincoln said, gearing up for the four-hour car ride.

"I'm so worried, Lincoln. Do people survive liver failure? Is he going to be okay?" Ann clutched her handkerchief in her hands nervously.

"I think they survive if they get a transplant. I've never experienced any of this before. I think the best thing we can do is pray," Lincoln said.

Her husband's unwavering faith had a way of reassuring Ann. "You're right. God, please help Damian and his liver. Help the doctors to act quickly and know how to help him. Please bring him through this. And help me to trust you and not be fearful." Ann sighed as she ended her prayer, looking out her window at the towering pine trees. It was in God's hands now.

She repeated her favorite verse to herself and then out loud— Jeremiah 29:11, "'For I know the plans I have for you,' declares the LORD, 'plans to prosper you and not to harm you, plans to give you hope and a future'"—clinging to it for Damian.

"I still have so many questions," Ann addressed Lincoln again. "How does a liver transplant work? Why San Francisco instead of UC Davis? Can anything be done for him if he has to wait for a transplant? Will he still be hallucinating? How long will he be there?"

"Why don't you write all your questions for the doctor down," Lincoln suggested.

Ann agreed. "Should we try to contact LB? Do you think he knows about Damian yet?"

"Yes, we should try. Do you have a number for him?"

"I have Milo's number, or at least his adopted mom's number. LB lived there a while back, when he first moved out on his own. They should be able to contact him."

Four Brothers: Mario, Damian, Milo, LB 2007

Nicole's wedding to Garry 2007, with Jacob, Raphael (1.5), LB, Nicole, Damian

NINE

California Pacific Medical Center

FEBRUARY 6, 2008

· · · · · · · · · · · · · · · ·

"No one can confidently say he will
still be living tomorrow."

—Euripides, Ancient Greek
Playwright c.480–406 B.C.E.

· · · · · · · · · · · · · · · ·

CALIFORNIA PACIFIC MEDICAL CENTER WAS IN THE
heart of San Francisco. Battling traffic to get there had been a
nightmare, but at last, Ann and Lincoln sat by Damian's side. He
looked pale and frail, but he greeted them with a weak smile. His
brain ammonia levels still impaired his clear thinking and speech.

A tall, dark-haired young man entered the room.

"Hello, I'm Dr. Wolff, one of the resident doctors here. I will be
overseeing Damian's care. It looks like we need to get him on the list
for a transplant. Did they explain his case of autoimmune hepatitis?"

"Well, not exactly. Something about how his body is attacking itself and his liver?" Ann said, trying to wrap her mind around all the big words. She wrote down the words the doctor said that she didn't understand so she could look them up or ask Kate about them later.

"Yes, essentially all the tests have come back negative, so the only thing we can assume is that it's an autoimmune response, similar to how his Crohn's disease causes his body to fight itself. We will start him on several steroids, hoping that one of them will suppress the overreaction and calm down his immune system. But if his body doesn't stop fighting itself, he will go into a coma and we won't be able to stop it. We need to get him on the liver transplant list as soon as possible," Dr. Wolff said.

"If his body is attacking his liver, won't it continue with a new liver?" Lincoln asked.

"One would think so. But because this liver has the infection, it's sending signals to the brain to continue an immune response. A new liver should stop those signals," Dr. Wolff explained.

Lincoln was quick with a follow-up question. "How likely is he to be eligible for a liver?"

"Well, he does have age on his side. Some people are on the liver transplant list for years. Most of the people on the list are over the age of fifty and have been alcoholics for most of their lives. Does he have any history of drinking?" the doctor asked them.

"No, he has chosen to stay away from alcohol as far as I know," Lincoln answered.

"Then he's likely to be ranked higher on the list. Then we have to wait for a liver to become available." Dr. Wolff took a deep breath and lowered his voice. "His condition is serious. At the moment, he has about one week to live, so we need to act quickly."

"One week to live!?" Ann gasped, then exchanged a meaningful look with Lincoln. "How did it escalate so quickly? What else can be done for our son?"

Stunned by the gravity of the situation, Ann stood up and flung her body onto Damian's in a tight embrace, as if attempting a game of tug-of-war with death. She clung tightly to Damian as a solitary tear slid down her cheek. She regretted having left him alone.

"The liver transplant is his best chance at life."

AS DR. WOLFF WALKED AWAY, HE HEARD THE COUPLE praying. He heard the dad ask for the Lord's will to be done.

God seemed so cruel to Dr. Wolff. Taking lives even when seemingly faithful people asked Him to spare the person, letting others live who didn't deserve to. Dr. Wolff was still a resident doctor; he hadn't become fully affiliated with the hospital yet, but he had already seen his share of deaths working under other doctors. It came with the territory. He could tell this would be a complicated case. He shook his head as he walked back to the nursing station to get the paperwork filed for the transplant.

Before he made his last rounds of the day, he checked back in with the liver transplant case.

"We've been on the phone with his insurance. They are demanding for him to transfer to the Mayo Clinic in Arizona," the nurse said.

"Why didn't someone tell me sooner? Get me on the phone with them. They can't force this." Dr. Wolff paced while he waited for the nurse to get the insurance company on the phone. He could not allow this; there simply was no time.

The nurse handed over the phone to Dr. Wolff. "This man needs a liver today. We don't have time for a transfer. Every minute we lose is precious time wasted," he said, making certain he was talking to someone with authority to make game-time calls. "His recovery support is here. His family is here. If we send him to Mayo, he will have no support. He's going to need follow-up care for years to come. Why put him out of state?"

"We have a better relationship for transplants with the Mayo Clinic," the insurer claimed. "He will be more likely to get the transplant he needs there, and it will be more cost effective."

"How is flying him by air ambulance more cost effective? Are we trying to save this man's life or save your pocketbook? This whole process is wasting precious time that we don't have. We are ready to move forward with getting him the transplant. He's twenty-seven; he is strong and healthy. He will rank toward the top of the list. We just need to get him eligible with your approval," Dr. Wolff advocated.

"I'm sorry, but we cannot approve him to remain at your facility. We need him to move to the Mayo Clinic in order to approve the transplant," the insurance agent said.

Dr. Wolff could not believe what he was hearing. He would take this to his uppers. He went in to check on the family and give them an update. They were sitting on the couch looking extremely fatigued.

"We're having some complications. His insurance company is forcing our hand to life-flight him to Arizona to be eligible for a transplant. I'm trying my best to argue against it. He needs to stay here, but he also needs to get on that list, so we may have to send him there. I'm so sorry this is happening. We are doing everything within our power to help him. I'm going to get to the bottom of this before I leave."

"Thank you for keeping us informed," Lincoln said. "If we have to fly there, we will."

As Dr. Wolff left, he could sense a powerful presence in that room. This couple truly seemed to be different.

Within the hour, the decision came through that they would comply with the insurance company's request because it seemed they had no other choice. Damian had several doctors advocating for his case, but nothing seemed to be getting through.

"Damian needs an advocate to watch over him and speak for his health needs," Lincoln told Ann. "I think one of us should stay here to be with him until they get him ready for flight, and one of us should get to Phoenix as quickly as possible to be able to meet him when he lands at the hospital."

"I'll stay here. You know I don't like flying alone," Ann said.

"You keep bringing the situation back to you. Damian is in dire need here. You might have to get stretched out of your comfort zone," Lincoln pushed back. "But I don't mind going. I'll do anything within my grasp to help Damian."

"You know I will too." Although her actions didn't always show it, Lincoln thought, but no time for an argument now.

Lincoln booked the next plane to Phoenix. As he boarded, he sent up another prayer for Damian and hoped he would make it to the hospital in Arizona in time to meet Damian there. Damian would fly in a helicopter from Cal Pacific Medical Center to SFO, where an air ambulance waited to transport him to the Phoenix airport and then to the Mayo Clinic.

Lincoln rarely felt angry, but watching time erode as he waited for all the decisions by the insurance company and seeing how this all came down to money boiled his blood. Would their boneheaded decision to save a little money put his son's life in jeopardy?

The short flight began its descent. Before he knew it, Lincoln was walking off the plane. The minute he turned on his cell phone, he heard, "ding, ding, ding, ding." Quickly scanning the messages, he gave a gleeful cry. The message read, "Don't get on the plane. He's staying in San Francisco. He is not going to Phoenix." The desperate attempts to reach him had been too late, but this was great news. The doctors had won the argument while he had been in the air. That meant Damian could get on the transplant list, finally, and stay where he was.

Lincoln went straight to the booking agent and booked a flight back to San Francisco. He boarded the same plane he had just arrived on as the same crew turned around and flew back to San Francisco. It was expensive, and—in the end—a waste of time, but at least Lincoln hadn't wasted any time getting back, and at least the process for Damian could move forward.

BACK IN SAN FRANCISCO, ANN AND LINCOLN DECIDED to go home to get some rest, then come back the following day. Damian had been ranked high on the list for a transplant in the Western United States. It was a waiting game for the next liver.

The ding of the elevator alerted them they had reached the first floor, and the elevator doors slid open. As they walked out, weary from the day, Ann looked up and noticed Connie and Larry making their way to the elevator. They appeared disheveled, but they were here to show their support for Damian.

"Hi, Connie. Hi, Larry. I'm so glad to see you here," Ann called out to them.

"LB brought us. He's parking the car," Larry said, glancing sideways as if he expected him to show up any minute. He eyed the elevator behind her as the doors closed. Connie stood by his side looking at the ground.

"Damian needs all the support he can get," Ann said, perking up at the prospect of seeing LB. "He is in a coma now—the doctors induced him, to preserve his vitals—but you can still talk to him."

"They better be treating him good. I've got to get up to see him," Larry announced as he pushed the elevator call button. "I'll set them straight if they're not."

"Thanks for being here with him," Ann said. "We're on our way home." She looked around wistfully for any sign of LB. She knew he wouldn't talk to her, but the thought of seeing him again brought her heart joy. She hadn't seen him since the wedding, and she could hardly count that; he never looked at her the entire time. As she and Lincoln walked out the sliding glass doors without any sight of him, she tried to imagine what it must be like for LB to see his brother like this. She knew they had a tight brotherly bond. Her smile brightened knowing that LB was making an effort to support his brother in this hard time. She walked slowly to the car, hoping he would appear, but LB remained out of sight.

The days seemed to drag on, commuting back and forth three hours both ways. Ann and Lincoln quickly learned to be there when the doctors made their rounds. That's when all the decisions happened, when questions were asked, and when the updates came through. They spent more than eight hours in the hospital room each day before heading home to check in on their youngest son, Jacob, who still lived at home, as well as Ann's mother, "Nana," who had moved in with them. Not to mention that Lincoln had a campground business to run—but they also couldn't ignore Damian or leave him. Someone needed to help make decisions with the doctors, and although he was an adult, he couldn't do that while in a coma. Ann leaned heavily on her nurse friend, Kate, for daily support.

THE OPENING OF THE DOOR JARRED LINCOLN AWAKE. Apparently he had dozed off. All the driving was exhausting. And so much waiting. The respiratory therapist came in to check on the ventilator that was keeping Damian alive.

"This is one sick, sick, sick boy. I can't believe this is the same guy I was talking to two days ago and he is this sick now," the respiratory therapist said.

"He's been on the waiting list for a liver for days," Ann spoke up.

"The good news is we're heading into the weekend and there's a big storm coming through the Sierras," the therapist said, moving around to Damian's other side.

"What does that have to do with Damian?" Ann asked.

"Well, there's a better chance someone will get in a car crash up in the Sierras and produce a liver for us," he said.

"What? You mean I'm praying someone will die so my son can live?" Ann asked, aghast.

"Well, I'm not a praying man, but you can do what you want," he said.

"I can't pray for that," Ann stammered.

"It's the only way he will get the liver he needs. The liver has to be transported within nine hours of the organ donor's death."

"You're sure there's no other way?"

"I've been in this job thirty-seven years. He won't live past the weekend if he doesn't get a liver, and the only way he gets a liver is if someone dies."

Looking up to heaven, Ann sighed with heaviness, feeling a deep grief in her heart. "God, you're going to have to teach me how to pray for this because I don't know how to do this. I want Damian to live, but I don't want someone else to have to die. God, show me your plan for hope in all of this."

TEN

The Surgery

FEBRUARY 13, 2008

. . . .

"Remember that hope is a powerful
weapon even when all else is lost."

—Nelson Mandela

. . . .

IT HAD BEEN SIX AND HALF DAYS NOW. SURELY THIS
man wouldn't live past today. Dr. Wolff was afraid to have such a
young man die on his watch. Who knew what it could mean for his
career? This man's parents seemed nice enough, but his colleagues said
they all do until it goes south and their greatest consolation becomes
money. Dr. Wolff asked the nurse for an update.

"His heart rate has been steady, but his liver failure is causing
deficiencies in his blood. His brain activity is also reading with
indiscrepancies," she said. "And he has been in a coma for six days
now. His vitals have been slowly deteriorating."

He thought that placing Damian at the top of the list would result
in a liver within a few hours to days. But then again, liver transplants
were so tricky because they required all the right circumstances to

align—plus, the donor had to be the right fit. What more could they have done for him?

Another nurse approached him at the station. "We just got a phone call. We have a liver match for Damian."

At last. But would it get there in time? The question loomed—looking at his vital signs, he wasn't sure Damian was going to make it through surgery. He needed to call in a team of experts immediately to see if they could stabilize him by the time the liver arrived. It might already be too late.

The next twenty minutes passed in a frenzy of frantic phone calls and desperate hope, as Dr. Wolff started bringing in the team that would be needed for prepping Damian for surgery. Thankfully, the parents were there already. He gave them a quick brief of the situation as the team entered Damian's room.

"His blood is not coagulating properly—it won't clot if we proceed with the operation. We're going to have to see if his body will take an injection of factor VII. He has to have enough platelets for surgery," the head surgeon said.

A team quickly followed the head surgeon's instructions as the surgeon continued, "There's too much pressure building up on his brain. We need to bring the swelling down. Bring in the cooling vests."

Another team started the refrigeration process. One pair worked together to get a cooling vest around his midsection while another nurse secured packs to his thighs. They needed to bring his core temperature down to about eighty-eight degrees. Cooling his body temperature would bring the swelling down on his brain, with the hopes that they caught it in time to avoid long-term damage. If everything could stabilize, then they could proceed with the transplant surgery.

"Is he cool yet? We need to see how much swelling the brain endured. Let's get a bolt in to measure the pressure."

ANN AND LINCOLN EXCHANGED LOOKS FROM THE corner of Damian's hospital room. "They're going to do what to our son?" Ann whispered to Lincoln as she watched doctors rushing in and out of the room. It seemed they had a whole army to help Damian. She was thankful, of course, but she couldn't help feeling a twinge of guilt, knowing another family was suffering right now, missing a loved one that they had just lost. She whispered a desperate prayer of hope, "God, please, let this work."

Was God really even listening?

Everything had been happening so fast. She had really thought he would be able to go home after a few days, just like all the other times. She'd never expected all this.

"Ann, you're biting your lip again," Lincoln said. He extended his hands to hers and clasped her fingers through his, encompassing her small hands in his own.

"I can't help it. I'm just so worried for our son."

A man drilling into Damian's skull startled Ann. "I'm scared, Lincoln. What are they doing?"

"They are putting a bolt into his head, something like a pressure gauge. It measures how much pressure is on the other side of the confined space, similar to how a tire pressure gauge works," Lincoln explained. He remained a pillar of calm and collected, reassuring Ann and soothing her fears.

One of the doctors brought out a big, shiny bolt and inserted it into the drilled hole in Damian's head. Ann watched breathlessly. "It looks like it belongs on a door, not a person," she whispered to Lincoln. Even in the most dire situations, Ann liked to lighten the serious mood if she could to suppress her angst. "It feels like we're in a revolving *House* episode."

Lincoln smiled warmly at his wife and held her hand tighter.

The head surgeon inspected the team's work. "Let's get a read on the pressure."

"The brain pressure is elevated, but the reading is still below the threshold for injury."

"Bring in the neuro specialist."

Minutes later, a lanky, graying man stepped into the room. He walked over to Damian, who had so many contraptions hooked up to him he looked more like an alien than a human. He looked up and down the test results, inspected the bolt for himself, and did one more pressure test. He analyzed the readings and all the information in front of him. He whispered to a few of the waiting doctors, then he walked over to the corner where Ann and Lincoln had been watching.

"The test results show that we reduced the brain swelling just in time. The tests read that the built-up pressure on his brain was not enough to cause injury." The doctor emphasized each word slowly. "But I don't like it. I don't like it one bit. There was a good lag of time between when they knew he had pressure on his brain and getting him refrigerated with the bolt in. How much did the brain swell before the refrigeration brought the swelling down? The test is only done after for the best results, so it could have been much higher. We will never know."

He paused, waiting a moment before heaping the heavy news on them.

"The choice is up to you as his parents. I can give the green light for the surgery, hoping on a chance we got to his brain in time before major damage occurred. *But*, I'm just telling you right now, he could wake up from this with a major brain injury. If any parts of the brain were pressurized too long without blood flow, those parts will be dead. He may or may not function normally, possibly suffering mental impairment. Honestly, from a doctor's perspective, I can't tell you one way or the other. It's your call."

Ann reeled for a moment. "How do we make a choice of life or death for our child?" She dabbed her eye with a Kleenex and took a deep breath, overwhelmed by the weight of the decision.

Lincoln put his arm around his wife's shoulder to comfort her. "We pray."

They grabbed hands and knelt their heads together, asking for God's wisdom. If it had been six hours earlier, it would have been an easy call, but with Damian's brain swelling, everything was changing so quickly.

But he was so young, with his whole life in front of him. And they loved him.

"We want to go ahead with the surgery. We're willing to take the chance that they caught it just in time," Lincoln said to the doctor.

The team whisked Damian into surgery to give him the new liver.

Ann and Lincoln paced the hallways of the now familiar hospital, waiting for Damian's return. Lincoln booked a hotel room next to the hospital for the night, anticipating the long wait. Soon after, Lincoln spotted Larry, Connie, Mario, and LB, who had heard about the surgery and came as quickly as they could. He told them everything he knew.

Mario started crying. "I wish we had been here sooner. Why couldn't the liver have come one day earlier? Do you think he will come out okay?"

"No one can tell. We have to wait and see," Lincoln said.

"We will be outside," Mario told him.

Meanwhile, Ann called Kate to tell her the update. She could hear the disappointment in her friend's voice as she recounted the story. It was obvious she did not agree with their decision to go ahead with the surgery when he had prolonged lack of oxygen to his brain. Ann started to question whether they had made the right choice, but she thought of Damian lying there on the bed so helpless. She felt it was right to do everything in her power to save him.

Late that evening, Dr. Wolff approached them.

"He's the youngest liver transplant our hospital has ever completed. He is in the recovery room now. I would go get some rest and come back in the morning to see him," Dr. Wolff said.

The next day brought confirmation that his body accepted the liver and the autoimmune response was resolved. With a brand-new liver, Damian had another chance at life.

Was it a heroic fix? Was his brain okay? They would have to wait until he woke up.

ELEVEN

The Wait

MARCH 2008

. . . .

"In the same way, the Spirit helps us in our
weakness. We do not know what we ought to pray
for, but the Spirit himself intercedes for us through
wordless groans. And he who searches our hearts
knows the mind of the Spirit, because the Spirit
intercedes for God's people in accordance with
the will of God. And we know that in all things God
works for the good of those who love him, who
have been called according to his purpose."

—Romans 8:26-28 (NIV)

. . . .

WHEN DAMIAN "WOKE UP" DAYS LATER, IT WAS
obvious he was not okay. His body was "awake," meaning his brain
caused his heart to beat and lungs to breathe without a ventilator, but
he showed no other signs of life.

Damian's eyes opened and stared vacantly at the ceiling. His body
was as stiff as a board, lifelessly still. The monitors showed he was
breathing, that all his organs were functioning properly, but from the
outside, it was unclear if he was alive.

Suddenly, his entire body started shaking as if having a seizure. It lasted just a few minutes and then stopped, his body lifelessly still again. Drool dripped down Damian's chin, and sweat poured down his forehead. Ann and Lincoln sat next to his bed, worried.

"He may be having a constant seizure. Sometimes seizures can cause stillness. We're going to run an EEG test," Dr. Wolff said.

Ann and Lincoln nodded, trusting the doctor and praying once more. The doctor was amazed at the consistency and kindness these people continually showed. This seemed to be a special family. He just wished he had more answers for them. This case was so unprecedented, even for experienced doctors. And here he was, a young resident, dealing with so many unknowns. Lincoln seemed so calm and collected, a solid rock in the wind. His strength and confidence seemed to flow to everyone around him, and Dr. Wolff benefited from it. Ann obviously leaned on her husband, but she sometimes seemed unaffected or less compassionate than her counterpart. She had a childlike giddiness about her.

"If it's a seizure," Dr. Wolff continued, "we may be able to find the right anti-seizure medication so he can come out of it."

A young man walked in then. He looked like a boy barely old enough to sit at the bar, let alone work in a hospital.

"Hi, I'm Ethan. I'll be performing the EEG test," he said sheepishly, appearing nervous to have spectators.

Ethan set down the bag of equipment next to the large contraption he had rolled in. Sitting himself next to Damian's bedside, he began the work of attaching electrodes to Damian's skull. Ethan's hand started shaking, then his entire arm shook as he lifted the first magnetic lead to Damian's head.

The lead slipped off, as Damian was sweating profusely. Sweat dripped off his head and pooled in a puddle on the bed below him. This would never work. Every time Ethan got a lead on, it would slowly drip down and off Damian's head.

Eventually, with great perseverance and eight towels, Ethan was able to get a read on the EEG.

The results showed no sign of a seizure. Damian's state was simply the way his brain was working. A seizure would have been better news because it could have been medicated. With this revelation, it was clear that Damian could be in this vegetative state forever.

Lincoln thought of the Terri Schiavo case where her brain functioning never returned and all that could be done was to continue to feed her and turn her so she wouldn't get bed sores. She had remained in a persistent vegetative state for fifteen years after a cardiac arrest that caused oxygen to be cut off from her brain for five minutes. Her case became widely known when her husband wanted to honor her verbally expressed desire to not "be kept alive on a machine."[1] The only thing keeping her alive was a feeding tube that provided artificial nutrition and hydration. When the husband tried to make the difficult decision to stop feeding her, Terri's parents took the situation to court, and the family disagreement skyrocketed into public debate. Many years, court cases, and controversial discussions later, Terri's husband finally received the backing of the court to end Terri's life. The whole time, Terri looked just like how Lincoln's son did now.

Six weeks after the surgery, Damian's eyes were still open and staring, stiff, looking blankly off, no movement of the eyes to show recognition, no movement of the hands or feet. Just stiff.

"When do we decide to turn off life support?" Ann asked Lincoln as they sat with Damian for their last hour before heading home. Weariness etched lines in Ann's forehead.

"How can you ask that so soon, Ann? The doctors haven't given up on him yet. And besides, there is no life support to turn off. At least

---

[1] Weijer C. (2005). A death in the family: reflections on the Terri Schiavo case. CMAJ : Canadian Medical Association journal = journal de l'Association medicale canadienne, 172(9), 1197–1198. https://doi.org/10.1503/cmaj.050348 (Accessed 2024 Jan 18).
  *A new documentary called Between Life & Death: Terri Schiavo's Story was released in 2023.

not in the sense you're talking about. There is nothing they are doing to keep his heart or brain going. He is doing that all on his own. God is giving him the breath of life right now. But his brain is showing no sign of activity other than just to keep him alive," Lincoln said. "His feeding tube is giving him the sustaining nutrition he needs, but cutting that off is much more controversial than a ventilator."

Lincoln's faith and confidence never wavered, even in the face of difficult decisions about life or death. His constant calm demeanor never changed, like a rock on the seashore pounded smooth by the roaring waves but unmoved. His calm strengthened and comforted Ann. Was she wrong to ask about the life support?

"So what do we do then?"

"There's nothing we can do but wait."

"Just keep waiting? What do I even pray for?" Ann's motherly heart hurt from the tumultuous emotional roller coaster. Did God really have a plan in all this?

"I've been reading Romans 8 over and over again. It says, 'The Holy Spirit helps us in our weakness. When we do not know what to pray, the Spirit intercedes for us through our wordless groans.' So we groan." Lincoln paused before continuing, "And today, we pray for rest. We're exhausted. This has been an exhausting several weeks. From here on out—with Damian's care and what it's going to take to get through this—we are no longer in a sprint; we are in a marathon. We need to have a marathoner's pace toward it; otherwise, our whole family is going to fall apart. We need to give the time and energy that's needed. We can't leave him and ignore him. But we also have to take care of our needs. And you look like you need a good night's rest. We will take tomorrow to rest up."

The first week they had driven the three and a half hours to the Bay every day except the night of the surgery when they booked a hotel. With the surgery done and the waiting game begun, they had transitioned to driving down every other day. Now they debated taking turns coming down. Who knew how long the wait would be. Of course they wanted to be there for him if anything happened, but they had to continue their normal life as well.

"I want to make it to Jacob's basketball game this week. I can't stand to be away from Damian too long, but we need to be there for Jacob too," Ann said, checking over their calendar while they sat with Damian.

Time in the hospital felt so different from normal time. It was kept not in hours and minutes but in nursing shift changes and doctors' rounds, medication time tables and vital check routines. Ann had found it difficult to track when she had eaten her last meal, or if they had eaten at all in a single day. Driving, waiting, longing, praying—it all melded together in the shock of the last several weeks. She could feel the fatigue in her body. Her brain felt a little bit slower too.

"Yes, I agree entirely. I think we should make it to Jacob's basketball game. What will it take to make that work?"

"It's on Thursday at four o'clock."

"Good, I'll work that day and be off in time to go with you."

"It's hard to have our child who has been on his own for several years all of a sudden need our full attention. At least we've been able to keep Nicole in the loop when we call her on our drives. It helps that she's married and busy with her nursing job."

"Imagine being Damian. It's even more difficult for him. I think we can manage juggling between everyone. Jacob understands. Besides, Jacob has that girlfriend he's chasing."

"You're right, like usual." Ann reflected for a moment on how selfish she had been to think of Damian as time consuming when he lay helplessly in a hospital bed. She watched his chest move up and down slowly, rhythmically with the breath of life. She thought for a moment about how hard Damian's whole life had been, riddled with hospital stays and health mysteries that eluded doctors. How had her heart grown so callous toward him when he became an adult? She had allowed blinders over her eyes and forgot about his health issue, only seeing the negative parts of his personality that agitated her. She felt regret pinch her stomach.

As they were talking, they didn't even notice the brown-haired almost-six-foot man slip into the hospital room. He stood in the corner, unsure of whether to advance or not. But the split second of indecision cost him.

Lincoln caught a glimpse of movement, and then his mouth widened to a hearty smile. "Hi, LB," Lincoln said. "Glad to see you here." Merriment danced in his eyes, erasing for a moment the weary lines of worry.

LB didn't look up. He grunted a low, "Hi," and shuffled his feet. He looked like an animal caught in a trap, as if he might suddenly dart back into the hallway, away from their stares.

"LB!" Ann's awareness of her weariness and regret vanished, and the corners of her mouth pulled into an exuberant smile. Her heart raced as she studied LB for a moment, feeling jubilant, and calculated if she should take the chance to hug him. She got up and started to cross the room.

"Come on, Ann. We should let LB have alone time with his brother," Lincoln said, picking up on the nonverbal cues. "We were just thinking of heading home anyway."

Ann stopped midway to LB, gave him a timid wave, and followed her husband out of the room, turning around at the doorway with a cheerful voice, "Goodbye, Damian. We'll be back in a couple of days."

LB REMAINED IN HIS CORNER UNTIL THEY HAD LEFT the room. Thankful he didn't have to speak to the people he had professed to hate on several occasions for a long list of reasons he still held to, he took a sigh of relief and sat down in the chair closest to Damian.

"Hey, bud. It's me, LB, your brother. Your eyes are open this time, but I still don't know if you can hear me," LB said, hoping, willing his brother to snap out of it and be the jovial, goofy brother he loved so much. "Just letting you know I'm here for you. The good thing is you're not really awake for all the recovery time, so your body will be all healed by the time you wake up. You won't even know you spent all this time in the hospital. I know how much you hate this place."

He held on to his brother's cold hand. It was hard to see Damian lying there lifelessly. Damian's chest moved slowly up and down, the only sign that he was alive. He looked deathly pale. LB wanted to just shake him and make him wake up. Why did it have to happen to Damian? He desperately wanted his best friend to wake up normal, with a future ahead of him—to get married and have his own kid, to feel the blessings of fatherhood that LB so enjoyed. LB reached into the future for Damian, and even uttered a small prayer for the first time in a long time.

It shocked him that Ann and Lincoln were there. According to the nurses, they were there often—and they lived even farther away than he did. Obviously, they cared about Damian. It hurt LB to even admit that. The monsters he had built them up to be in his mind weren't capable of actually caring for him or his brother. They were hypocrites, awful people who gave their kids away to the system. He had justified in his mind how terrible they were when he had his son, Raphael. That sweet, precious baby could never do anything that would prompt LB to send Raphael to boot camp or a group home. He was a parent now, and in their shoes, he would never do what they did to him. He would always fight for his son.

And yet, there they were, showing up for Damian time and time again, challenging his views. They were there for the exact same reasons he was, out of concern and love for Damian.

He tried to shake it off. He knew he was right about them. After all, he doubted they would have done the same for him. He wouldn't let this soften him. He had been building this wall for too long now.

MORE WEEKS PASSED, MOSTLY THE SAME FOR DAMIAN.

Dr. Wolff walked toward Damian's room with a heavy heart, knowing the conversation he must have. As he stepped into the room, he noticed weariness etched into the mother's face and graying hairs pushing their way through her hairline. He hesitated before drawing attention to himself, as his eyes rested on the father, who slept in the corner chair with a sudoku puzzle in his lap. He noticed one of the brothers also sat in the other corner, closest to Damian. Dr. Wolff busied himself at the computer for a moment, then sat on a stool close to the bed, opposite Ann. Lincoln roused in the corner, hearing the abrupt movement.

Clearing his throat, Dr. Wolff began, "We are here at another crossroads in Damian's health, where the decisions come down to your choice. We can continue down this path where we wait and see. His liver transplant was successful, but he has not stirred out of his coma in eight weeks. He continues to breathe on his own, but he might never wake up to his former self. As you know, the one thing keeping him alive is his feeding tube. At some point, he has to leave the hospital. We want to start talking about your options.

"We ran some scans on his brain activity, to try to understand what is happening. It appears the most damage that occurred was in the frontal lobe, which deals with reasoning, rationalization, and making decisions. There is also damage to parts of the left temporal side of the brain. The ramifications remain unknown, but this could affect his speech, as both the Broca's and Wernicke's areas may have been damaged. Those areas work together to help recall and deliver

137

words. The part that appears undamaged, at least as far as the scan goes, is the back and core part of the brain, which means if he comes out of this state, he could have memory recall. The brain is tricky to nail down, and as of now, his brain is entirely unresponsive.

"We have all been racking our brains to understand why so much pressure built up so quickly. One theory is about his brain shunt he had installed at birth. The shunt helps remove extra fluid so pressure doesn't build up, but it also stunts the growth of the cranium. It's possible, as a result, he lost his shock absorber in his brain that would absorb extra pressure. It's hard to pinpoint exactly what happened. If we had gotten the liver one day sooner, it could have been an entirely different story."

Mario had been sitting quietly taking it all in. His ears seemed to perk up when he heard that last remark. "Then why didn't you do something sooner? Why didn't you refrigerate him sooner to bring down the swelling? Why didn't you detect the pressure buildup in his brain? Why didn't you do more for him while he was waiting? You could have saved his life if you did something one day sooner." Mario stormed out of the room after making his angry declarations.

Ann looked embarrassed at Mario's outburst. "Sorry for that. Don't worry about him. He will be okay. We don't hold it against you. We know you did everything you could to help Damian."

"It's okay. It's normal for people to blame us when things go wrong or unexpectedly. I do want to make you aware of the possibilities to come. Of course, no one can predict the future. Damian could remain in this exact vegetative state forever, dependent on a feeding tube for survival with little to no interaction with the world. People rarely recover from this much brain damage. He could 'wake up' in the sense that eventually his eyes could register movement, possibly even regain use of his limbs. We're not sure, in part because we have no idea how much time elapsed during the brain swelling, so there is no way to tell exactly how much damage occurred. He likely won't walk or talk again. He may never feed himself or communicate at all. As his parents, his care will likely fall onto your shoulders," Dr. Wolff said. "At some point, he has to leave the hospital. I'm not sure if you plan to bring him home. We can start looking into long-term care facilities. Whatever you choose, the journey will not be easy."

Lincoln looked at Dr. Wolff with his piercing blue eyes, filled with valor and determination. "We are prepared to care for him if and when that becomes necessary. We believe our God can bring him back to us if it's within His will. He must have a reason for keeping him alive this far. We firmly believe our God is still in the miracle business."

"I've never met people quite like you, who truly live by their convictions," Dr. Wolff told them. "Send those prayers up. I'm here to witness what happens."

"The wild ride of this situation with Damian is unlike anything I've experienced in my life up to this point," Lincoln said. "I've never run into situations where there are seemingly no options, but either to stay or walk away. I know with my convictions I must stay. I must be here for Damian. I've had to learn to lean more into God to trust Him in a whole new way. I'm expecting God to show up because He says He will never leave us. I believe God's truths are absolute, so I trust Him with my whole being. I feel His presence with me always, so I have nothing to fear."

Ann added, "I'm praying we all will get to see God answer in a real way." Lincoln averted his eyes from hers.

After Dr. Wolff left the room, with his eyes attentive to Damian, Lincoln said, "Ann, I'm ready to do what it takes to help Damian, but I'm not sure you're there yet. Are you still questioning if we should take him off life support? Are you praying for God to bring Damian back to us? Sometimes you seem indifferent about whether he lives."

"Of course I want our son to live. I admit I've started to feel hopeless. I keep hoping God will miraculously have Damian sit up and start talking to us. But his situation seems so unchanging. I keep asking God what His plan is in all of this. Hearing how grim his situation may be, that Damian might never be the same, even if he does wake up, makes me even more hopeless. I do trust God, but I just can't see Him in all this." Ann wrung her hands, and her lip quivered as she spoke. "I don't want to take him off life support if there's any chance he will come back to us. I agree with what you said earlier. I want to stay and be here for Damian, whatever shape that takes."

"It's okay to have doubt, Ann. God is big enough to handle it," Lincoln said and drew her in for an embrace. He whispered into her ear, "We will face whatever comes together."

DAMIAN LIVED.

Slowly, defying all odds, Damian came out of the lifeless state.

It started with erratic twitching and movements.

Then he started thrashing and banging around in the bed. He still had a blank look on his face. His eyes were open but did not track movement or show signs that he could register the world around him.

His head started to move around, still without any focus.

One day, Mario sat in the room visiting with Ann and Lincoln. He noticed Damian's head moving and shouted a gleeful, "Damian, you're moving." Then to Ann, he said, "I can't believe I was here to witness this first sign of movement. The least I can do is to be here by his side, even if he never comes out of it. I just want my brother back."

Damian's case was unprecedented, but he appeared to be making progress. It happened slowly. Dr. Wolff ordered a physical therapist to start range-of-motion exercises. In the scenario that Damian did return to walking, they needed to keep his body in shape. The body starts curling in on itself, the doctors explained, if it isn't used in its normal functions. The feet start going flat and the toes go down, shaping to the flat of the bed, so that he would be unable to walk.

Damian's visitors were eager to do "something." Ann and Lincoln watched the physical therapist work every single joint down his body, starting with the neck and head, working out the arms, and wrists, and down to his legs and feet. The physical therapist explained that the more often they did this, the more likely he would be able to walk and do normal things again when he was ready. Ann enjoyed teaching Larry Navarro how to do the exercises, pleasantly surprised that he had come for another visit.

"It may all be pointless," Ann said as she showed the movements to Larry. "He might never walk again, but at least we have a way to pass the time while we're with him."

Overhearing her remark, Lincoln said, "Ann, it's more than just a way to pass the time with him. We have to keep our hope. It's giving him the ability to keep his mobility. It's an act of love."

Every week brought more movement. Four weeks after he started waking up, the nurses strapped Damian into a chair so he could sit up. It's good for the body, the nurses explained, to be vertical to prevent pneumonia from lying all the time. They had to use straps so Damian's body didn't slump over. Damian sat, staring blankly and drooling.

Lincoln looked over at Damian, then at Ann, then out the window at the sunshine beckoning him to bask in it. "Hey. I have an idea. It's such a beautiful spring day. Why don't we take Damian for a walk?"

"Great idea. I would love to get out of this room."

"Well, regardless of what you want, I'm sure Damian would like the fresh air."

"You're right. He's been cooped up here for ages. I should think more about how all this must be for Damian. They just gave him his medications, so he should be good for another three or four hours." Ann hit the call button on Damian's bed and scolded herself for being so thoughtless again.

After explaining their plan, the nurse quickly brought in a specialized wheelchair outfitted with extra straps to help Damian sit up. The three of them worked together to get Damian into the wheelchair. She slowly disconnected the IVs with the reassurance that they would return before his next medication and feeding.

"That looks like it should do the trick. Well then, we'll be back," Lincoln said to the nurse.

Nurses stared at them as they pushed Damian out through the hallways for the first time. It was shocking. He had been in the same bed for nearly three months now, but today, Lincoln pushed right past them. He and Ann went down the elevator and walked right out the front door.

"I was thinking of taking him to that park on a hill, the one we've walked to before," Lincoln suggested.

"Are we supposed to take him that far?" Ann asked.

"It's close enough to us. He needs some sunshine on his face. He needs to enjoy the birds and the air. He's been cooped up in there for months," Lincoln said, pushing ahead confidently.

Ann and Lincoln chatted happily as they walked up the steep hill. The park looked down over the bay and the Golden Gate Bridge. A little breathless when they arrived at the top, they parked Damian's wheelchair next to their bench and let him soak in the sights of the park. The sun streamed down on Damian's blank face, and a lovely breeze caressed him.

Birds chirped in the trees overhead. Dozens of families played in the park, some on the play set, some playing soccer. Others were throwing balls to dogs, the dogs chasing happily and barking at each other. Stimulation and life buzzed all about, a stark contrast to the bleak hospital room where time simply ebbed away. In the blink of an eye, a delightful hour had slipped away. It was restoring Ann's soul to get out and breathe in nature; to be reminded of God's goodness and hope for Damian. The sunshine on her back and the green grass beneath her feet grounded her in trusting God's plan. She prayed the same restorative qualities might transpire in Damian.

"Damian, I suppose we should get you back before you're missed," Ann said, looking over at Lincoln, who also seemed refreshed. She hesitated before leaving this moment, but she knew the next medication window was coming up quickly.

On the way back, she noticed a homeless person lying on a sidewalk bench. She felt a wave of sadness envelop her. She suddenly remembered her dad and wondered what he would have done.

"Do you think we should bring him a blanket or some food?" Ann wondered out loud.

"Who?" Lincoln asked.

"That man. He looks like he could use it. I was just thinking about what my dad would have done."

"Right, we can see if we can find him again when we're leaving to bring him something."

Ann nodded her head.

The trio made their way back to the hospital, back up the elevator, onto Damian's floor. The head nurse approached them from behind her desk.

"Where have you been? Where on earth did you take him?" She stood with her hands on her hips, questioning them.

"We went to soak in the sun," Lincoln responded.

"Where did you go? Where have you been for so long? My nurse thought you were going to take him to the patio outside the front door," she questioned.

"Oh, we just went to the park up the hill," Ann said a little sheepishly.

"Park? What park? There is no park around here." The nurse raised her hands up in question.

"The one with a dog park right on top of the hill," Lincoln said, lifting his shoulders and arms in surrender.

"LaFayette Park? That's at least two blocks from here. You can't do that. You can't just leave the hospital, especially with someone like Damian. He is in the hospital's care. Something could have happened. Don't do that ever again," the nurse scolded them.

"Sorry, we didn't know. We just wanted him to get out and experience the sunshine. I think it did him good," Lincoln apologized.

The nurse escorted them to their room to reattach Damian, then skulked away.

Soon after, Dr. Wolff came to the room to second the head nurse. But as he walked away, he said, "Just so you know, I think you had Damian's best interest in mind. Who knows what the sunshine might wake up in him."

Before they left the hospital, Ann bought a sandwich and tucked it in her purse. She asked Lincoln to drive down the street they had walked earlier that day. When she spotted the man, she instructed Lincoln to pull over. She hopped out of the car and delivered the sandwich without a word, then scurried back to the car to begin the nearly four-hour drive home.

TWELVE

Awakening Frankenstein's Monster

LATE APRIL 2008

. . . .

"There are only two ways to live your life. One
is as though nothing is a miracle. The other
is as though everything is a miracle."

—Albert Einstein

. . . .

THE VERY NEXT DAY, LINCOLN DROVE DOWN ALONE
to sit the day with Damian. Damian sat in the chair next to him, this
time without a strap. His muscle tone grew stronger each day that he
sat up, though drool still dripped down his face, and he stared, not
looking at anything in particular.

"Damian, do you remember the glorious sunshine yesterday? You
probably almost forgot what that felt like, to get the warmth of the
sun on your face. Did you like that? Did you see all the kids playing? I
remember when you were a kid, playing away. You have always loved
to swim, from the day you came to our house. You were over the

moon about that pool we had. Do you remember that? And you liked kicking the soccer ball around. You loved to be active when your body allowed it," Lincoln said, sending up a prayer at the same time. "Lord, let his body be active again. Restore his youthfulness and agility."

Whenever Lincoln came alone, he brought his Bible with him. He had been reading out of Isaiah, so he continued. Lincoln read through the first three verses before movement caught his eye.

Damian started sliding down in his chair. Like a teenage boy in the back of a boring high school class, he slid his bottom toward the front of the chair, slouching down.

"You're going to slump right onto the floor. Stop that, Damian." Lincoln put down his Bible and went over to help him sit up right in his chair again.

Damian let out an exasperated groan, "Hewgh." It was the first audible noise Lincoln heard him make. Lincoln examined his son with a cautious hope growing within him. Was something stirring inside the shell of the body that looked like his son but had been lifeless and unresponsive for months?

"Well, I'm sorry you're upset with me, but I'm not going to let you fall on the ground," Lincoln said, chuckling a bit. Lincoln returned to his place in Isaiah, " . . . Saith the Lord . . . I will give you wings like Eagles . . ."

Slowly, slowly, Damian's bottom started moving toward the edge of the chair again.

"You're doing it again, Damian." Lincoln stood up again to prevent him from falling.

Damian did the same thing three more times, with Lincoln adjusting him back to sitting up straight. The final time, Damian managed to get his bottom all the way to the edge of the chair before Lincoln could move. Damian's body slumped over the hump of the chair with his feet touching the ground and his legs bent like a frog.

Then, abruptly, Damian stood up.

Completely surprised, Lincoln gaped at Damian standing on two feet. His heart leaped with unexpected hope. Then, seeing the vacant look in Damian's eyes, his heart lurched with fear, for it appeared he had awakened Frankenstein's monster. Before either man moved, three nurses ran into the room.

"What's going on with Damian? His heart tones skyrocketed on the monitor," the head nurse said in alarmed tones before assessing the room. All three stopped in their tracks as they caught sight of Damian. The three stood staring a moment, then the head nurse looked accusingly at Lincoln. "What are you doing?"

"I didn't do it. He did."

"Oh my, oh my. Let's get him down. Make sure he doesn't fall," the head nurse said in a shrill voice to one of the others. "His heart can't handle the physical exertion after lying in a bed for so long."

The three of them worked together to get Damian back onto the chair. It took a great deal of effort; Damian seemed determined to stand. Once the commotion settled, the nurses asked how it happened.

"I was just sitting here reading the Bible," Lincoln explained. "And then he slumped to the edge of his chair several times and made a grunting noise. I kept putting him back up, but he kept sliding down and eventually stood up, all on his own."

"Okay, let's watch what he does," the nurse suggested.

Damian slumped down again and stood up by himself with all of them watching.

"You see, he wants to stand," Lincoln said.

"We see that. We just don't know what to do about it. He's been comatose for so long. He still isn't registering that he can see. His eyes appear to be vacant. This seems dangerous. I think we should call the doctor," the nurse said, while keeping a firm grip on the back of Damian's hospital gown.

"Not to mention the fall liability," another nurse muttered quietly and went to get the doctor.

They coerced him to sit down again, but Damian popped right up. The cycle continued until eventually he grew tired of it, and they eased him into bed.

The next day, Damian stood up again, repetitively. Within two days, Damian stood up, took a step, and then walked right out of the room. He walked past the nursing station. Jaws dropped. No one could believe what they were seeing. Here came this man, who'd been in bed for months, thought to be in a continually vegetative state, now walking the hallways unassisted. Lincoln walked beside Damian, who was shocked himself, as he observed the whole scene. Damian walked slowly, shuffling his feet along the corridor without any sign of emotion or mental clarity, simply a vacant stare straight ahead, head cocked, arms limp at his sides, and an open mouth with drool spilling out of the corner continually.

Ann walked on the other side of Damian. She had to come see it for herself. It was a miracle. And terrifying. He was like a zombie.

"What do we do with him?" Ann asked Lincoln once they got him back into the room.

"I don't think any of us knows. Our best bet is to keep him safe while he experiments. But we don't want to stifle anything because obviously something is happening. His brain is communicating to the rest of his body. His brain is awakening at last," Lincoln replied.

"We can't miss a day with him now, there's too much action," Ann said. "Do you think something clicked when we took him to the park?"

"I think it just might have. Who knows how the brain and body works. But it's almost as if Damian has been trapped inside all this time and all of a sudden he feels the warmth of the sunshine, hears the laughter of children, sees a whirl of activity all around him, and something deep inside of him said, 'I've got to figure a way out of here. I have to get up and moving or I'm going to die in here. I'm stuck in here. I've got to get out,'" Lincoln said. "And I think our prayers have been working too."

Thus began Damian's journey. Continually trying new things, exploring, pushing the boundaries, surprising everyone with his agility, Damian continued to grow and change daily. Day by day, his movements became less stiff and looked more like walking. His eyes began to move just a little. His limbs regained strength and flexibility, although sometimes flailed in jerky movements out of his control. Then one day he uttered a throaty babbling sound.

Dr. Wolff came into the room on his rounds. "Damian has surprised us all. I'm in disbelief at how he has clamored against the odds and is making a rampant comeback. None of us expected this much progress. I'll be the first to admit we were entirely wrong about him."

"Like you told us, no one can predict the future," Lincoln said. "Especially with brain injuries. We have trusted God to show up for Damian all along the way, and he has certainly surprised us. We will continue to wait and see."

"I'm not going to put any limitations on what Damian can and can't do, although I'm sure others will throughout his rehabilitation process. Now that Damian is showing obvious signs of life, like being able to walk, we will likely look into a rehabilitation facility. We will hope to transfer him to a place specifically for those who have suffered a brain injury like his. It looks as though your journey will be a long one once he leaves here."

"There are other people like Damian?" Ann asked out of curiosity.

Dr. Wolff cleared his throat before answering. "Well, not exactly like Damian. I haven't seen this type of case where liver failure causes the brain to swell. Most often it's a motor vehicle accident or a stroke that impairs brain activity. I'm sure as you go along Damian will be quite the unique case. But know that we are always here to help with his unpredictable health conditions along the way. I would love to follow his care as best I can."

"We appreciate your compassionate care throughout this whole process. Thank you for being willing to do everything you can to help him. You have made this journey bearable for us," Lincoln said to him, with Ann echoing her thanks.

"I was more willing to take extra measures because you were focused on Damian's care from the beginning and not looking to hold things against us," Dr. Wolff said. "For us, it's a two-way street of respect, and I can see the integrity of your words backed by your actions. I have never seen a family so strong as yours. You have been so supportive of your son all the way through this, the ups and downs. Your dedication is tremendous. Watching the miracle of Damian has been life-changing for me. I can see your prayers work. I'm starting to believe your God is real."

THIRTEEN

Move to Care Meridian

MAY 2008

. . . .

"'I wish it need not have happened in my time,'
said Frodo. 'So do I,' said Gandalf, 'and so do
all who live to see such times. But that is not
for them to decide. All we have to decide is
what to do with the time that is given us.'"

—J.R.R. Tolkien, *The Fellowship of the Ring*

. . . .

"WHAT DID THE DOCTOR SAY TODAY?" KATE ASKED ON
the other end of the phone.

Ann looked over at Lincoln in the driver seat as she put the phone
on speaker. They were on I-80 headed home from another eight-hour
day at the hospital. Damian had been in the hospital almost four
months now. The fatigue showed in the circles under Lincoln's eyes
and the forced smile he managed to give her.

"He has been steadily improving every day since waking up. They
are ready to move him to a care facility in the Bay Area for people
with brain injuries. It's called Care Meridian," Ann said.

Lincoln chimed in, "We talked with his insurance today to make sure it's a good fit. His COBRA insurance expires in three months, but they will pay for him to be there for ninety days. They have specialized brain injury people who will work with him, teaching him basic life skills again."

"I can hear the hope has returned to your voices. That's great news he will be getting out of the hospital. It's a long journey ahead of you, but I'm praying that he will make progress in this new place," Kate said. "I know you won't give up on him. You two have got to be the most faithful people I know."

"Thanks for calling. It means so much to have your constant support," Ann said.

As she hung up, she looked over at Lincoln again. "How are we going to keep doing this? What about Jacob? Are we giving him enough time?"

"God will give us the strength we need. We're going to trust Him each step of the way," Lincoln said.

Ann trusted God. He had, after all, undeniably moved on Damian's behalf. But God still didn't seem to answer her prayers the way she expected Him to.

Her faith in God started the moment she stood in the shadow of that cross. She clung to her childlike faith through all of life's circumstances, including her father's death several years ago. Although she had rarely seen a direct answer to her own prayers, God's presence in her life was undeniable. She continued to believe her life verse— Jeremiah 29:11—with renewed vigor as she said to Lincoln, "If God kept Damian alive, then He must have a plan for him. He has given us hope to get this far. I know Damian has some kind of future ahead of him."

Damian's move to Care Meridian brought hope to the family. Every day, he made new strides. He was surprisingly active, regaining use of all his limbs and vocalizing sounds. As time went on, he no longer had a vacant stare, but appeared to see the world around him. He began to make more eye contact. Stretches and movement with his physical therapist helped Damian gain full use of his body in a controlled way. All that constant movement the family had done while he was in his vegetative state kept his body limber and ready for use.

His occupational therapist, Lucas, thrust Damian into real-life situations to help him adapt to the world around him. The first huge accomplishment for Damian was eating with a fork, although he was still mostly fed through a feeding tube. Lucas took Damian out on walks in the community, and even into stores. Damian tried to grab everything in sight, but Lucas patiently showed him how to keep his hands off the breakable merchandise and maneuver through the aisles without touching everything.

One day, Lucas was working with Damian, teaching him to stay out of the street, respect the moving cars, and cross at the crosswalks. Damian usually stayed within reach but managed to wrestle away and sprint up the hilly street through a residential neighborhood. Damian ran faster and farther than Lucas could. Lucas came back sweaty and out of breath, clutching Damian's shirt, just as Lincoln strode up to the home.

"Wow, he can really get away from me now. This is getting to be dangerous. He is definitely outpacing me he's so fit."

Everyone celebrated the small victories and milestones Damian had as he became more and more aware. The speech therapist, Vivian, said Damian could parrot words. She said she was unsure if he actually grasped the meaning of them, but he would repeat, "tree tree tree tree tree," or "car car car car car."

Vivian also told them about his manic moods where he would be completely uncontrollable and needed two or three people to calm him down or strap him into a chair. In these moods, he was agitated, jumpy, and angry, which often led to physical outbursts. He would slap or shove the people in the room, throw objects, flail his arms, kick aggressively, twist and shout. He yelled, screamed, or muttered repeated syllables. His periodic impulsive behavior was entirely unpredictable, explosive, and often dangerous. Ann and Lincoln had only observed a mild version of this jittery rage that Vivian described in their visits thus far.

Damian's manic behaviors prompted his care team to increase his psychotropic medications: Ativan and Haldol. Although Damian was making significant improvements with all the therapy he was receiving, he also needed to remain safe. He was a fit twenty-eight-year-old man, extremely strong and without cognition to be aware of his capabilities. It was a difficult scenario; in order to control his wild moods, they had to increase his drug dosages. The drugs caused him to be more sedated, which also slowed his ability to learn. It was a delicate balance of encouraging his growth while controlling his outbursts.

Ann or Lincoln, or both, visited at least three times a week, sometimes taking Damian on outings to the park, or down to the beach. Ann often hoped to see LB but had glimpsed no sight of him since the hospital.

Walking into Care Meridian felt routine. When Damian had almost completed his ninety days, Ann visited the facility with Kate for an overnight stay. Kate had been her lifeline through this entire time with Damian, helping her make sense of it all. And now Kate was there to help Ann observe Damian before making the decision to either take him home or find some other option.

"Hi, Ann. Who have you brought with you today?" the receptionist, Fiona, greeted her.

"This is my friend, Kate," Ann replied. As she spoke, she signed in at the desk and retrieved the identification badges required. "Have you had any more developments on possible placements?"

"No, Damian is a tough placement. He is too young for a majority of facilities, and not too many facilities are willing to take on his level of care. It's hard to place a one-on-one case. Taking him home won't be easy either. I just know he can't stay here past the ninety days," Fiona replied.

"Well, that's why we're here. We want to see what his care looks like through the night," Ann said. "So we know what we're in for, if we do take him home."

They walked back toward Damian's room. His respiratory therapist was just leaving. Damian's room was a constant whirl of activity, between the physical therapist, the occupational therapist, speech therapist, the nurses who took care of his feeding tube and twenty medications, and everyone else. At 7:00 p.m., the night shift came in. Two helpers were assigned to Damian overnight.

"Our plan is to stay up all night to watch his habits," Kate said to Ann. "You have to be honest with yourself about if you can actually do this."

As the evening drew on, Damian was wide awake. The two nurses got him up to play ball with him. Damian would pick the ball up and roll it back. Then, he had his first blowout poop. The runny poop dripped down off Damian, splattering the floor as he walked.

"Watch intently everything they're doing," Kate instructed.

The two helpers worked together skillfully. One of the nurses pushed a call button; the janitorial staff swept in quickly with the mop and sanitation bucket to clean the poop that was mucked all around the room. While that was happening, the nurses walked him to the nearby bathroom, where they stripped him and showered him off, both holding on to him so he wouldn't slip. They toweled him off and then began the rigorous process of dressing him, which he fought every step of the way. He flailed his arms as one held his body and the other put the loose-fitting shirt over his head. He kicked and kicked as they sat him down to pull on his underwear and pants. But they continued to work as a team, patiently waiting for him to calm down before they continued.

"Ann, I don't think I could do this. His level of care is extremely high," Kate leaned over and whispered to Ann.

Ann thought to herself, *If Kate couldn't do it, there's no way I could do it.* She watched closely as they finished the dressing process. They seemed to manage it as a team; maybe if Lincoln was helping her, it could work. "But like Fiona said, I just don't see any other viable option. And he's my son."

Thirty minutes later, the janitorial staff had the poop mess clean, and the nurses were laying Damian down for bed again.

Everyone got a little bit of rest until the commotion of his next blowout bowel movement. Damian appeared to sleep very little.

"Is this a normal night?" Ann asked one of the workers. "I thought he would sleep more and poop less." Ann treasured her sleeping hours. And Damian was so aggressive in his resistance to get dressed. Taking care of him appeared to be beyond her capabilities. At full height, she stood almost an entire foot shorter than Damian. Wrestling someone taller and stronger than her was not something she practiced in her life of comfort and ease that she—and her waistline—had grown accustomed to.

"It depends. Sometimes he sleeps; other times he is awake all night. He doesn't have a sleeping pattern. Are you sure you want to try to take him home?" she said.

"I don't know where else he can go," Ann said, already feeling panic rise within her.

"His care is a challenging case," the nurse replied.

"I think once he gets home and settled he will calm down," Ann said, trying to reassure herself.

On the third blowout poop, the janitor started talking to Ann before leaving the room. "I wouldn't take him home if I were you," he said.

"Where am I supposed to take him then?" Ann asked.

"Once you take him out of the medical setting, they don't have to take him back. No matter what you do, don't take him," he warned as he leaned his body weight on the end of the mop.

"What do I do then?" Ann asked.

"Just leave him until *they* find a solution," he said and then walked out of the room with his mop bucket.

Seeing the stress lines on Ann's face as he walked away, Kate said, "He does have a point. You do have to take that into consideration. Just keep watching what they're doing and keep being realistic with yourself about if you can do it. It might not be the answer you want, but you have to be honest. It will be much harder to get him back here once he gets home."

ON THE WAY HOME IN THE MORNING, KATE LOOKED over at Ann. "So what did you think?"

"I don't know. It seems like a lot, but maybe Lincoln and I could do it," Ann said. "I really have no idea what I'm doing."

"If you're serious about it, you could hire a nurse to help you at home. I know someone who might be able to help you out. And you could think about asking Nicole to help you?"

"I would never ask Nicole to help. I don't want her to be in the position of seeing her brother exposed like that. I don't want to put the burden on her. She has way too much going on anyway. She is finishing nursing school and just got married," Ann said.

"Well, she could help with the nutrition and medications part that you feel so worried about," Kate pointed out.

"It's just not her responsibility," Ann stuck to her answer. "I don't want to put this on her or Jacob. They don't need to be affected by this. Jacob's going into his senior year. Lincoln does want to have a meeting with the Navarro family to see if anyone wants to help be a part of bringing him home—mostly to give LB a chance to voice any opinions he has about his brother's care."

"Not to discourage you, Ann, but I don't think you will be able to manage him at home. And people may say they will help, but when it comes down to it, they have their own lives that come first. I would refuse to take him home," Kate said.

"What other option do I have? They can't find another placement, and we can't afford to keep him there," Ann said. "It's forty thousand dollars a *month* without insurance. That's half a million in a year. We're happy to pay for him, but who has that kind of money? Medi-Cal won't cover Care Meridian, and we're worried that the type of place Medi-Cal would cover would stick him in a wheelchair in a corner and sedate him with drugs. That is if anyone would agree to take him. So far, the skilled facilities Care Meridian reached out to won't accept him. There just doesn't seem to be a good option."

"Have I steered you wrong thus far?" Kate asked.

"No," Ann admitted.

"Like the janitor said, once you get him home, you're stuck with him. They won't take him back. The hospitals won't take him. You can't just walk him back into a rehab facility. But if you leave him there, it's their responsibility to find something that will work for him," Kate reiterated.

After the overnight experience, Ann and Lincoln took Damian on a few outings to see what it was like to have him in their care. They spent as much time as they could watching the therapists work with him and taking him places to glean as much as possible. As they watched, they thought to themselves, *These are normal people—yes, highly trained—but we could do what they're doing.* But Damian was a moving target, constantly changing and learning new things, making his care highly unpredictable.

AN ATTRACTIVE BRUNETTE ANSWERED THE DOOR FOR Ann and Lincoln at Brooke's house in Roseville.

"Hi, I'm Stacy," the brunette said, stepping aside to allow the newcomers inside. "You must be Ann and Lincoln. I've been hearing so much about you."

"And how are you related here?" Ann asked, stepping inside the doorway to a nicely furnished hallway.

"I'm one of Damian's cousins. I've always liked him," Stacy said with a genuine smile.

"Wow! I had no idea he had so many family members he was in contact with. I'm almost in tears seeing how many people are here who love Damian," Ann said. *I should have known that. Why didn't I know that? Why didn't I know such an important thing about my own son?*

They followed her into a large open living room where the Navarro family mingled. Damian's three brothers sat around the room. Mario, the oldest, sat close to his girlfriend, Tish, on the love seat, and Milo lounged in an oversized chair in the corner. LB sat on the ground with Raphael, who was toddling around, the object of most people's attention. Connie was outside with Larry, who was talking to another relative. And a few other faces filled the room who were unfamiliar to Ann.

"This must be Brooke, LB's fabulous girlfriend. I'm so glad to meet you at last," Ann said, extending her arms to hug her as the hostess walked up to greet them.

"Yes. Thanks for coming out here to our house. We all want to help Damian however we can," Brooke responded, receiving the hug. "Damian has always been kind to me."

Brooke motioned for everyone to sit down in the assorted couches and chairs crammed into the living room. LB remained on the floor, leaning against the couch, focusing all his attention on Raphael so as not to make eye contact with either Ann or Lincoln. He looked noticeably uncomfortable.

Brooke signaled for Lincoln to begin. "Let's open with a word of prayer. We don't have any answers, but our God does. God was important to Damian, as most of you know, so I think it's appropriate to ask Him to help us sort all this out," Lincoln said, bowing his head and saying a quick prayer.

"As you all know," Lincoln then addressed the room, "Damian's health has taken a wild turn. I know most of you have visited him at the hospital throughout his time of liver failure, liver transplant, and now awakening a new Damian. We have no idea what his future holds. He has relearned how to walk and a few basic skills. He has said a few words, mostly repeating sounds without any meaning. Currently, his care is very intensive. He is in a place called Care Meridian where he has six or more therapists working with him. However, his insurance is running out to stay in the facility, and after that, the cost is astronomical to keep him there. Which is why we are having this meeting."

LB still hadn't looked up, but the rest of them looked concerned. Just then, Larry barged through the door and made a scene as he sat down, spilling a splash of his beer on the carpet.

"Really, Larry," Brooke said in an exasperated tone, grabbing a towel.

Mario spoke up, "Is there somewhere else that can take him? Somewhere less expensive?"

"We have been looking into that," Lincoln answered. "So far we haven't found any care facilities that would be willing to take him. The best thing would be to keep him where he is, but after his insurance runs out, the options seem to be falling onto the family for his care. Since you are his biological family, we wanted you all to voice your opinions if you think something different should happen than what we are proposing. We also wanted to see who is interested in being a part of his care team. What are you able and available to do?"

"What is the care going to look like?" Brooke asked. "I'm not working, so I have time."

Pointing at Raphael, Ann said, "Well, you do have three little people dependent on you already, especially that cute one who is into everything. But we would love your help if you can spare it. I spent the night at his facility last week. A lot of his care involves cleaning up poop. And administering his medications every four hours."

"I'm not afraid of poop." Brooke laughed. "I have a toddler, as you pointed out. Where are you thinking he would live? Are you thinking he could rotate houses? Or is that even possible?"

Ann and Lincoln had spent many hours talking about it already. Although Damian's siblings all loved their brother, none of them realistically had the time or patience to take Damian into their homes full time. None of them had a stable income or home that could easily accommodate another person. If anyone was going to take over full-time care of Damian, it would have to be them.

But they called the meeting together for LB's sake, to give him a space to voice his opinion if he had one. Ann loved her sons and was willing to do anything for them. Being in the same room as LB brought her immense joy.

"Unless someone here feels they truly want to house Damian in their home, Lincoln and I were planning to bring him home. We have the most space and availability. I think it would be difficult for him to be constantly changing locations. But in terms of how to help, we're still making a plan. Perhaps coming up one afternoon a week to sit with Damian or just sit with me while I take care of Damian. Something like that," Ann said. She looked at Raphael sitting in LB's lap, longing to hug them both. "What we do know is that we love Damian and we want to surround Damian with people who love him to give him the best chance at recovery."

"We want to help you however we can," Stacy, the cousin, said. "Can we help in getting your home prepared for Damian? I'd love to come up and see your house. Damian always talked about how much he loved it. I think it's right for him to be there, in the place he loved."

"What are you getting at, Stacy?" Larry interjected.

Ignoring Larry's comment, Ann responded to Stacy's question. "If you want to come up next weekend, I'm actually feeding the staff for the Fourth of July and could use some extra helpers. I feed about fifty people for three days. You could come help me serve them and check out the house too."

Brooke stood up from her chair and said, "I will gladly come help next weekend."

Stacy echoed, "Me too."

Then Brooke looked pointedly at LB and put both hands on her hips. With a stern voice, she told him, "LB, these are good people."

Everyone but LB laughed, lifting the mood of the whole room. The meeting ended with that—everyone laughing and resuming conversation with the people around them. Mario quickly escaped out the back door with Milo and Larry, heading to the cooler and joining Connie. Brooke marched over to LB, looking intent to tell him the rest of what was on her mind.

LB HELD RAPHAEL ON HIS LAP. LOOKING AT HIS SON reminded him why he needed to stay safe behind the walls he had built. How could anyone give their kid away to the system, and not fight to keep them? They had walked out of his life, just like his biological parents did. All this love for Damian was a show; they would give up on Damian soon enough. As soon as Damian became too much to handle, they would ship him off to an institution. Just like they had given up on LB and sent him away when he posed a challenge.

But at the same time, how could LB reconcile this constant showing up for Damian when he thought they didn't care? He pushed out the thoughts that threatened to bring the walls crashing down and built them up just a little bit higher, reminding himself of the true villains they were. He refused to look up until they were gone, even as Brooke made all kinds of accusations at him.

Ann and Lincoln prepared to leave. Stacy and Brooke made plans with Ann to come help with the staff feeding. Ann wrote down her number for both of them and gave Brooke a hug before leaving. "I'm so glad we got to meet the mother of my grandson at last. I knew I would like you."

"LB had me convinced I wouldn't like you." Brooke laughed jovially. "Boy, was he wrong. I wonder what else he could be wrong about."

Damian at Care Meridian after starting Haldol

Outing from Care Meridian before Haldol: (above) Damian with Lincoln, (right) Damian with Ann

FOURTEEN

We Need a Rescue

JULY 2008

. . . .

"Adonai, El Roi—the LORD, the God who
sees me, Hagar's words. . . When we stumble
onto hard roads, he finds us and comforts
us. . . . Or does he call us to them?"

—*The Chosen, Dallas Jenkins (Genesis 16:13)*

. . . .

AS ANN AND LINCOLN DROVE UP THE HALF-MILE
driveway with Damian in the back seat, Kate's words echoed in Ann's
head. On the way out of Care Meridian, at least four people had
asked them, "Are you sure? Are you sure you want to take him home?"
After hundreds of conversations going back and forth about it, they
felt it was the only option. It would be challenging, yes, but he was
family, and family doesn't belong in an institution. Maybe bringing
him home would help clear his head and restore his brain. With all
the improvements at Care Meridian, they hoped he would make a full
recovery. But here she was questioning it again.

Lincoln parked the car outside their fifteen-year-old home they built on top of a hill overlooking the valley. The horizon stretched to the coastal mountains and down to Sacramento on a clear day.

"We're home, Damian," Lincoln announced as he unbuckled him from the back seat.

He helped Damian out of the car. Damian had all kinds of things attached to him; he had bandages on his arm and head, and an IV cord for food and medications attached to his back.

Damian got out of the car, took two steps, then ran.

Before Lincoln could react, Damian's legs broke into a sprint, faster and faster, down the driveway.

Ann and Lincoln looked at each other, shocked.

Gasping, Ann said, "He can run?"

"Not run, sprint," Lincoln corrected.

"Hurry, hurry. Back in the car. He'll be lost. He has no idea where he is," Ann said, scrambling back into the passenger seat.

By the time Lincoln clambered back in the car and steered down the hill, Damian was out of sight. The half-mile driveway had never felt so long. Had he wandered off into the hillside of oak trees? Lincoln kept his eye on the road while Ann scanned the outlying land.

"There he is. He made it all the way to the gate. He's fast," Lincoln remarked, screeching the car to a stop.

After wrangling Damian back into the car, Lincoln wiped his own drenched forehead. In contrast, Damian did not have a single bead of sweat from the ordeal. His mental state had a long way to go, but his physical body had gained greater strength than Lincoln had imagined it would.

This time Ann had the wheelchair waiting just outside the car door while Lincoln held on to Damian's body as he climbed out of the car. It took both of them working together to get him seated in the borrowed specialty wheelchair and strapped in.

"Fuck fuck fuck fuck fuck fuck fuck fuck fuck."

"What did you say, young man?" Ann stood glued to the spot, her eyes bulging out of their sockets.

Damian's whole face turned red with anger, and his eyes squinted, his feet and arms flailing. "Fuck fuck fuck fuck fuck fuck fuck fuck fuck."

"Are you upset we put you in the chair?" Lincoln asked calmly.

"Fuck fuck fuck fuck fuck fuck fuck fuck fuck."

"This can't be happening. Get him to stop, Lincoln," Ann said, covering her ears. She sunk her forehead into her hands. Thinking back over the last few months, she tried to remember if she had seen any behavior remotely like this, and if so, what to do about it. She was drawing a blank. That sinking feeling in the pit of her stomach tripled in size.

Lincoln talked in a quiet, soothing voice to Damian. "Damian, calm down. You're home. I'll unstrap you, but you can't run. Damian. Look at me. Do not run." They had no idea what Damian could or could not understand.

Holding on to Damian's shoulder, Lincoln unbuckled Damian from the chair. They just needed to make it a few more steps to get into the house. With a quick spin and a jump, Damian broke free again. His agility surprised Lincoln. But this time Damian started walking toward the edge of the cliff. Ann trotted behind them, but her short legs were no match for Damian's long, quick stride.

Damian veered off right at the last second, continuing around the small loop at the top of the driveway. Lincoln breathlessly kept his pace right beside him. He allowed Damian to be free to explore at arm's length, like he had seen the occupational therapist do with him several times in the city. Ann waited at the "Y" of the driveway for them to loop back around.

Damian's arms swung as he walked, almost as if he were marching, while yelling indiscernible sounds at the top of his lungs, mixed with, "Fuck fuck fuck fuck fuck fuck fuck fuck fuck." He marched around and around the circle driveway, as if Jericho might fall down. Then he shook his hands to the sky.

It really might have been a type of Jericho to him. At the care home, he had seemed angry, but not like this. Now that he was home, Ann and Lincoln wondered if he might be thinking his chances for getting out of his mental state were over. His mind could have woken up to the reality that he was trapped in a body with no means of communication. It was like there was a wall between his inner and outer self, and he would be able to speak clearly if he could just climb over the wall.

Which is exactly what he did next. He walked over to the porch, and with one leap, hopped onto the ledge surrounding the deck. He stood, six feet above the ground below. Before Lincoln could grab him, he hopped down on the ground, completely fearless.

Learning quickly from his mistakes, Lincoln ran down and grabbed him around his midsection. He managed to walk Damian into the house, with Ann quickly locking the door behind them.

"I'm calling Care Meridian. He never acted this way before. Something must be wrong," Ann fretted.

"Wait, I think he just pooped. I'll need your help," Lincoln said, still catching his breath from the constant activity.

Poop was an all-hands-on-deck operation. They had watched the nurses taking care of him and had even helped with the process a number of times. But now, in their own home with a seemingly out-of-control man who had superhuman strength, the task seemed daunting at best.

Damian's body constantly had to battle Crohn's disease, which meant that his poop was never completely solid, always some variant of diarrhea. When his Crohn's was under control, it was a mushy solid but still runny. When it was out of control (not medicated properly), it was brown liquid that splattered his chair, the wall, the people around him, and left a dripping path to the bathroom. Not to mention the acrid smell.

Right there in their kitchen, Damian's first bowel movement oozed out of his diaper and onto the floor. Ann stared blankly for a moment before she realized she needed to jump to action. They walked him into the bathroom just off the kitchen to shower him down. They stripped him down and got his diaper off, his arms flailing the whole time with more angry shouts.

It dawned on Ann that they hadn't thought through all the details. Cramming into their one-person shower with Damian, they struggled to get him clean. He had become so vocal, shouting, "Fuck," the whole time.

Lincoln toweled him off while Ann ran to find a change of clothes. He was too skinny for most of the clothes they had brought home from his apartment. Everything looked baggy on him, and his pants had nothing to grab on to, so they fell down to his feet. She looked for something tight fitting and ran back to the bathroom.

Now for the task of getting him dressed. Damian was like an oversized toddler, especially when it came to getting dressed. More like a baby, as there was zero cooperation. He squirmed and fidgeted. One person had to lift up each leg to get his pants on while the other held him still. Then he had to sit down to get his shirt over his head and through his arms. His shoes were especially difficult. While he was kicking, getting the shoe over the foot then tied was nearly impossible. It all took at least ten minutes each time, sometimes longer.

This is exhausting. Ann felt the day would never end. Next on the agenda was figuring out the feeding tube. And they couldn't forget his twenty-plus meds, which they had to administer strictly every four hours. They practiced once with supervision, but she felt a little intimidated. That reminded her—she should call Care Meridian.

"Hi, this is Ann. I think something's genuinely wrong," Ann said, fidgeting with the piece of paper in her hands.

"Hi, Ann, what do you mean?" Fiona answered.

"Damian is throwing a giant tantrum about everything. He's been shouting the F-word nonstop. He seems very agitated. We never saw him act anything like this. I think he's sick or upset or something. We don't know what to do," Ann told her.

"No, he did that all the time when he was here," she said.

"He did?" Ann asked, the shock rising.

"Yes, I thought you knew. He had manic outbursts often. He would shout the F-word."

"Why didn't anybody tell us?" Ann asked.

"We thought you had been here enough to experience what he was like," Fiona replied.

"He was mostly drugged when we experienced him there. Well, what should we do?" Ann asked expectantly.

"The best thing you can do is find a home for him to live in," Fiona said.

"But we want to keep him here, at home. Don't you have any suggestions?" Ann's desperation grew in her voice.

"You can get his Ativan and Haldol increased and see if that helps."

"So we just have to drug him to get him to stop?"

"That's all I can suggest. Good luck," Fiona said before hanging up the phone.

Ann slumped to the ground feeling hopeless. She had no idea it would be like this. If she had known it would be like this, she would have asked for more time, more training. Had they made a mistake in bringing him home? *God, give me strength.* She just wanted to make it to bedtime.

"Ann, he just pooped again," Lincoln called from the living room.

DAMIAN POOPED TWICE MORE BEFORE 10:00 P.M., AND they were ready to call in reinforcements.

Bedtime didn't go as planned either. Damian refused to get into his bed. Instead, he paced back and forth, back and forth. Ann and Lincoln felt helpless.

"We can just lock the door, and maybe he will settle down while we get some rest ourselves," Lincoln suggested.

They did just that, and had settled into bed when they heard a loud thump.

"I'll go check," Ann said.

Anticipating his arrival, Ann had decorated Damian's room with some of the things from his old apartment, including a beautiful inlaid table Damian made in woodworking class in high school. Photographs from his childhood and his guitar decorated the walls. When she got to the room, she saw shattered glass everywhere. Damian had taken a photo frame off the wall and hurled it across the room, shattering it into glass splinters that covered the floor.

"Oh, no. Damian, come over here. I don't want you to get hurt," Ann hissed.

Lincoln appeared over her shoulder and sighed.

"We're going to have to empty his room, I suppose. I'll play ball with him for a while, see if I can get him to calm down. You go get some rest after you get the glass swept up," Lincoln said.

If this is just the first day, how are we going to survive? Ann thought to herself as she swept.

Much later, she lay in bed trying to go to sleep, but she just kept imagining endless days stretching before her with a manic man who looked like her son but acted like a deranged one-and-a-half-year-old.

Jesus, help, she kept repeating, hoping to lull herself to sleep. She had to re-energize herself. Summer was Lincoln's busy season at the campground. Tomorrow, she would be on her own. She was already dreading what the morning would bring.

THE SUN STREAMED THROUGH THE WINDOW, dancing on Ann's face, lightly awakening her. Had she really slept until 9:00 a.m.? She savored that moment of sun, hope dawning onto her day. Today could be different. Damian might poop less or have a breakthrough, even say, "Truck," instead of the F-word.

Damian's second day home started off as expected—poop, breakfast, pills, more poop. Then she got a phone call.

"Hi, Ann," Bart, Lincoln's older brother who helped run the campground, said through the telephone. "I wanted to come visit Damian, now that he's home. Would that be all right?"

"Sure, we would welcome the company," Ann said.

Ann wheeled Damian out to the spacious deck, overlooking the green lawn and the stretching valley below.

"Damian, you're going to have a visitor," Ann told him.

Damian made some grunting noises and strained as though he was trying to communicate, but Ann couldn't make anything out.

Nana joined them on the deck, settling into a comfy rocking chair. Nana lovingly stroked Jackie, the cat who sat on her lap. She had been a stray cat that wandered to them, possibly from the campground. The cat purred loudly and drooled profusely when she received attention. She was an outside cat, but a well-loved part of the family. Close to Nana was Damian's wheelchair. The wheelchair was a loaner from a man who passed away at Care Meridian. The weighted adult chair fitted with a lap strap kept Damian and everyone else safe.

"Hello, Damian," Bart exclaimed as he walked onto the deck, giving him a pat on the back. "You made it home all right, did you? Did they treat you okay in the hospital? Any pretty ladies?"

Damian stringed together some syllables, "da da da da da da."

"Well, it's good to see you back here. Although you need to get some meat on those bones," Bart said.

"He doesn't look like much, but he is super strong," Ann said. "And fast as anything!"

Bart's attention turned toward Ann to ask her how she was coping with him being home. As they were talking, Damian used his feet to inch closer and closer to Nana.

He scooted right up next to Nana, raised his arm, and with a clenched fist, hit the back of her head.

Moving quickly, Bart grabbed Damian's hand before he could hit her again. "Don't you ever hit her again," Bart scolded Damian.

As Damian looked up at Bart, a wave of shock passed through his eyes, which quickly turned into rage. He wrestled his hand out of Bart's and started to scream.

Damian flailed his arms and then began bouncing up and down, thrusting his feet onto the ground so that his whole wheelchair was bouncing. He looked like Tigger bouncing across the porch, somehow propelling his hundred-pound body to move the sixty-four-pound wheelchair as if it weighed nothing.

Screaming and thrashing, Damian continued his fit for what felt like an eternity. Ann finally called Lincoln to come home and asked Bart to leave.

"Mom, you had better go inside. I don't want you to get hurt," Ann said to Nana.

As she turned back around, Damian tipped his wheelchair over; he ended up lying face down on the ground with his wheelchair on top of him. Damian stopped yelling for the first time in twenty minutes. Ann could see his face muscles relax and fatigue take over. His body went limp after so much exertion. He had finally worn himself out.

Ann bent over to unbuckle the straps and heaved the chair up and off Damian, just as Lincoln ran to her side.

Together, they lifted him up from under his arms and carried him into his bed.

Ann sighed. At least she would get a break for two to three hours while he slept off his mania. And another glimmer of hope, Kara, the home health nurse Kate had recommended, would have her first four-hour shift tomorrow. She was only available twice a week for four hours, but four hours sounded glorious.

THE DAYS DRONED ON, A SEEMINGLY ENDLESS CYCLE of catching sleep when they could while caring for Damian twenty-four hours a day. Ann hadn't imagined how much tireless work it would take to care for him. At Care Meridian, he had five or six therapists working with him, plus his feeding specialist, an RN to track his medication, a different person to change him in between poops, not to mention the janitorial staff. Now she was supposed to be all of those combined with no training. No wonder she was exhausted.

Had she given him his morning medication? The details seemed to be blurring in her mind. They couldn't go outside anymore. Damian ran down the hill five times in the first week they were home. Any time he got out, he just started running. And then he would hit the back of the car when she pulled up to get him, refusing to get in. Once she got him in, he would kick the back of the seat and pull her hair as she was driving or try to grab her arm. He would yell and yell. She kept thinking to herself, *Thank God we live in the country with no one around. If we had neighbors, they would surely think we were torturing the poor man.*

Ann called their local doctor, and he shared his opinion that it was perhaps too soon for Damian to come home and gave them a list of organizations to call. No offer to help call the homes, just a list. And, of course, no advice insofar as how to pay for it all. They had said if he remained disabled for two years, he would qualify for better insurance.

She felt so alone. It helped when Kara came, but her time always ended so quickly. At least she could call Lincoln at any moment and he could be home in five minutes, but she didn't like bothering him at work. Ann was used to his long work hours. She had, after all, been the main caregiver for her four children, making most of the parenting decisions and fulfilling their needs. Jacob was her only other child at home, but his social activities in his senior year kept him so busy she hardly saw him. But this was so different. She found herself in need of help, in a more dire way than ever before.

Brooke had come with Stacy to help feed the staff the weekend before bringing Damian home, but when she asked when Brooke might be available to come back, Brooke had looked at the ground, avoiding eye contact. And then when Ann called Brooke earlier that week, Brooke had made a flippant excuse, so Ann took the hint that help would not materialize. Mario also had an excuse as to why he couldn't drive out that week. Work was piling up for him, he had said with slurred speech.

She didn't want to involve her friends; it was just too much for them. Besides, Damian seemed more anxious when anyone paid a visit. His anger and frustration were so extreme—in his manic moods, he would bite, scratch, spit, kick, hit, flail, push, pinch, and yell. They had to modify his wheelchair with anti-tip bars so he could be contained safely. He constantly pulled his feeding tube out and if she couldn't get it reattached she had to drive him down to the ER. Getting him dressed had become a nightmare; he simply did not want to cooperate. Every day felt like they were barely surviving.

That morning had killed all of Ann's hope. The stench that greeted her nostrils when she opened the door almost made her gag. Damian stood, teeth clenched, a fiery look in his eyes and arms stretched over his head covered in brown, painting the walls with fecal matter. Broad, brown hand strokes covered the wall, the floor, and the bed. She shut the door for a moment to compose herself, took a deep breath, and prepared to plunge into the cleanup. Hours later, when she sat down alone at the kitchen table, Damian resting, her despair deepened.

How had her life come to this, an unending cycle of dealing with poop and spending her entire day with an anxious, jittery man who had her nerves on edge? She had given up all her former church responsibilities and social outings to stay home with Damian. She saw the days stretching before her like a desolate desert as far as the eye could see in every direction, with no hope for reprieve, no oasis in sight. Overwhelming fear gripped her. *Is this how I'm going to spend the rest of my life?*

A knock at the door interrupted her thoughts of hopelessness. Ah, it was Kate.

"How are you managing?" Kate asked.

So thankful to hear her friend's voice, to see someone who could have a conversation with her and wasn't going to hit her, Ann rushed over to hug her. Ann opened her mouth to speak, but no words came. Then the floodgates opened, and Ann felt she had never truly cried before that moment. The tears spilled from her eyes in a river, telling the story of her hardship.

"You . . . were . . . so right, Kate," Ann squeaked out between sobs.

Wrapping Ann in her arms, Kate said, "No, Ann, I wasn't. What you are doing for your son is beautiful. You are giving yourself entirely. But it looks like you need help. I'm calling in reinforcements."

"I should not have brought him home. It's too much. I can't do it," Ann said, her sobbing giving way to the occasional hiccups.

"It must be overwhelming. We are going to get you more help. You need another home health nurse—I thought Kara would be more available. You can't do this all alone."

Kate helped Ann make a quick call to the local doctor that she worked for. They set up an appointment for Ann to see the doctor for her own overwhelming feelings and asked for another home health nurse to be sent out for Damian as soon as they could find someone. Then Kate sat with Ann and listened to all her stories.

FIFTEEN

The Rescue Plan

AUGUST 2008

. . . .

"In the most dismal place, at the longest
point of night—just before sunrise—the
morning star shines its glimmer of hope."

—Donna F. Ivery, Sleep, Pray, Heal

. . . .

ANN SAT IN THE CAR, WILLING HERSELF TO GET OUT
and walk into the office. *Is something wrong with me?* Ann never
imagined she would be in a place where she would have to accept *this*
kind of help. Kate told her it was normal, that everyone needed help
at certain points in their lives. Ann wasn't so sure. But her hopelessness
had grown so much, nothing seemed to ease her despair. She talked to
God, but Damian was just as angry as ever. Nothing changed.

Kara and Lincoln were home with Damian so she could come
to this appointment. She sat in the car, took a long, deep breath,
and felt as though someone else was opening the car door while she
hovered above, as if watching herself go through the actions. She

plodded toward the office door, checked in, and sat down in a chair, still feeling disembodied.

"Ann, I'm Dr. Eugene. I'm happy to see you today. Follow me." The kind man with dark curly hair and a genuine smile invited Ann into his office.

Ann's tongue felt as though it were glued to the roof of her mouth. She sat in the uncomfortable silence that her own lack of words seemed to create. She couldn't remember the last time she didn't have *something* to say.

"So, tell me about what's been happening in your life."

"I just feel sad all the time," Ann began and then couldn't think of what else to say.

"Have you had any major changes recently?"

"Everything. Everything has changed." Ann felt a ball of anger mixed with bitterness crawl up her gut, into her chest, and up and out. Then the words came rushing out like a waterfall spilling over the edge of a cliff. She told him about Damian and being thrust into becoming his caregiver, that her life had become an endless desert. Tears spewed, and she hiccuped. "It's just so overwhelming. He needs so much help. And I need help. I feel like I've lost myself. I just can't do it another day."

"Have you thought about hiring someone to help you take care of him?"

"We have one nurse, but she has very limited availability. It's not nearly enough help. We're waiting for another nurse. And my friends have offered some help, but I just don't think he should be their problem. I'm the one who decided to bring him home. I should have listened and kept him where he was."

"Let's talk about your feelings of responsibility. If people are offering help, why aren't you taking it?" Dr. Eugene leaned back in his chair with a pencil in his hand and a thoughtful expression on his face.

Ann sat at the edge of her seat, and her arms flew up with indignance as she spoke. "I'm the one who brought him home. I should be able to handle it."

"But you can't. Let me ask you this, what if this were happening to your friend?"

Ann leaned back in her chair and thought for a moment. The fingers of her right hand curled into a fist that tapped her mouth lightly. "Well, I think I would assume they had it under control. I would offer to be there for them, but I wouldn't expect to get tangled up in it all."

"Do you believe you deserve to have help?"

"Yes. Well, I don't know." Ann's forehead wrinkled, and she fixed her eyes on a trinket on Dr. Eugene's desk.

"Why?" Dr. Eugene tapped his fingers together, his eyes intent on Ann's face.

"I guess I just grew up believing the less help I asked for, the better." Ann's curiosity in the trinket grew, avoiding the intense gaze that might saw open the depths of her soul.

"Do you hang on to a sense of control?"

"What do you mean?"

"If you ask for help, you make yourself vulnerable and show weakness, but if you continue to do things on your own without help, you keep an illusion of remaining in control of your circumstances."

"Yeah." Ann's eyes dropped to the ground, and her voice was almost a whisper. "That sounds like me."

"So if you have a difficult time accepting help for yourself, it's common to also resent others who need help. This could be the stem of where your overwhelming emotions about your son are coming from. All of a sudden he needs an exorbitant amount of help, yes?"

"Yes. And he's so angry. He dislikes it as much as I do." The fire in Ann's eyes returned, and she met his gaze once again.

"And how does that make you feel?"

"He is so jumpy and jittery. I feel like my nerves are on edge all the time. I've never felt this way. We've always had a peaceful home. Our home has always been a place of refuge for me and others that we've welcomed in. Now I dread every minute of being home, and yet I'm stuck there in captivity—helping my son who can't help himself but hits and kicks and bites me when I'm trying to help him."

Dr. Eugene paused and leaned back in his chair once again, allowing space for her to continue. His knowing eyes studied her face. "It can't be all bad. What's one good thing about him being in your home?"

"What? Something good about being stuck with someone who is so constantly angry and raging and poops an insane amount?"

"Are you angry at him for needing your help?"

"No, why would I be angry at him? I'm just thankful he survived."

"Good. There's something you're thankful for."

"Yes. I mean, he almost died. His liver failed. He is way too young for his life to be over. I love him. I admit, I was hard on him before the brain injury. I regret that now. I see how difficult his life must have been. He groans in pain when he has bowel movements. It's awful to watch. I can't help but cry sometimes, knowing how debilitating his pain has been his whole life, without me realizing. I thought he was lazy, but he was in so much pain. I was so wrong. But I didn't expect him to come back to my home."

"Yes, you didn't expect him to need you to this level. And how could you? Often, the mark of successful parenting is your fledgling leaving the home, building his own nest, possibly never to return. But now he has returned. And it sounds like you might have some resentment, not toward him, but the situation. You expected your life to be different at this point, no? You have a senior in high school, your baby, and then you should be free to go on adventures with your husband. You put in the childrearing work, and it should be drawing to an end. And now here you are—stuck—caretaking for your adopted son who has suddenly become quite needy and aggressive. It's normal that this is overwhelming. It's normal that you're sad. You're grieving your life—what you thought it would be."

Ann sighed deeply, feeling understood. "Maybe you are right. I am begrudging him for changing my life so completely. I feel like this will be the rest of my life, taking care of him and not having a sane thought to myself. I feel like my life that was full and vibrant was robbed from me."

"All those feelings are normal. I do want you to think about if you are taking on more responsibility than is yours to take because you don't want to accept more help. Being in need of help is not weak; it is part of being human. We all need each other in this life. The way you're thinking about the situation could be making it more difficult for yourself. But that doesn't mean that it isn't a hard situation, just that you need more help in your corner."

Ann remained silent.

"We can explore more next time. We're out of time for today. I want to prescribe you antidepressants."

Ann hesitated, feeling that pit in her stomach grow again. "I don't know. Are you sure that's the best way to help me?"

Dr. Eugene was already scribbling on a piece of paper. In a matter-of-fact tone, he said, "We will start on a very small dose and see if it helps. It's almost impossible to take care of another person if you're feeling hopeless for yourself. This will just take the edge off and bring some equilibrium to your hormones."

Ann took a deep breath, letting it all sink in. "I'm willing to try anything at this point. I just know things can't stay the same."

"Good. They will have the slip for you at the front. I look forward to our next conversation." With that, he rose and escorted her back to the front desk area.

As Ann walked out of the office, she noticed she felt lighter in spirit. *Why was I so worried to come here?* It felt good to be heard and understood. She felt the smallest glimmer of hope return.

"GOOD MORNING, ANN. YOU HAVEN'T BEEN AT CHURCH in weeks. How is Damian doing?" Jean Pearson asked on the other end of the phone.

Church? Ann thought to herself. *How am I supposed to go to church with a raging, unpredictable man?* She wondered why this woman from church was calling as she replied, "Yeah, he is a handful."

"The doctor said you called to get Damian's drugs adjusted. He said Damian keeps having uncontrollable episodes. I am a home health nurse, and I'm coming over to help you," Jean said.

"Thank God," Ann said, feeling relief surge through her body. "How soon can you get here?"

Half an hour later, Ann welcomed her through the door and then went back to finish making her sandwich. She had been making the sandwich for more than twenty minutes, unable to focus, distracted by other tasks. She felt at the brink of insanity.

"Where is Damian now?" Jean asked.

"He was in one of his manic moods. He is in his room," Ann said.

Leaving the sandwich makings—again—they walked toward his room, and heard loud thumping and yelling as they drew closer. Listening closely, it sounded like banging on a window. Ann nervously opened the door.

Disaster had struck, like a tornado had picked up everything from its place, whirled it in the air, and threw it down with a thud. The dresser was tipped over with all the drawers open. Clothes littered the floor, the bed, and the ceiling fan. The old-fashioned shaving tub, one of the few items left from his former life, lay on its side partially blocking the door from opening.

Damian jumped on the bed, arms in the air, yelling a string of syllables.

As soon as he saw the door open, he jumped off the bed and ran for the opening. His body moved so quickly and unexpectedly it caught Ann and Jean off guard. He squeezed through the opening and escaped into the hall.

Family photographs lined the hallway leading to Damian's room. As he ran toward the wall, he clenched his fist and punched the glass of Ann and Lincoln's wedding portrait. Poised to strike the next hanging, Jean caught his arm in midair.

"Damian, *no*," Jean said in a stern voice. "You can't wreck your home. Stop."

She firmly escorted Damian to his chair in the living room, where she and Ann worked together to get him strapped into it.

"I'm calling the doctor. This situation is unsafe," Jean said with an authoritative tone. "Someone is going to get hurt, and most likely, it will be your mom. One of you is going to throw your back out trying to control him, or he's going to hurt himself. He is not ready to live at home. We need to find him a placement. I'm going to help you. In the meantime, Ann, you've got to take everything out of his room. He needs to have only a bed. He is too strong, and he might hurt himself or someone else as he tries to throw everything."

"Then it will look like an institution, being so bare," Ann protested.

"Unfortunately, that's how it will have to be—until we either find him a proper placement, or he can show us it's safe. He will have to earn the extra furniture back," Jean said.

Damian's chair started bouncing up and down. He was still furious, foaming at the mouth.

"How often does he have episodes like this?" Jean asked.

"Pretty much every day. It usually lasts anywhere from a few minutes to a few hours. Sometimes he will exhaust himself and finally fall asleep. Other times he is just sitting in his chair staring out the window or at the TV. I think that's when the drugs kick in," Ann answered.

"How do you control him?"

"We don't," Ann said. "It's impossible when he gets into these moods. He kicks and hits and scratches. He knocked his chair over until we got anti-tip bars added a week ago. We just have to get him into his chair, which is always a two-person job, and wait for him to stop."

"Is there anything that triggers an episode to start?" Jean asked.

"Not that we can see. It just comes on." Ann shrugged.

"Okay, I am going to help you," Jean said again. "I'm going to start calling places myself until we can find something. But first, we have to finish making that sandwich of yours. You must take care of yourself to be able to take care of Damian."

Jean walked her back to the kitchen and guided her step by step through taking the bread out, then the meat.

"It sounds like he is starting to calm down," Jean remarked. "How is his sleep?"

"He never sleeps more than three hours, at random times throughout the day," Ann said with a glazed look. "Sometimes at night he wakes up and paces for a few hours, then sleeps for a while."

"I'll go get him down in his bed. I want you to sit down and concentrate on eating your sandwich," Jean said. "I'll start a load of laundry too."

Alone again, Ann's mind wandered back to the hopeless state she was in. *Why does it never stop? He is so skinny. How can he poop so much? Will Jean actually be able to help me?* She could not live her whole life like this. Even in the wheelchair, she wasn't safe from his biting, kicking, and screaming. The constant rage and edginess wore on her nerves. She questioned whether the antidepressants were working. Or had she remembered to take them?

When Jean returned to the kitchen, she said, "Good. At least you got some nutrition. I want you to make taking care of yourself a priority. I'm going to be checking in at least three times a week, and more if I can make it. I'll be checking his vitals and helping you however I can. When I'm not with you, I'll be making lots of phone calls until we find somewhere for him to go."

THE WEEKS DRAGGED ON AND ON. SEVERAL TIMES, Jean called with excitement in her voice. "I think we have a placement. Start packing."

Ann would hang up and start packing things for Damian. This always ended in Jean calling back a few hours later with the same story. "Upon getting more details, the home feels under qualified to take on a case like Damian."

It felt like they had run into a fifteen-foot iron wall. They kept hitting the same roadblock. Damian simply did not fit the mold for any care facility. The mental health world considered him a medical patient because of his liver transplant and feeding tube, while the medical world considered him a mental health patient because of his brain injury. There were mental health facilities and medical facilities but not one that issued help for both. And of course, even when they found one . . . would they be able to afford it?

Hopelessness threatened to overtake Ann. She began to feel there was absolutely no way out with every door slamming shut. She started calling the facilities herself, trying to explain the situation, hoping someone would hear her desperate pleas and say yes.

Every phone call was the same. "Your best bet is to have him admitted into a hospital."

GOD GAVE ME DIARRHEA

"I can't just walk my son into a hospital and say, 'I want to admit my son. Sorry. I can't handle him.' They wouldn't take him unless he was sick," Ann said to Jean, thinking to herself, *This is just like what Kate said. Once I took him home, it would be impossible to bring him back.*

"Well, he has to get sick," Jean said.

So Ann's new dilemma was: Should she pray for her child to be sick? Or just wait until he got sick? If she could make it that long.

Ann called every facility she found listed in Northern and Southern California, Nevada, Arizona, and New Mexico. No luck. No help.

It was a Tuesday night, the night Ann and Lincoln had been hosting Young Life teenagers for a boating night. Ann wanted to get out of the house, so she left Lincoln with Damian and went down to see their friends who had been carrying on the ministry in their absence. She was desperate enough for another break she had reached out to her friend Martha to come sit with Damian the next week so they could both participate in the last few weeks of summer.

Ann got into a conversation with Bobby, one of her friends who happened to be a police officer. She started out sharing the basics, but soon she was sobbing, sharing how completely overwhelmed she was and how no one could help.

"You know, people do it all the time. They can't handle their relatives, be it a father or brother or whoever it is. They leave them on the street corner by the hospital. I have to pick up cases like that all the time. They throw in the towel and let them be somebody else's problem. If a police officer picks him up, they will take him to the hospital. The hospital will have to admit him because of the bylaws they have. It's that easy. And you're not the only one who's ever done it," Bobby said.

"I could never do that. Just leave my son somewhere, hoping someone will take him in. What if something happens to him? What if someone bad takes him? What if he walks in front of a car? All kinds of things could happen to him," Ann said, shocked at the idea of it.

"The other option is to call the sheriff when he gets manic to take him in on 'fifty-one-fifty.' Then he would be sent to a mental health facility," Bobby suggested.

"I'm afraid of the violent people who are in those types of facilities. He might become even more violent or get hurt. And they would have to medicate him so much he wouldn't be able to continue learning and growing," Ann said. "But . . . at this point, I would send him anywhere that would take him. That said, we've already called lists of mental health facilities. They don't want to take him because of his feeding tube."

"Looks like you're stuck praying he gets sick so he can be admitted," Bobby said with a shrug. "Once he's in there, he becomes the hospital's responsibility. You can walk away, and they have to find a home for him to go to. You can finally rest."

"If that's what I have to pray for, then . . . that's what I'm praying for. And we're praying it right now," Ann said determinedly. "God, if you're listening, I really need you. Like more desperately than I've ever needed you. If you truly care about us in the smallest details, I need you to help me get out of this situation. I can't do it alone, God. I'm afraid to pray this because you might actually answer, but I need my son, Damian, to get admitted to the hospital. If he must get sick for that to happen, can he get just sick enough so he needs to go to the hospital but not too sick that something serious happens? I can't do it anymore. I haven't slept in two months. Please, God, just give us the help we need."

Ann prayed that prayer, believing that God would act in some way, trusting that He was who He said He was and could work a miracle on her behalf. Damian was already walking proof of that. But this time, *she* needed God to show up for her, in the most desperate way she had ever needed him.

When she told Lincoln about her prayer back at home, he said, "God sees how desperate we are. I don't think we should pray for him to get sick, but let's just pray that God will provide us the help we need in any form that takes."

Ann cried on his shoulder and then relaxed as Lincoln stroked her back, trusting that God would find a way.

FRIDAY MORNING OF THAT SAME WEEK, ANN WOKE UP in the same hopeless state. She had been up all night with Damian. He had terrible diarrhea, worse than she had ever seen it before. It was pure brown liquid that shot up his diaper, covered his backside, his chair, and sometimes the wall, the ground, everything in proximity. Sometime in the night, she just strapped Damian to the toilet and fell asleep on the ground next to him. His system was obviously in shock. He usually pooped six to eight times a day, sometimes less, but this seemed constant—two or three times every hour. How could one scrawny person poop that much?

Lincoln took over Damian's care for the morning until Jean could get there. Determined to seek help, Ann called the next five facilities on the list. She was nearing the end of the options in nearby states, but she couldn't think about that right now.

Finally, Jean arrived to help. Lincoln was wheeling Damian back from the sixth bathroom visit of the hour. She was just in time to help with his morning medications. Damian had seven medications that had to be administered in the morning, another five in the afternoon, and eight in the evening. Each capsule had to be crushed with the marble pestle and mortar and given through his feeding tube. It was a process Ann still felt unsure of. Thank goodness Jean was there.

"Damian looks ashy and pale," Jean observed.

"He's been having constant diarrhea. I think he's sick," Ann said. "He looked like he might even throw up."

Jean pulled out her nursing kit and ran a few tests on him. "Yes, he's sick. He has a low-grade temperature too." Just then, Damian had yet another bout of diarrhea explode up his backside. "Oh my, yes, this is a bad case of diarrhea. We need to get him to the hospital."

"Really? You mean he's sick enough to go to the hospital?" Ann exclaimed, almost too afraid to hope. Was this God's answer to her prayer? Of course she believed God answered prayer, but usually it happened more gradually—the kind you look back on two years later and realize, wow, look how God answered that. But she had never seen God work this fast on her behalf. "I'll call them to let them know we're coming."

Ann hung up with their doctor and slumped her head to the table. "He said he would call in a medication for Damian. They don't want to admit Damian into the hospital because they're afraid we're going to walk away and leave him." Feeling defeated, Ann's feeling of hopelessness returned, seeing as that was, exactly, the plan.

Jean said, "That's outrageous. He needs medical care. If he gets any worse, or even stays the same for much longer once you start the medication, the hospital will end up taking him anyway. We'll see what happens, but soon, we'll just have to show up without calling. It's harder to refuse you in person. I'll stay the rest of the day to help monitor him."

After another forty-eight hours of the same, Ann had enough. Nothing seemed to ease the diarrhea—if anything, it had gotten worse. "Lincoln, we're going down there. Let's get packed up and go." Ann started to race around, grabbing anything she might need, and then suddenly stopped with her hand in midair. "But what if he has diarrhea on the way?"

"I guess we can tarp the back of the car. Who knows, if he's covered in it, they might be more likely to take him," Lincoln said, chuckling to himself.

On the way down to the local hospital, Ann whispered a prayer over and over again, "God, please let them take him. Please let them take him."

They made it to the emergency room, got him checked in, and waited and waited until they finally got into a room—where they waited some more, to see a doctor who would determine if he was sick enough to be admitted. Thankfully, they were at least in a room, even if it was a triage room, so everyone would stop staring at them as though they were doing something to hurt Damian. The return to a hospital seemed to get Damian into a manic mood. He was yelling and kicking. It took all of Lincoln's strength to keep the wheelchair in place and on the ground.

Ann looked up at the sound of the door opening. A doctor she hadn't met before walked in, which surprised her. With the amount of times they had been in this hospital over the years for Damian's Crohn's and even recently to help with the constant reattaching of Damian's IV, she thought she'd met everyone.

The doctor walked briskly over to them, saying, "I'm going to be frank with you. I've been instructed not to admit him." A yell from Damian interrupted him. "But to start with, we're going to have to get him to calm down. Then I will at least diagnose him."

A nurse came in shortly to give Damian a dosage of Ativan to try to get him to calm down. They couldn't give him much because he already had some in his system from his home medications. Lincoln left to get some coffee for them both. Alone with Damian, Ann couldn't hold back anymore. She started to cry. She thought for sure leaving him at the hospital would be the answer. She couldn't imagine bringing him home right now. Slow tears turned to sniffling sobs, which turned to wailing. She cried and cried until her eyes had no more tears to cry. Then she just sat there, red eyed, hiccupping, waiting for the doctor to return.

Damian finally settled into a manageable state. Ann sent up one more desperate prayer, "Please, God, let them admit him."

The doctor returned to do his check on Damian. Ann sat nervously as he did his tests, taking in the information he sought. He had paperwork in his hands. Then, surprisingly, the doctor sat down in the stool close to Ann.

Looking into her eyes, he said, "I want you to know my job is on the line. The head of the hospital does not want to be responsible for Damian's care. However, I'm watching you take care of your son. It's clear to me that you're doing the best you can and it's not good enough. It's not going to be good enough. I've seen a few families who are at their lowest and simply can't take care of their family members anymore. Often, they just get left here. It's expensive for the hospital to take these cases on, but your hysteria shows me that the best thing for you is for us to help you. I'm going to admit him."

Was it really true? That last statement was still sinking in as Ann said, "I don't want you to lose your job."

The attending nurse at the computer asked, "Are you sure you want to do this?"

"Beyond a shadow of a doubt. I have to help this family. I see they are at the end of their rope. They need help. I'm admitting him and will face the consequences," he said. "You are going home tonight and getting a good night's sleep. I'll take care of the details, and we'll call you when we get it figured out."

Ann's tear ducts opened up again, but this time it was happy tears. She cried and cried again, feeling true relief for the first time in months. God answered her prayer. God saw her need and answered her. She hadn't felt His tangible presence like this since she was a little girl, standing in the shadow of the cross. God would find a way to help Damian, and she could finally rest. She knew without a doubt

Damian's sickness was not random; it was exactly what she had asked for: something curable that would get him the help he needed and get her the relief she required.

She started sobbing again, unable to believe that God could answer a prayer in the form of diarrhea.

Lincoln wrapped his arms around her, tears also streaming down his face. "We finally get the relief we need. God answered our prayers for help. They will take care of Damian. Let's go home and get some rest."

When Ann got home, without Damian for the first time in two months, she could feel the weight of the pressure lift off her shoulders. She thanked God again. She knew now it was in the hospital's hands to find a placement for him. No more phone calls, no more all-nighters. The door of hope stood open.

"I have met the God who sees me. Thank you, God, for the doctor who was willing to risk his job to give me the reprieve I needed. Thank you for giving me rest. Thank you for the extreme diarrhea. And please heal Damian quickly. Bring us answers and a place for him." Ann prayed on her pillow before drifting off to sleep.

Damian improved over the next few weeks, but the hospital never pressured the family to bring him home. When Ann asked the doctors about it, they said, "Yes, normally we try to pressure the family to bring him home. But we know it's not possible for you right now."

Ann knew in her heart that God had intervened yet again on her behalf, showing her that it was all too soon to bring him home. Her worries that it was a weakness of hers that she couldn't handle it were squelched as she saw them continue to advocate on her behalf.

The hospital kept them informed of what long-term solutions they found. So far, nothing.

SIXTEEN

The Shining Beacon of Hope: Donna Watson

FALL 2008

. . . .

"I cannot change the world, but I can cast a stone
across the water to create many ripples."

—Mother Teresa

. . . .

DONNA WATSON LOVED HER JOB. EVERY DAY WAS just a little bit different; she never knew who she would find at the hospital. As the social services agent, she scouted at the hospital for new patients for a senior care home in Live Oak. She especially loved the Alzheimer's patients; they were usually so sweet, thinking of her as their mother. She certainly wasn't old enough to be their mother, but she had some motherly qualities, and among them was a natural knack of making anyone feel comfortable. Her eyes seemed to dance with spunky merriment as she laughed and talked easily with anyone she met. Her hair was beautiful too, dark brown, all the way down her back. She was Native American, belonging to the Maidu tribe.

Donna walked into Rideout for her routine check for new arrivals. She stopped to check in with the nursing staff and saw one of her old friends.

"Any new patients I should know about this week?" Donna asked her friend.

"There is a new case down that hall. He's been here a few weeks already. They're desperate, looking for anyone to take him," the nurse replied.

"Oh, that skinny kid you keep sending me inquiries about? Yes, I've seen your three referrals for him. My boss already said, 'Hell, no,'" Donna said. "We're a senior home. We don't take anyone that young."

"Well, he's a unique case. I thought you might be interested. Just take a look," she urged.

Donna didn't have to go looking for him. She had passed the interesting case out walking the halls of the hospital with his dad. *Hmm, the family involvement is good.* She looked at the list in front of her; the caseload for today was especially high. She resolved to look into it again next time.

SEVERAL WEEKS LATER, DONNA NOTICED HE WAS STILL there. She decided to ask a few more questions. She found his nurse, but no sign of the family.

"What happened to him?" she asked.

"The short of it is he had liver failure, which caused brain damage," the nurse explained. "He woke up like this. The family hopes he will make more improvements if he can get past his anger. He says a few words, mostly cuss words. He's been here over a month now. They can't find a care facility that will take him. He's on heavy drugs to keep him this calm. The doctors don't have much hope for him recovering his faculties. His brain damage was severe, but he does have room to improve."

"I'm curious. I'm going to talk to my boss again," Donna said. "Maybe we can. I mean, why not?"

Back at the care home, she walked straight to the boss's office. "Hi, Cindy. Remember that case you already said no to? The kid who was too young, with a brain injury? At first, I thought it was totally crazy, but the more I've seen him, I'm starting to warm up to the idea."

"How young are we talking?" Cindy demanded.

"Twenty-eight, I believe," Donna replied, scanning the paperwork in her hands for confirmation.

"Absolutely not. Don't even think about it. Our youngest resident is forty-six. And even he is too young. We are a senior care home. Let him be somebody else's problem. And besides, wasn't he manic?"

"Yes, he is at times," Donna said.

"This is exactly the kind of case we need to pass on. We have to let somebody else that has broader shoulders and more experience deal with someone like him," Cindy said with finality in her voice. "Obviously, I wish we could help everybody. But we are primarily an Alzheimer's care facility. We won't have the right therapy for him."

Almost a month later, Donna couldn't ignore that he was still there. Every time she had visited the hospital, she had seen his mom or dad with him. Clearly, he had strong familial support. They obviously loved him enough to spend their time with him. She had a feeling they wouldn't just dump him in the care home. It was worth having a conversation with them. She talked with the head CNA and got the information to contact the parents.

AS ANN PULLED INTO THE HOSPITAL PARKING LOT, SHE heard her phone ringing in her purse. Spotting an open space, she quickly parked and scrambled to find the ringing silver object, which always seemed to hide in the deepest crevices.

"Hello."

"Hi. This is Donna Watson from Live Oak Manor. We are considering bringing your son to our facility."

Ann didn't leap with excitement. She had experienced continual moments where places got her hopes up, only to ultimately decide on a rejection. This would likely turn out to be the same. "All right," she said coolly.

"I would like to come visit him in the hospital if that's all right with you," Donna said.

Oh gosh, no one is ever going to want to take him if they actually spend time with him, Ann thought to herself. *I couldn't handle him. Why would someone else be able to?* "You can if you want to," Ann said, feeling the situation wouldn't go anywhere anyway.

"Good. I'll check back in with you after my visit this week. Thanks," Donna said in a chipper voice.

That lady is in for it, Ann thought. *She sounds so positive, but I'm sure she will change her mind once she meets him.*

Ann visited Damian every afternoon that week. On Wednesday, she asked the nurse if anyone had been in to see Damian.

"Yes, the woman from Live Oak Manor was here today. She spent four hours with Damian this morning. She sat here and talked to him. It was like they were having a real conversation; he was quiet and calm the entire time. When she left, she told me, 'I'm going to help this family.'"

"What?" Ann stammered. "You mean she met him, and talked to him, and still wants to help him?"

"Yes, she said she would do what it takes," the nurse said, returning to check on Damian's vitals. "Oh, and I met his brother earlier this week too."

"LB?"

"That sounds right," the nurse said flippantly before leaving the room.

As Ann sat in the chair to process these good bits of news, her phone started ringing again.

"Hi. It's Donna Watson, from Live Oak Manor. I met with your son today. I see something in him that's good," Donna said through the phone. "I want to help your family."

Was Ann hearing correctly? "Really? Can you share that something good you see in him? As his mother, I would love to hear that."

"He was quietly sitting, and I was quietly talking to him. While I talked to him, he looked at me like he could understand me. I think he understands everything that's happening to him and he's just trying to figure out how to cope with it," Donna said. "He wants to be able to communicate."

"Wow, you must have caught him at an especially good moment," Ann said.

Donna laughed uncomfortably. "Ann . . . don't you also see something good in Damian?"

Ann shifted her weight and bit her lip, the question taking her by surprise. "I guess I have been so caught up in how difficult he can be my vision has been clouded."

"I can understand that. I've heard how he has spurts of manic rage."

"So you know about that and you still think you could take Damian's care on at your facility?"

"If not us, then who?" Donna pointed out. "I've noticed no one is jumping at the bit to take him from the hospital. But I do have this one teeny, tiny problem."

This was what Ann had been waiting to hear. "And what's that?"

"Well, my boss hasn't agreed to it yet. She turned me down the first time I asked her about Damian almost a month ago. I have to work on her," Donna said. "I can't give you any timelines right now."

Ann hung up the phone with Donna and sat stunned for a moment, reflecting on what Donna had said. She saw something good in Damian. *How could I have been so blind?* Now that she could rest and have distance from Damian, she should have arrived there on her own. She felt guilt rising up in her chest, for all the things she had thought about Damian. For judging him so harshly before his injury when he couldn't keep a steady job instead of seeing how debilitating his Crohn's was. And then only being able to see him as the person who took her freedom away. She thought about what her doctor had said, about resenting Damian because he needed her help. Had she continued to allow that to cloud her vision of him? Ann felt hot tears stream down her cheeks as she opened her mind to a new way of seeing.

She breathed a silent prayer in the hospital room sitting next to Damian, "God, give me new eyes. Give me compassion for my son. Help me to see him as you see him. Rid me of my contempt and haughty heart. I have been blinded by pride, by my own harsh judgements. You only ever give me grace upon grace. May I extend that now to Damian. Forgive me for being so blind to see the good in him." She barely dared to have hope to utter the last few words, "God, if Donna is the one who can help us, please make all the details work out."

She knew God was capable. He had shown her the meaning of hope in action, and she clung to it.

DONNA BELIEVED IN GOD TOO. SHE HAD SEEN GOD defy the odds in wild situations and trusted God would work this one out. She reminded herself, one person walking with God is the majority. She felt God working in this situation with this family. When Donna spent the morning with Damian, she heard God whisper to her to trust Him. She felt Damian was special, that he would teach her something, and he would be an asset to the care home in some way. She sensed God's presence was strong in him, although he seemed to be angry at his situation. Who wouldn't be? His able mind and body were stolen from him so prematurely. Donna had mentioned his situation to her daughter, and her daughter knew exactly who she was talking about. Her daughter had been following the family updates on Facebook because she had gone to school with Damian and remembered him being a super athlete on the swim team.

Donna marveled at how God worked, in incredibly intricate ways. Now she could make a difference in this young man's life. If only she could get through to Cindy.

She walked prayerfully up to the office, choosing her words wisely. "Cindy, I've done some more investigating. Before you say no, I want you to consider what I'm proposing."

"Is it that boy again?" Cindy asked, glancing up from the stacks of paperwork on her desk.

"I feel we are the right fit for him. I spent some time with him. I talked with his family. They are extremely involved with him. Their love and dedication to him is incredible. The mother said they'd called more than a hundred places—there's no place out there for him. I truly feel we can help him. And he might even help us expand our services. If not us, then who?"

"We don't have therapy or care set up for young people. It's all geared toward people over sixty. We won't even know what to do with him. And we'll be stuck with him for who knows how long? He could live to be seventy for all we know, or older. We're not equipped for fifty years of responsibility," Cindy said. "It's too much. That's my final say."

BUT, OF COURSE, IT WASN'T. EVERY COUPLE OF WEEKS, Donna returned to Cindy with a new approach to the request. Every time, Cindy came up with three or more conditions that must be met in order for her to consider it. What about the fall risk? He would need a one-on-one. He would put our other residents at risk. He had too many psychotropic drugs. The concerns went on and on. Donna resolved each condition.

In the end, Cindy said, "I still don't want to. All our staff will quit on us."

So Donna set up a staff vote where she presented Damian's case to them and asked if they would be willing to care for a twenty-eight-year-old manic man with a brain injury. The staff did show apprehension, but of the over fifty employees, only two voted no to working with Damian.

The success of the vote led Donna to the seventh try. Donna was persistent, and like the persistent widow in the Bible, she had worn down Cindy. On the seventh request, Cindy said, "Fine, Donna. Let's see what it would look like to bring him to our facility. I want to meet with the parents first."

Excitement surged through Donna. She called Ann right away. "Ann, I have good news. I think I finally wore her down. She wants to meet with you. It was the seventh time. I asked her seven times to consider bringing Damian to our facility. She said no every time until the seventh. The number seven in the Bible means perfection. This is an act of God. God is telling us he needs to be here. I think Damian's going to get the help he needs." Donna fought the urge to jump up and down while the words spilled out.

Tears glistened on Ann's cheeks on the other end of the phone. "I think you're right, Donna. I'm amazed. You are Damian's guardian angel. Donna, thank you. You've helped me remember the good in my son. I can't thank you enough."

Soon, the meeting details were arranged. After months of being in the hospital, Damian might finally have a way out—and to a place that could actually help him. Ann and Lincoln arrived at Cindy's office, hoping for the best, expecting the worst.

"It's a pleasure to meet you," Lincoln said, extending his hand to Cindy.

She accepted his handshake and gestured at the two chairs opposite hers. "Sit down. Make yourselves comfortable. Let's talk about this son of yours."

Ann shared most of the story, including her own despair while caring for him. She shared how no one was remotely interested in his case until Donna Watson came into the picture. She raved about how wonderful Donna was.

"Yes, and Donna seems to think the two of you are wonderful too. Wonderful enough for her to come back to my office repeatedly to ask me to consider helping you. I'm still feeling leery of committing to his care."

"Just because I know it's on your mind, I want you to be assured we don't intend to dump him," Lincoln said. "We want to be very involved. We will even come every day at the beginning. We want this to work for everyone. We just know we can't do it on our own right now."

"I appreciate you saying that. Of course, him being dumped here is one of my main worries," Cindy said, straightening her posture. "But also, I need to know—is he combative? How often is he manic? Will our older residents be safe around him?"

Ann's eyes met Lincoln's, remembering the time Damian punched Nana. Lincoln cleared his throat before answering, "He has moments of calm, but he is very angry. I liken it to going through the stages of grief. I believe he's grieving right now the loss of his life as he had imagined it. He often gets into a fit of rage. But he can be contained to his room during those times. Other times, he is calm and simply wants to roam. Unless he is in a rage, he has not shown signs of intentionally hurting others."

Cindy handed a document across the desk to them. "Before we can officially agree to bring Damian into our facility, I need you to sign this contract."

Lincoln and Ann read over the contract. Ann pointed to the line that read: "If the care facility cannot manage the patient, responsibility for the patient returns to the family." They exchanged another worried glance.

Ann spoke in a shaky voice, "I'm sorry, ma'am. We would really love for this to work out, but we can't sign this document. We already tried taking him in, and we couldn't handle it. I couldn't handle it. That's why he went into the hospital. That's why the hospital is trying to place him. We would like to one day be able to care for him at home. But if you tried and one week later said, 'We can't handle it,' and made us take him back, then we are back in that pickle we were in before he went into the hospital."

Lincoln backed Ann up, "Like I said before, we don't have any intention of abandoning him. We're here for the long haul. We don't just say that; we truly mean it. If you need more resources, we will try to find ways to get you more resources to help care for him. But, at the same time, we can't take him back. My wife is struggling too much. If agreeing to this statement is required to get him in, then I'm sorry, he can't come in. Because I can't promise something that I can't keep, and I can't keep that promise. As a Christian, I can't sign this document knowing it's not true."

Cindy looked at the two sincere faces sitting across the desk from her, amazed that these people were every bit as wonderful as Donna had described. She picked up the document from her desk and ripped it in half.

"We don't need it after all. I appreciate your honesty. I trust that we can do this. We'll take him."

Cindy agreed to bring Damian into the care facility until he was well enough to go back home, if that became an option later down the road.

Ann and Lincoln felt it was a miracle. Nobody else was interested; no facility was designed for a "Damian." But they thanked God for Donna and her first timid maybe.

SEVENTEEN

Live Oak Manor

JANUARY 2009

. . . .

"We must let go of the life we have planned, so
as to accept the one that is waiting for us."

—Joseph Campbell

. . . .

ANN GLANCED AT LINCOLN, FEELING HER HEART
thumping in her chest wildly as they pushed Damian across the
threshold of Live Oak Manor. In her mind, it was a question of when,
not if, something would go wrong. It was Damian, after all, and what
if they changed their minds about taking him?

Lincoln easily pushed Damian to his new room. Ann had
adamantly insisted Damian must be in a solo room. *Or else he might
be found flinging poop while the other person slept.* Two turns and down
the hallway, the seventh door on the left.

"Here we are, Damian. Your new digs," Lincoln said soothingly,
praying silently that this would be a smooth transition for everyone.
It felt good to be out of the hospital setting. Of course, the care home

still felt like a medical facility, but slightly cheerier than a hospital wing.

Ann spun around the tiny room, akin to a prison cell, taking in all the bare walls and adjacent bathroom. "I deem this room Damian-proof. Here we go. You can get out of your chair and check it all out," Ann said, as she began unbuckling Damian's chair.

Damian stood up swiftly and began pacing the floor. He wandered into the bathroom. Ann started unpacking the meager belongings they brought for him. Mostly clothes filled the bag; he didn't need much else. She brought a plant to put on his bedside table and a canvas of the photo of the four siblings taken at Nicole's wedding to liven up the walls of the austere room.

Damian sauntered back into the bedroom and right out the door. "We'd better follow him," Lincoln said, noticing as Damian's backside disappeared out of the doorway.

Ann and Lincoln trotted to catch up to him. The hallways were eerily deserted; perhaps the residents were napping. Damian found an open doorway and meandered inside the social room. Several couches lined the room, with an elderly gentleman sitting on one. Damian walked over to a round five-foot table with four chairs around it, the perfect size for card playing. One center post held the table up with four claw-like feet sprawling out from it.

Damian slowly leaned onto the table, watching it sway a little as he did. Before Ann crossed the room, Damian hopped himself onto the edge of the table. The table started wobbling, about to flip over, but quickly Damian scooted toward the center, now sitting in the middle, balancing the table. With agility like a cat, Damian leaped to his feet on top of the table. Finding the spot where the table could wobble without tipping, Damian used his body weight to surf the table back and forth.

Ann's eyes widened in alarm, looking at Damian, then at Lincoln. "Damian, today is not the day to try out new dangerous skills. Come down this minute." He had never done anything like this. Of all days, day one in his new home. The table swayed back and forth, balanced but dangerous. And his surfing form was perfect.

Suddenly, a flashback image of Damian in seventh grade popped into Ann's mind. Damian wore a Hawaiian shirt with three of his best buddies from middle school standing on the stage during the annual talent show. "Kokomo" by the Beach Boys played as they surfed the stage with their best suave seventh-grade-boy moves. His body flowed back and forth to the beat, completely immersed in the music. Ann felt the corners of her mouth tug into a smile, remembering Damian as a goofy seventh grader who loved life and music. She felt a wave of love for Damian overcome her. He had always tried to please her and make jokes to get her to smile. How could she have forgotten so much about her love for him as a child and teen, before her frustrations?

An old, crackly voice snapped Ann back to reality. She whirled around in surprise, believing they had been alone in the room.

"Young man, you're not supposed to be doing that. They don't like that one bit around here. You better get down," the frail elderly man sitting on the couch said.

Alarmed that the whole table might come crashing down on this frail man, Ann doubled her efforts to coax Damian down. Lincoln scooted around to the back side of the table while Ann held the front of the table to stop it from wobbling. Damian, however, remained in the middle, determined to explore his newly found agility. In the middle of the table, his legs were just out of reach.

"Damian, someone is going to see you. Get down now," Ann pleaded with urgency.

"He's going to get himself in trouble. He's going to get hurt," the peanut gallery commented.

Even if they could reach his legs, he moved so fast. He kept on surfing the table. Finally, Lincoln stood on a chair and was able to grab on to one of his arms. He slowly helped Damian sit down on the table and scoot off without him falling or crashing down.

"Damian, you can't do that." Lincoln said, holding on to him before he tried it again. "This is your new home."

That set him off into a violent rage. Damian started whirling around, trying to twist out of Lincoln's grasp. "Fuck fuck fuck fuck fuck."

The old, crackly voice spoke up again, "Young man, they don't like that either. Watch your language."

"He can't control it," Ann spoke up, becoming suddenly defensive of her son. "He doesn't know what he's saying." And even if he did, he had a right to be angry. Ann's compassion for Damian grew as she thought about how she would feel if she was told this was her new home. Ann's heart broke knowing Damian's history of being placed in new homes—at a young age, getting torn from the familiar and constantly forced into a place that was now supposed to be called home. God answered her prayers daily to truly see Damian in a new way. This violent rage set off by his "new home" must be linked to his childhood.

Lincoln held Damian with his arms around his midsection to keep him from getting too close to the man on the couch. He didn't want Damian to hurt a resident—especially not during his first hour of his first day. "Ann, go get his chair so we can get him back to the room."

Ann returned as quickly as she could, and the two of them worked together to wrestle Damian into the chair. Throwing punches, flailing, wiggling his body, kicking, screaming, Damian resisted with his whole body until they finally got him buckled into the chair.

"Goodbye for now," Ann called out to the man on the couch as they pushed the screaming Damian back into the hallway and to his room.

Safely inside with the door shut, Ann said, "This is not going so well. I'm worried about how Damian will cope with this being his new home. I was thinking about how he must feel when he's told those words. Maybe it triggered his childhood trauma of constantly being moved to a new home."

"You have a good point, Ann," Lincoln admitted. "I'm amazed at how your compassion for Damian has grown. You have an intuitive ability to understand him. I think you might be right. Let's try to get him settled down and stay with him as long as he needs us. It continues to surprise me how much Damian might understand about what's happening. I know his anger must stem from wanting to be able to tell us how he feels about it."

"What if this isn't the best choice for him?"

"I don't see that we have any other options right now. It's within close driving distance to our home, so we can be here often. We won't leave him alone. We will walk through this with him."

After twenty minutes of shouting and bouncing his wheelchair, Damian slumped over, panting and frothing at the mouth with fiery eyes and veins popping out of his neck. His rage could be off the charts, but it left him exhausted.

"Finally," Ann said. "We can get him into his bed." They worked together to get him out of the chair and stretched out on the bed.

"Let's go walk around and check out the place while he sleeps for a while," Lincoln said.

They closed the door quietly and slipped down the hallway. More people were milling around now.

"Lincoln, look," Ann whispered. Mostly Alzheimer's patients filled the care home. Ann pointed at one of the vacant faces she saw walking past her. "They look creepy. It looks like nobody's home."

"Ann, don't call them creepy. Let's try talking to one of them," Lincoln said.

A woman absentmindedly walked past them. "Hi, I'm Lincoln."

The woman stopped and stared at him. "Do I know you?"

"No, we're new around here," Lincoln said. "What's your name?"

"I'm Wendy. Do I know you?" the woman answered.

"Our son is going to be here in the home with you," Lincoln told her.

"Do I know you?" The woman answered. "I'm Wendy."

This conversation was going nowhere. "Oh good. Here's one of the CNAs," Lincoln said, turning away from Wendy to catch her attention. "We have Damian sleeping right now. We're going to go back and check on him before we head out for the evening, but don't hesitate to call us if you need us."

"I'll come to check on him with you," the CNA said, leading the way to the room.

Ann opened the door, cautiously, hoping to see Damian still in the bed where they had left him. He was indeed on the bed. However, he was standing on the bed, covered in poop, jumping up and down, painting the walls with his diarrhea.

"Oh," was all the CNA managed to say, gawking at the scene before her.

"Damian!" Ann exclaimed, scampering toward the bed. "Get down this minute."

Lincoln sat on the bed and grabbed him around the knees. "We've got to shower you off, Damian."

Damian resisted, but with the three of them working together, they got him stripped and into the shower. The CNA called in reinforcements to take care of the poop covering the walls and bed. Within half an hour, they had him showered, clothed, and the room sanitized, quite a bit quicker than the process at home, where they usually had to also steam clean the carpet and do it all just the two of them. Ann sat down in a chair, breathing heavily from the activity, an ache going up her back.

"Thank goodness he is not our sole responsibility anymore," Ann said to Lincoln. "I think we should go now before anything else happens."

"I think you're right. They have our number if they need to call us back in," Lincoln replied.

BACK AT HOME, LINCOLN DRIFTED OFF TO SLEEP while watching the news. Ann turned the lights out and headed to the bedroom, noticing the clock read 11:07 p.m. *Thank goodness they didn't call us back in. Damian must be doing okay,* Ann thought to herself, thankful she could get the rest she needed.

Before she made it to bed, the phone rang. "Hello," Ann answered, a bit groggy.

"Hi, yes, is this Mrs. Young? We need you to come back. We can't get Damian to sleep. He keeps jumping on the bed. He's getting more agitated and manic the more we try to help him. If you could please come back, we don't know what else to do," a desperate voice said into the receiver.

Willing to do whatever it took to make this work, Ann and Lincoln jumped back into the car and drove the hour-long drive to the care home. When they arrived, Damian was jumping up and down on the bed, just like a toddler.

"His brain continues to awaken. Today, we opened the next stage of toddlerhood. He wants to stand on top of everything and bounce," Lincoln said as he watched Damian with the three staff members, who stood clueless about what to do with him. "Jumping is new to him. He surfed and jumped today. What's next?"

Lincoln always had a way of finding the humor in a situation and defusing angst. Ann loved her husband for that.

"We can take care of him from here," Ann said, dismissing the CNAs back to their posts. Unlike the hospital that typically had one nurse to every five patients, in a care home, the ratio was one CNA to eight or nine patients. If three CNAs were in here taking care of Damian, that left the rest of the CNAs working extra hard to make the rounds for the other residents, even if it was the middle of the night.

Although they had to unexpectedly return, Ann was thankful they were in a setting outside their home. It felt more public, not suffering alone in her own space, surviving Damian's moody whims. Speaking in soothing tones to Damian, they slowly calmed him down.

"Damian, it's okay. These are good people. They are going to help take care of you. I know it might be scary being in a new location, but isn't this better than the hospital? Look at the fun you've had today on this springy bed. You are safe. You are cared for. And we will visit you every single day, just like we have been," Ann spoke to him.

Damian jumped up one last time and then hopped down onto his bottom. "That's right, Damian. Let's get into bed," Ann encouraged him.

After about an hour, they coaxed Damian to calm down and had him in his bed asleep. Not wanting to risk the drive back, they stayed through the night with him.

AFTER GETTING THROUGH THE FIRST TWENTY-FOUR hours at the care home, Lincoln realized they needed to check back in with Cindy. He left Ann with Damian to go find her. Damian had pushed the boundaries even more than he expected, right off the bat—which, he was sure, left the staff baffled at what they had just signed up for.

Knocking on her open door, Lincoln poked his head in and said, "Hi, do you have a few minutes?"

"Yes, please," came the urgent reply, as she emerged from behind a newspaper.

"So you've had a little over twenty-four hours of Damian's care. He's quite a handful," Lincoln said, taking a seat in the closest chair.

"Yeah, that's an understatement," Cindy said, rolling her eyes and sitting back in her chair with her arms crossed.

"We want this to work for you, for us, and for Damian. He's exploring his territory, and he needs constant supervision. You have a staff that assigns so many patients per CNA. For a while, he's going to need one-on-one care," Lincoln said. "Occasionally three-on-one care for special circumstances like showering him."

"Yes, it's obvious he needs one-on-one care," Cindy agreed.

"Okay, let's make that happen," Lincoln said. "I know his Medi-Cal won't pay for one-on-one coverage. How much extra would it cost on top of what the government pays to get the care he needs? We will help cover that as long as we can afford it."

"He's going to need twenty-four hours of one-on-one care. Rather than charge you the full normal rate, I'll just charge you what the care costs us. If you can pay for twelve hours of care, we will pay for the other twelve hours. How does that sound?" Cindy asked, twirling a pen in her hand.

"Yes, we can support that," Lincoln said. "When we are here, we will come sit with him and give the staff member a break for that time. But you can have them on staff so if we can't be there for whatever reason you still have the coverage. If we can, that gives you one more CNA on the floor to help with everybody. We will try to make it here every day for four hours or whatever we can give."

And so it began, the frequent and often comical trips to the care home. Ann and Lincoln didn't always come together; they would often alternate, but they tried to be there most weekdays. Weekends were often crowded with visitors for the other residents, and they preferred showing up in the quieter moments.

Oftentimes, they took advantage of the freedom to do fun activities the CNAs may not have time to do with him. Walking around the outside courtyard area with Damian to get sunshine and fresh air quickly became a favorite pastime. Or they would say, "We're going to take him out to the McDonald's drive-thru to get fries. We'll be back in a while." Ann and Damian's favorite place to go was the Starbucks drive-thru. Damian became a mini-celebrity at Starbucks when one of the workers found out his story. They gave him his vanilla bean Frappuccino for free. Damian showed excitement through his movements and vocal cues. Ann smiled, seeing her son making improvements and being enjoyed by others who celebrated the good in him with her. The treat, for Ann, was an added bonus.

Ann knew her Damian—whom she loved—was still inside there somewhere. And now that she was caught up on rest, she felt life wasn't so out of control. She loved being able to take Damian on outings because, like anybody, he could realize there's hope outside of where he was by getting out and seeing things. It was a win-win for the care home; they got an afternoon break, and he came back refreshed.

As Damian's brain continued to awaken, he explored his world just like a toddler would. A toddler starts crawling, then walking, and exploring in new ways, doing new things they hadn't done yesterday. Well, that was Damian.

Walking into the lockdown Alzheimer's unit was always an adventure. Ten to twelve residents in wheelchairs lined the wall adjacent to the front desk to see the hub of activity. It was a social hour, discussing the comings and goings. A person with Alzheimer's had lost the ability to filter, so whatever was on their mind spewed out.

One day as Lincoln walked in, he greeted the ladies out front with a, "Hello." As he breezed by, he overheard two ladies talking. "Do you see the size of that man? He's a big guy."

The second lady replied, "Man, I don't think I'd want to be his wife. Imagine making love to him."

Lincoln chuckled to himself as he walked up to the front desk.

Greg staffed the front desk. As the sole RN who worked at the facility, Greg administered the medicine to all the residents. Because he sat down at a desk, the residents constantly walked up to him all day long, yelling at him to call their mother or brother.

"Call my sister. She never comes. I haven't seen her in months. Can you call her and find out when she's coming?" Minnie said to Greg.

"No, we can't call her today. She was just here yesterday," Greg replied, continuing his work lining up the pills in order. Then, pointing to the board behind him, he said, "See, look. Here's a picture of you with her yesterday."

Minnie wailed, "I haven't seen her for months. You're lying. She wasn't here yesterday."

"She was here. This is the two of you together," Greg said, handing her the photo, then looked up from his work. "Hello, Lincoln." He greeted the newcomer with a big goofy smile. "Damian's learned something new again," Greg said, trying to hold back a giggle.

"Oh really?" Lincoln replied. "What's he doing today?"

"Damian has learned to love to run," Greg said.

"Run? Like running away from you? He's been good at that for a while," Lincoln said.

"No, run, just for the joy of running." Greg had a big smirk on his face.

"Tell me more," Lincoln demanded.

"Running down the hallway like this with his arms pumping. As fast as he can. There's old people with their walkers walking down the hallway, and he's running around them like he's running sprints down the hall," Greg said, chuckling to himself. "We can't have running."

"Okay, so we need to find a way to get him outdoors to run maybe," Lincoln thought out loud.

"Yeah, I think I'll have the CNA take him outside and let him run," Greg agreed.

"That's so strange. On his own, his brain says, 'I've got to run,'" Lincoln said. "Incredible."

GREG'S UPDATES ON DAMIAN'S NEW SKILLS BECAME A fairly common greeting for Ann and Lincoln.

"You'll never guess what Damian's doing now."

"Oh?"

"Damian has learned to skip. He's skipping now," Greg said.

"Did someone teach him that? Or did he learn on his own?" Ann asked.

"I don't know. You never know with the CNAs. They like to have fun with him and try to do things to make his world a little bit more joyful. But he learned to skip, so now he skips. He's skipping down the hallway," Greg reported, always getting a good laugh about Damian's latest developments.

Almost every time they came, Damian had learned something new and interesting. The next time it was jumping on one foot. And then discovering the code pad on the door to break out and pounding the keys incessantly. And then spinning in circles.

WHILE HE OFTEN BROUGHT JOY TO THE PEOPLE taking care of him with his energetic, exploratory, youthful self, the residents were not so sure about him. Oftentimes, forgetfully, the little old ladies would say, "Hey, you're not supposed to be in here. You're too young to be here. What are you doing here?"

The residents had never seen anything like Damian. With Alzheimer's, the brain often kicks into fight-or-flight mode. One resident had formerly been in the Navy. He was a nasty grouch, and he did not like Damian one bit. He had already tried to force Damian to leave by locking Ann and Damian out on the patio. One day, he was eating his dinner, with Damian and Ann hovering close by.

"You know he's too young to be in here," the former Navy SEAL said to Ann.

"I know," she replied, keeping her eye on Damian. Damian stepped closer to the man's food. She knew that if Damian saw any food that he wanted, he would take it. But the good thing was he finally was eating regularly enough that the doctor said they could take his feeding tube out. This had come as a relief because he would regularly pull it out, chew on it, or fling the long tube around his head like a lasso as he was walking the halls of the care home.

"If you touch my food, I'll stab your hand," he said to Damian, brandishing his dinner knife in the air toward him. "Don't you dare."

"Damian, let's walk over here," Ann said, guiding him away and down the hall.

As they roamed the hallways, suddenly Damian's diarrhea struck. The power of the diarrhea dropped his whole diaper and pants down to his ankles off his skinny bones. It was always a bother to keep his pants up. Even with a belt, he was so skinny his pants often slipped right off. So there he was, naked in the middle of the hallway, with his pants and diaper around his ankles, covered in poop, standing in a pool of diarrhea.

"You don't belong in here, sonny," Mrs. Cooper, one of the patients, said. "This is our home. What do you think you're doing, getting poop all over it?"

Several residents popped out of their rooms, gathering to see the spectacle. Ann stood gaping for a moment, distracted by the audience. Indecision stuck her feet to the ground. The question at hand was how to best get him back to the room. Strip him here and try to clean it? Or pull the poopy clothes back up, drip a trail of diarrhea to the room, and then clean it up? She chose the latter, to get away from all those staring eyes of disapproval as quickly as possible. The CNAs could clean up the trail, and she could get a head start on Damian.

Minnie, another one of the beloved split-personality residents, followed her into the room. "So when is Damian going home?"

"Well, he's going to go home when he gets better," Ann said, trying to get the poopy situation under control.

"He's not going to get better. He's going to be like this forever," Minnie said.

"Well, then we'll find out how to manage as we go along," Ann responded.

"But where will he stay?" Minnie asked. "He can't stay here."

"I don't know. I don't know any more than you do," Ann said.

"Well, you should find out. He's your son," Minnie told her.

"I suppose so," Ann said absently. She had gotten the mess cleaned and now began pulling a shirt over Damian's head.

"I just love you, honey. So glad we could have this little chat. You're so sweet," Minnie said.

Then suddenly the alternate Minnie kicked in. "Hey, you. Get out of here. You don't belong here. This isn't your room. What are you doing to him? Get out of here, NOW!" Minnie started screaming.

"All right, Minnie, I think it's time for *you* to go now," Ann said, pushing a button to call for help.

SEVERAL MONTHS LATER, AS ANN AND LINCOLN strode confidently into the care home, Cindy popped out of her office and motioned the two of them over. "Ann, Lincoln. Could I have a word with you?" Cindy said, trotting to catch up to them in the hallway.

"Sure, of course," Ann replied, stopping mid step and whirling around. "What is it?"

"Well, it's just that we have our insurance inspection coming up. It's quite a process; they look into every hazard and inspect the building. It sometimes takes several days," Cindy explained.

"What does that have to do with us?" Ann questioned.

"As you know, Damian can be very unpredictable. Do you think there's any way Damian could go home for a long weekend with you? Just so we could feel comfortably secure that he's not going to do who knows what during the inspection. I know it's a lot to ask, but it would help us out."

Before Ann could answer, all three of their heads turned to investigate the cause of the sudden onslaught of shrieking and laughter. Down the hallway, an outbreak of commotion caught their eye. "Oh, my," Ann said. "Is that Damian?"

Sure enough, Damian had escaped his shower and ran stark naked out of his room. Still drenched, he slipped on the ground. As Cindy, Ann, and Lincoln moved closer to the action, Damian stood again and twisted just out of reach of the three CNAs chasing him. Damian moved quickly with great agility, hopping and twisting, running down the hallway, a wild, naked man on the go.

All the residents popped out of their doors, hearing the commotion. Several disapproving faces stood in their doorways. But Henry, the former golf player, stood there laughing, doubled over. He thought the whole scene hilarious, belly laughing with his hands on his knees.

Lincoln looked over at Cindy. She stood there watching the whole thing with her mouth gaping open. Chuckling at the irony of the moment, Lincoln said, "Yeah, I entirely agree with you. We will take him home that weekend."

Cindy walked away, shaking her head in disbelief. Lincoln trotted to catch up with Damian and help get him contained and clothed.

PLANNING FOR THE WEEKEND AT HOME PROVED TO be a good reminder of all the ways they would need to renovate their home before bringing Damian home permanently, the option they still felt was the best long term. They talked about adding a bathroom extension designed specially for Damian, all tiled with a drainage system in the middle. The bathroom would also be fitted with its own laundry capabilities.

It also served as a good reminder of how they needed to hire more help if they brought him home, hopefully for all his waking hours. Damian being at the care home had shown Ann that his care legitimately required two people to help him a majority of the time. That was where they had gone wrong last time. They were so consumed in the crisis of his care they hadn't been able to find more hired help. His continual raging anger had been the biggest reason Ann felt she couldn't handle his care before. The poop, the medications, the feeding, the cleaning—she felt she could do those if only his anger lessened. Spending the weekend with his jittery nerves again showed Ann he was still too angry to consider bringing him home.

As time passed at the care home, Dr. Pearson, the main provider for Live Oak Manor, became particularly interested in his case. Working with Alzheimer's patients, he specialized in how the brain works. He especially understood how strong medications altered the mind.

Because of Damian's wildly angry manic episodes, Damian was on heavy psychotropic drugs. When he was in Care Meridian, he started on Ativan to control the loud and aggressive episodes, which worked for a while to calm him down but quickly showed to not be enough. On Ativan, his mind remained sharp, and he could learn new things, but when it became necessary to start Haldol, a mind-altering drug for strong psychosis episodes, it significantly slowed his brain's ability to learn and grow. Damian needed to be on Haldol constantly, which caused him to be absent-minded, sluggish, and drooling, like a walking zombie. Eventually, the Haldol became less effective. When Damian came into Live Oak Manor, he was on a regular dosage of Haldol and Ativan, as well as several other medications, but both did little to calm his moments of rage.

"We have to get him off the Haldol," Dr. Pearson said one day. "Haldol long term is never good. It's just like any other opioid drug, where you grow accustomed to it and you have to take it all the time, but you no longer get the benefit of it."

But Lincoln said, "He needs it so badly because he's so manic even with it. He can hop his whole wheelchair across a room even on Haldol. I would rather him not need it, but I can't imagine how manic he might be without it."

"That shows me that the drug is not doing its job effectively. Which means we should find alternative solutions."

The doctor slowly worked on getting him on other drugs to replace both Haldol and Ativan over the next several months. With the changes, Damian became more clear-eyed and aware. The clarity of mind allowed for more opportunities for growth.

ONE DAY, ANN PICKED DAMIAN UP FOR AN OUTING. She had been amazed at his new verbal developments that seemed to result with the reduction of drugs. He was parroting more words and even occasionally said, "Yes," in reply to a question. They had started speech therapy again. Today, she decided to reward him with a trip to the park.

First, she drove to get their customary Starbucks. Damian lit up with excitement in the back seat, bouncing up and down. "Yes yes yes yes yes." She got him a vanilla bean Frappuccino without the coffee and herself a peppermint mocha.

She drove to the nearby playground and unbuckled Damian. He bounded out of the car, with his drink in his hand, spinning, and chattering loudly, "Yeah yeah yeah, no buddy, no."

She guided him toward the swing to see if he would enjoy swinging. As he sat on the swing and she pushed him, his whole demeanor lit up. He was enjoying himself, and she was too. The sunshine felt warm on her skin, and she couldn't help but smile.

They walked around the loop of the playground; sometimes Damian broke into a skip. All too soon, it was time to return him. "Damian, we have to go back now." Ann motioned toward the car and guided him by the hand.

"No no no no fuck fuck fuck fuck fuck." Damian spun wildly away. He yelled and spun in furious circles. He started foaming at the mouth and pushed Ann away when she tried to grab his torso. He had fiery eyes and veins popping out of his neck as he broke free again. He threw wild punches, then ran over to the swing and flung it as hard as he could.

Ann stopped to watch him for a moment, waiting for his rage to calm. He was taller, faster, and stronger. She might have to call in reinforcements. Thank goodness there was no else in the park.

Ann hurried to the car to grab his chair and pushed it back toward him. With coaxing and patience, she finally got him into the chair. Both of them panted loudly for a moment.

"Damian, I can't do this alone again. That was too much," Ann said as she pushed him toward the car. He yelled another string of profanities and contorted and rocked his body, almost tipping the wheelchair over. At last, she got him to the car and safely inside, where he continued to bang on the car windows ferociously.

THAT EVENING AT DINNER, ANN RECOUNTED THE story to Lincoln.

"I learned so many things. Outings to the park alone are out of the question. And he was being sweet, in a way I haven't seen before. I think, because of the reduction of drugs, he is starting to feel like himself and have more awareness of the world around him. But at the same time, he is still so angry. My heart hurts knowing he has such intense anger with no relief. He's angry almost all the time. He does get excited by outings, but his anger is all-encompassing once it takes over," Ann said.

"Yes, the intensity of his rage does make caring for him like running an unending marathon. That's why we will have to have around-the-clock help if we manage to bring him home again in the future," Lincoln agreed.

"I think we will be ready sometime. I did have a sweet moment with him before the manic rage. I know he likes being out of the ward. I can't deny that. But I also like having a stable life, freedom to go places and still have him in our lives. I've loved plugging in with Young Life finally. I'm enjoying getting to know the high school students. If he comes home again, that would be out of the question. I want to at least wait until Jacob graduates high school this year so I can keep making it to all his events. God is going to have to undoubtedly convince me if he wants Damian home again."

"The one thing about bringing him home is we might get to see LB again. We haven't seen him since the family meeting. That doesn't mean he hasn't been to see Damian; we just haven't run into him." Lincoln stopped speaking with sadness clouding his eyes.

Mentioning LB brought a sudden chill to Ann's heart. She wished with her whole being she could bridge the wall he had built between them and bring back the son who had stolen her heart the moment he came into her life. It hurt to know he hated them so vehemently, and couldn't even look at her. "Yes, I've noticed we haven't seen him again. Seeing him frequently after so many years reminded me how much I miss him. I don't know if anything will get through to him."

"Let's not give up hope. God never gives up on us, after all. If God wants to bring him back, He will." Lincoln spoke with renewed spark in his eyes. "I also want to keep trying to access the inner Damian. I know he's in there. I've been looking into some new communication tools. The thing I do love about him being at Live Oak Manor is it gives us time to decompress and get creative with the time we do spend with Damian. And every time I go, I feel like I learn more about how to communicate with Damian. I've learned how to slow down and listen to his nonverbal clues and body language that show his discomfort, anxiety, or even excitement."

"You're right," Ann said. "I feel like I have learned how to be more patient with Damian and work with him. If you slow everything down, he is more eager to cooperate. Sometimes."

"Yes, he has to get to a place where he can accept the brain injury for what it is. If he can ever get to the place of accepting his new body and brain, I think he will be much more cooperative," Lincoln told her.

With tears in her eyes, Ann prayed out of the depths of her soul for Damian, "Lord, this seems impossible right now, but if Damian has to stay this way or even as he comes out of it, let him experience joy. True joy and contentment. Remove this anger and frustration from him. Bring the spirit of acceptance over him."

She prayed that prayer often for him, especially when she was with him in his manic episodes. She knew it would be a miracle for him to experience uninhibited joy.

A FEW MONTHS LATER, ANN DROVE HOME FROM AN evening volunteering with teens at Young Life club. She reflected on the evening of fun, laughter, and Jesus and how good it felt to be back in ministry. She had given up everything because of Damian, but now that he was in the care home, she had time and energy to give in a life-fulfilling way again. Every Monday, she was taking a few teens to club to enjoy the silliness, singing, and Jesus talks.

Weary from the evening, she thought, *Oh, I'm so glad I don't have to deal with Damian when I get home.*

Just when that thought crossed her mind, a voice that was not her own interjected.

"You just spent the last part of the evening loving other people's kids. But your kid is in a care home. It's time to bring him home."

But God, I've done everything you've asked of me. I'm doing your ministry.

"That's not what I'm asking you to do right now. I need you to love your son."

Ann reflected on the last several months, where she had felt new life breathed into her without the burden of Damian. She thought about how excited she was to jump into this ministry. With Damian in the care home for almost a year now, it was as if she had said, "Oh good, now I can just relax and focus on what God wants me to do." But God didn't want her doing ministry work right now. He wanted her to do a different kind of work, the work that he had designed for her in this time and place.

But God, isn't it enough to just keep visiting him at the care home? They take great care of him there. And he's close by. You answered so many prayers just to get him there.

But she knew bargaining wouldn't get her anywhere. She could petition all she liked, but she knew what she ultimately had to do.

Ann kept driving, and another thought struck her. LB's words from their countertop talk echoed into her mind as strikingly similar to what God had just told her. *"You don't care for kids; you just keep kids in your house. You care more about other people's kids than your own."* Was it true? Did she care more for kids outside of her home than her own?

The two moments in time suddenly seemed remarkably similar. Here she had an opportunity to obey God and bring her oldest son home instead of leaving him in the hands of an institution. She felt remorse overcome her, wishing she had tried to fight harder for LB, knowing how he viewed getting sent to a group home, how he had begged her not to send him, and now seeing the results nearly ten years later. She could have answered differently to the judge, even petitioned to bring him home. At the time, she felt powerless to the hands of the system, and hopeless without the knowledge of how to get through to LB. But if she had slowed down her life to make more time for him, could it have been different? Her heartache from the last decade intensified. *I miss him, God.*

Tears threatened to blur her vision. She pulled her car off to the side of the road. In the darkness, she ruminated on the events of the past, her current feelings, and her selfish tendencies that had come into her awareness in the last few years with Damian. She asked God for forgiveness. *I wasn't able to bring LB home, but I can bring Damian home. I can't undo the past, but I can choose to love Damian with my 'yes.' I won't question your perfect plan. I know I can't do it alone. I will rely on you to be my strength.*

EIGHTEEN

Divine Encounters

APRIL 2008

. . . .

"Until we can receive with an open heart, we're never really giving with an open heart. When we attach judgment to receiving help, we knowingly or unknowingly attach judgment to giving help."

—Brené Brown, *The Gifts of Imperfection*

. . . .

DAPHNE SAT ALONE ON THE COLD METAL BENCH IN her jail cell on her twenty-second birthday, at a new all-time low. How had her life come to this? One dabbling led to another, then before she knew it, she had to steal to fund her addictions. The first time, she got the "slap on the wrist" and was then released. However, the federal offense of stealing mail two weeks later landed her a much higher consequence. Between six years in prison or six months in jail followed by a drug rehab program, she chose the latter. Ideally, the shortest rehab she could find.

"You have a visitor," the jailor called out, unlocking the cell door and leading her to the visitation window.

Daphne sat down across the window from her mother and noticed the familiar passionate glow in her mother's eyes that meant she might burst with news. Daphne felt her stomach tie in a knot as she waited for her mom to speak, wishing it was her boyfriend who came to visit.

"Daphne, I've been dying to tell you everything. A woman saw the write-up about you in the newspaper and wants you to come to her rehab program in Madera. She wants to come to interview you to see if you would be a good fit," her mom, Barbara, said in rapid fire.

Cutting her off at the pass, Daphne interjected, "How long is it?"

"Thirteen months, I believe. It's an all-women's Christian program, and it's free," she added.

Daphne groaned. "Thirteen months? That's like a life sentence. I think I'd rather just do my time in prison."

"Your older sister and I both feel this is where God wants you. I know God still has a mark on your life for good. This has just been a rough patch. I want you to consider it. Your options are pretty limited anyway," Barbara said. "And I have something else to tell you. I'm leaving Fresno to move to Loma Rica near Marysville. Your uncle Dave pastors a church there, and I feel convinced God wants me to move there."

"You're leaving me and my sister? To move how far away?" Daphne raised her eyebrows and looked down her nose at her mother with squinted eyes.

"It's five hours. Sometimes God calls us to do things that don't make any sense in the moment. I don't want to leave you, but I know God has a reason and will reveal it in His perfect time. I'm trusting you to Him. I love you." Barbara got up to leave before the officer approached to enforce the time limit.

Daphne walked back to her cell feeling more alone than ever. Her mother's words echoed in her mind. *God doesn't care about me anymore. I screwed that up a long time ago.*

She threw herself on the ground, then lifted her head to rest it on the bench in her cell, tears leaking out uncontrollably. She longed for someone to bring her a hit of something, anything. She sobbed for what felt like eternity.

As her sobs gave way to heavy breathing, she felt a calm and peaceful presence rest on her. God's peaceful presence flooded her body with warmth, and illuminated her cell with His light. Her former darkness of minutes ago melted away, and she felt God's presence renew her faith she had grasped on to as a child.

God did care about her and see her, even in a jail cell. Daphne looked at the stack of unopened letters in the corner of her cell, all from people she had never met. She hadn't wanted to read them until now. She opened letter after letter and cried again, overwhelmed by the love shown to her by strangers.

Suddenly, in that moment, her life made perfect sense.

Realization dawned that God brought her here to jail to get her away from the people she had chosen to mingle with. She had made one mistake after another when she was around them. They were still out there living the same lifestyle, but she had a second chance. God nudged her with His loving presence. *"Fear not, for I have redeemed you. I have called you by name. You are mine."*

Daphne knelt and lifted her arms up to the heavens. She breathed in God's presence, drinking it in with joy. She uttered a prayer up to heaven, "Thank you for providing a way out. I see now that you never left me. I shut you out. If this rehab program is the path you want me to walk, I'll do it with gladness. I'm leaving the drugs behind. I forgot what your presence felt like. I don't want to leave it again."

After that life-altering moment, anything she faced felt bearable with God's help. At the end of her jail time, she was released to the Madera Rescue Mission rehab program.

The year in rehab passed quickly, with classes on the Bible and relapse prevention, where Daphne learned to set boundaries with the people around her so she wouldn't fall into the same habits.

Her problems had all started after she moved to Fresno at age twenty, shortly after she had rejected her boyfriend's offer of marriage. He had stayed in Paso Robles while she fell into the wrong crowd. But when she was arrested, the only number she could remember for her one phone call was his. She had begged him to call her mom to tell her where she was and help her. He had immediately agreed to be there for her throughout her time in jail and beyond.

And now, as she approached the end of her year in rehab, he was talking about marriage again—which surprisingly did not feel as scary as it once did.

God continued to encourage Daphne with His constant presence. But now, two months away from her release date, she had to secure a job as her key to freedom. And who would take that risk? On paper, she looked like a train wreck. Convicted felon, thief, drug addict— the list could go on.

She reminded herself that's not how God saw her and prayed for a miracle.

ONE SUNDAY MORNING, ANN SAT IN HER CHURCH pew and reflected on how everything in her life had significantly changed since Damian's injury, which had happened more than two years ago now. For one, they left the community church where she was the secretary for fifteen years. God paved the way for what was needed by leading them to this tiny little Baptist church six months before Damian's injury, and in two-and-a-half short years, it had already shown her the meaning of church through constant support. Of course, their church attendance had been sparse the past two years, being so constantly busy with Damian's care, but the small community never stopped caring about them and showing their support via phone calls, meals, prayers, and friendship.

Originally, she thought God brought her to the church to build up their children's program, especially since she had already created a long-standing children's program in their last church called Thank God It's Tuesday, which continued without her.

At the time Ann was leading the kid's ministry, her knowledge was all in the box. She remembered saying to the kids, "God is good. He loves you. You can put your hope in Him," without truly grasping the meaning. But to have a traumatic experience turn to good, to witness Damian come through the clutches of death, and then to see God work out a solution to help her at her lowest point when all odds were against it, that was hope in action. You *see* hope instead of hearing about it. He became her God who sees her.

She thought she was coming to this new church to minister. But God had different plans. Plans to lure her to Himself. She wasn't there because they needed her; she was there because *she* needed *them*. She needed them to show up for her in her time of greatest need.

She thanked God silently during the closing hymn. As the service closed, she praised Him for showing up for her time and time again.

Ann felt a tap on her shoulder. After turning around, she said, "Good to see you, Barbara."

"How are you doing? How is that wily son of yours? When are you going to bring him to church with you?" Barbara asked.

"He's doing good. It's hard to believe we're already coming up on a year of him being at the care home. We are thinking of transitioning him home soon," Ann answered.

"Do you think you're ready for that?" Barbara asked with lines of concern etching her forehead.

"I'm nervous about it, honestly. It was so hard last time. I reached my all-time low. But, you know, God showed up for me in such a real way. I know He will again. And we are more prepared this time. We're finishing up our remodel—we extended his room and put in his own bathroom with all tile flooring, to make it easy to wash him down. Also, we're hiring more help. That's where we went wrong last time. I felt so alone," Ann confided.

"Really?" Barbara's whole demeanor changed, from genuine concern to excited interest. "Are you open to hiring anyone? My daughter, Daphne—you know, the one we've been praying for—she's been looking for an opportunity to move closer to me. She's willing to do anything. She just needs a job. No one will hire her because she's been to jail, and now rehab. She's ready to be released on probation, but she just needs a job, any job as a condition of her probation. She truly has a good heart, and I know she's changed."

"Well, usually I don't take a chance on someone I don't know, but I do know you, and I trust you." Surprising herself, Ann continued, "We will absolutely hire her if she wants the job."

Within a few weeks, Ann found herself writing a job offer letter based on Barbara's recommendation. She would advocate for Daphne to be released on probation to come work for her. She planned to visit Daphne in her drug rehab the following week, but the hiring process was already set into motion. Ann thanked God for guiding her path; each step of obedience opened a doorway and a way forward. She felt confident God would take care of the details and that Daphne would bring joy into their home. Her God never failed. He continually challenged her and opened her eyes to His ways, ever pursuing her with His love.

MEANWHILE, DAPHNE SAT IN HER PROGRAM STUNNED that a complete stranger would take such a chance on her. She silently thanked God for answering prayers and lining up every detail as she argued with her probation officer.

"I'm not releasing you to Marysville, California. That's the drug capital of the state. You've come so far, you've invested all this time, you've learned so much. Why would you want to move there?" the officer probed.

"I know it doesn't make sense. But the Lord called my mom to move there. I'm doing good. I'm done with drugs. I'm ready to serve the Lord and live my life. And God has lined it up for me to move up there with my mom. She found a job for me," Daphne explained.

"Yeah, this job—they don't even know you. They know you're a drug addict, and they're going to trust you to take care of their disabled child?" he questioned, browsing over the paperwork she had given him, including the character reference from Ann.

"Yes. It's what God is lining up," Daphne said with confidence.

"I'm not going to make it easy for you. For your own sake, you'll have to come back to take a drug test every week for the next two years," he said. "You'll be spending a lot of time in the car—it's a four- or five-hour drive."

"If that's what it takes to walk the path God has for me, I'll do it," Daphne said with confidence.

IN MID-JULY, BEFORE DAPHNE'S GRADUATION, ANN AND Nana brought Damian to meet her. It was a brief encounter during her visiting hours. Daphne had absolutely adored Ann and Nana when she met them a few weeks ago. Meeting Damian, however, made everything feel more real and daunting. He shouted a few times and paced in a circle, seemingly agitated. Suddenly, she wasn't so sure she was cut out for the job. She had never done anything remotely close to caring for another person full-time. Would he hurt her? Or could she somehow hurt him? She realized she wouldn't get to meet Lincoln before working for him. Was he as kind as Ann, or would he be overbearing? What if she wasn't cut out for this kind of work? The questions loomed in her mind as she tried to stay present in the moment of meeting her new employer.

"So when do you get released?" Ann asked as she steered Damian away from a potted plant.

"Next month. It feels like I've been waiting for this day forever, and now it's so close. I can't wait to actually hug Chris. He wants to get married in September," Daphne said. She closely watched Ann navigate Damian's twirls and twists, keeping him contained to one corner.

"Wow. That feels soon. I hope you've known him a while," Ann replied.

"We will have known each other for six years. We dated before, but then I just wasn't ready to get married. I couldn't be happier that he waited for me, even after I rejected him. And he was so sweet the whole time I've been in here. He sent me coffee and chocolate while I was in jail to make it all bearable. He called me and visited me. He's been amazing. He knew he wanted to marry me since the day he met me."

"Well, if we can do anything to help with the wedding, we are happy to," Ann offered. "I used to be a florist, many moons ago, but I still love doing it when I can." Damian made another twist and got out of her reach. "I think we had better get Damian back home before anything happens."

After saying goodbye, Daphne stood in place wondering what kind of things Ann was referring to when she said, "before anything happens." She realized she should have asked more questions about what the job was actually like. She got carried away thinking about her freedom and her love. Damian looked very agile and strong for being so skinny. She thought the disabled son with a brain injury would be in a wheelchair, drooling and lifeless. Damian was clearly not that. He looked perfectly normal—skinny, yes, but healthy. She could hardly tell anything was wrong until he babbled.

What had she signed up for?

DAPHNE GRADUATED FROM THE PROGRAM IN AUGUST 2009 and started work for Ann and Lincoln immediately. She moved in with her mom in Loma Rica for one month until she got married to Chris at the end of September on Ann and Lincoln's deck. Everyone from the church donated the food, the music, and the flowers. Daphne felt incredibly blessed as she stepped away from her old life and into God's path set before her.

Lincoln accompanied Daphne for her first shift to pick up Damian from the care home and bring him back to the house. He explained Damian's story up until that point and what his care was typically like. She listened intently as he described the frequency of his bowel movements and the cleanup process it entailed. *Yikes.* Lincoln then described how Damian got to the care home in Live Oak and how they would be bringing him home full-time soon. Hearing his whole story brought tears to Daphne's eyes. Damian was too young for this to happen, too young for his life to be robbed from him. She realized her mother must have felt the same way about her, throwing away her own life with addiction when so much potential lay before her. She thanked God for her own second chance at life and felt a keen desire to help Damian live the fullest life he could while in her care.

Working together, the two of them managed to get Damian into the back seat. His anger raged. He beat the back of the seats in front of him with his fists. He started kicking the front seat where Daphne sat. He yelled and yelled. Daphne started to get nervous. Maybe he didn't like her? Was he always like this? Lincoln pulled into the Starbucks line to get Damian a drink. Daphne took mental notes as she watched Damian calm down, sipping out of the clear cup with a green straw.

The next surprise was the rancid smell of Damian's poop. Back at the house, diarrhea oozed out of Damian's diaper. She had to keep herself from gagging as she cleaned him up with Lincoln's help. The smell was worse than anything she had smelled before. The new bathroom wasn't done yet, so it was quite a process, with the three of them barely fitting in Ann and Lincoln's bathroom. She wanted to get some fresh air, so Lincoln advised she take Damian for a walk around the property. But Damian was fast. She could barely keep up with him when he walked.

Lincoln had hinted that Daphne would be getting him alone on her next shift. By the end of the day, she was more than nervous about that prospect.

FOR SEVERAL MONTHS, DAPHNE DROVE IN THE SUBURBAN to Live Oak Manor three times a week to pick Damian up, bring him to the house for several hours, and then return him. She slowly fell into a rhythm with Damian. As everyone got used to Damian's care in Ann and Lincoln's home, they did an overnight stay, and then another. Then the time came to bring him home full-time, after being at the care home for about fifteen months.

All the details were hammered out. Daphne worked full-time Monday through Friday. Rachel, one of the CNAs from the care home who worked one-on-one with Damian, filled in the weekend hours. That left Ann and Lincoln responsible for the early morning hours, evening hours, and the middle of the night wake-up times. Ann told Daphne she felt confident knowing she had support built in at home so that this time it might be bearable. Ann's confidence in Daphne boosted her own. She thought about the many hours she had spent with Damian up to this point and felt she had learned to read his moods quite quickly and understood the basics of his care. She wasn't as experienced as the other CNA, but her developing love for Damian guided her.

AFTER DAMIAN HAD BEEN HOME FULL TIME FOR almost three weeks, Ann and Daphne were standing in the kitchen together while Daphne cooked Damian eggs over easy. Daphne asked, "Ann, are you going to leave? Am I doing okay with Damian?"

"You're doing fabulous," Ann said.

"Well . . ." Daphne hesitated. "You can go somewhere if you want to."

For a moment, Ann just stared at her, confused. "Oh, I suppose I can. Are you sure you're going to be okay with him?" Ann asked, unsure of how to feel. The last time they brought Damian home, doing anything without him was completely out of the question. She had felt stuck at home in an endless abyss. They had been in survival mode. What were these new possibilities opening up before her?

"Yes, I'm going to be fine. That's why I'm here," Daphne said. "You could use the break."

Just like the first time you leave a baby behind and think about them the entire time, Ann got in her car, drove to town, and worried about how Damian was doing. But, oh, how wonderful. She could just walk into the store, alone. It was freeing.

But she could only bring herself to go to two stores before she rushed home frantically to check on Damian, certain that something had gone wrong.

Ann walked in the door, expecting chaos. Damian was sitting in his chair, smiling and babbling, while Daphne made him a grilled cheese.

"How did it go? How did he do?" Ann asked.

"Well, he pooped, and then I got him down for a nap. He was just typical Damian," Daphne reported. "He was a bit agitated, but we walked outside on the deck, and he eventually calmed down."

After that, life felt like it could begin to normalize. They settled into the new normal with Damian being a part of their lives, but not their whole lives. Ann felt relieved. For the first time, Ann could acknowledge willingly that she needed help and slowly came to accept that help. In allowing Daphne to care for Damian five days a week without her, she was learning to let others help her, an incredibly humbling and difficult lesson.

Before, she had only trusted Lincoln to help her. Kate, Kara, and Jean had shown up in her times of most desperate need, but she never wanted to give them too much to do because of her own stubborn self-reliance. Even in the care home, when she was there with Damian, she took most of his care on herself and had a hard time letting go. God was showing her a different way, a way that opened her heart to more freely receive others' acts of love and service, something that had always been uncomfortable for her. This heart expansion created room to love Damian and not resent him for needing her help when he was difficult. Daphne quickly felt like part of the family.

THEY SETTLED INTO DAY-TO-DAY ROUTINES WITH Damian. In the evenings, Ann completed his grooming, cutting his hair, clipping his nails, or shaving his beard while he watched *Jeopardy* with Nana. Watching a show kept him somewhat still, but brushing his teeth was another story. Anything that entered Damian's mouth became a chew toy, so keeping his teeth clean was a difficult feat. During the day, Ann taught Daphne and Rachel how to continue the work of his speech and occupational therapies. One of the goals was to help Damian's dexterity. Working with a specialized cube, Damian practiced buttoning and zipping, in the hopes that one day he might help with getting himself dressed.

Another experiment was getting a guitar for Damian to play, hoping perhaps his muscle memory would take over and his fingers might remember chords.

"Damian has surprised me. He seems to light up when we hand him the guitar," Daphne said to Ann one afternoon as Damian was loudly moving his fingers back and forth over the strings.

"I wish you could have heard him play before his injury," Ann told her, looking thoughtful. "He would play for hours and hours. I would never tire of listening to him. I remember I could hear him while he played in his bedroom upstairs, and I would have to bang on the door for several minutes to get him to come to dinner. When he started playing sometime in high school, it was like a whole new world opened up to him. He even had a band at one point."

"Wouldn't it be incredible if this was the avenue that opened his world back to him?" Daphne asked.

"I keep thinking it might be just the thing. I know he comprehends more than he lets on. He is such a booger. We visited his speech therapist yesterday. She asked him to say, 'Shirt.' She got a knock on her door and had to step out into the hallway. Right after she left the room, he said, 'Shirt shirt shirt shirt shirt shirt.' When she came back, she asked him to say it again. He just looked at her, silently. So she said, 'I'm going to try to leave again. Tell me if he says it.' The minute she walked out of the room, he said, 'Shirt shirt shirt shirt shirt.' That little stinker wouldn't ever say it in front of her. But she was amazed at all the brain processes going on. First of all, he said the right word but was choosing to purposely not say it when he was asked to. She said it showed his sense of humor was still intact and he had motivation to learn."

Daphne laughed louder as the story progressed. Then she looked over at Damian, who was now lifting his guitar over his head, threatening to throw it at her. She rushed over to his side and grabbed the guitar. "Damian, you don't have to be so upset. I'm not laughing at you. But it is funny. You do understand us, don't you?" She looked into his steely blue eyes trying to find recognition in them.

"I can't believe the doctors thought you would stay in a vegetative state forever," she continued. "They should see you now—running, jumping, shouting, holding a fork, sitting still to listen to a book, and even strumming a guitar."

"We actually have an appointment with Dr. Wolff in a few weeks," Ann said. "He is always amazed to see Damian. He is such a kind man, following Damian throughout his health journey. And now he is big-time at his hospital. Damian has made huge amounts of progress that he never thought he would make."

DURING HIS TIME AT THE CARE HOME, DAMIAN HAD become less agitated, with more moments of calm. This trend continued when they brought him home. When it had once seemed impossible to reduce his long list of medications, they had worked with the doctor at the care home before bringing him home to take him off a few more. Eventually, he no longer needed the strong psychotropic drugs except for a small dosage at bedtime to improve sleep, meaning most of his medications were dedicated to keeping his Crohn's under control.

Damian's growing docile state opened the door to make more improvements.

The biggest miracle and improvement happened when he participated in getting dressed rather than fighting the entire process.

It happened overnight. The day before he fought every step of the process, dragging ten minutes out to feel like forty. A few weeks ago, Lincoln got a hernia trying to get him dressed and had to go in for surgery. Then one morning, Damian sprung out of bed and waited by the dresser. Ann came in, prepared for the drudgery of the process. She talked absent-mindedly to Damian about what color he might prefer and how they were going to get through the day together. She had everything laid out on the bed, ready to begin the fight. But the fight never came.

"Damian, you're helping me?" Ann said in absolute shock. "That's it, yes. Put your arm into the hole, and then the other one." Damian grabbed on to his shoe, showing interest. He easily slid into his pants. She then took the shoe and held it steady on the ground. Damian wiggled his foot into the shoe, putting pressure on his heel as she slid the shoe on.

"Am I dreaming? Damian, this is a miracle. If you know how to participate like this, we can do so much more, go to more places. Good job, Damian. I'm so proud of you."

Ann couldn't wait to tell everyone of the newest development. This would help alleviate a huge amount of daily stress. She waited with bated breath to see if he would retain the advancement the whole day.

When he continued helping in the process weeks later, she wept with happiness, thanking God for the unimaginable breakthrough.

AND THEN DAMIAN EXPERIENCED JOY.

Ann put on a cartoon for Damian while she was dusting the house. She looked up in confusion when she heard the noise for the first time.

Then, there it was again, a catatonic, "heh heh heh heh heh," escaped his throat.

Is he choking? Ann thought to herself. She inspected his mouth to see if any unknown object caused him to choke. Then she noticed his eyes glued to the television. "Heh heh heh heh heh heh."

"Is it funny, Damian?" Ann asked. While watching him intently, she turned the TV off. His eyes crumpled, and he frowned. Then she turned it back on to the slapstick-humor cartoon scene. The low chuckle returned. "Heh heh heh heh heh."

Wow, he's laughing. For the first time since his injury. He has genuine joy in this moment. Ann smiled to herself, acknowledging a small answer to her prayer.

His laughter continued to evolve, and when somebody else was portrayed as going through misery—getting whacked or in a car crash—he would be belly laughing.

One day, Kevin, the neighbor who had helped build Damian's bathroom addition, brought his three elementary aged children over. The kids loved Damian and immediately started playing ball with him. When one of the girls missed and hit her brother in the head, Damian started laughing uncontrollably, bringing tears to his eyes.

The boy laughed heartily along with Damian. "Miss Ann, can we get Damian out of his chair? Can we bring him outside?"

"What do you think, Kevin? Would that be okay?" Ann asked before agreeing.

"Yeah, no problems here. Damian looks like he could use some sunshine. The kids will take good care of him. I'll go out with them to make sure Damian behaves himself."

Before she knew it, Damian was up and out of his chair, following the children outside. One of the girls ran onto the trampoline. Damian walked up the wooden steps behind her, ducked his head to get through the netting, and found himself on the black bouncy circle. His eyes lit up as he steadied his feet underneath him and then used his arms to wind up for a big bounce.

Joyous laughter rang into the air. The three children and Damian bounced and bounced with glee, falling over from laughing so hard.

Ann watched from a distance, taking in the miracle before her eyes. For the first time in years, Damian was participating in life as an equal. The children didn't see him as "other" or "disabled." They simply saw him as a playmate who brought joy, and in doing so, they released the joy from him in its fullest capacity. She watched Damian come to life as he played and laughed, regaining that childlike joy. God was healing his heart from all the rage and allowing Damian to re-engage in life in a new and different way. Ann felt herself beginning to accept that even if Damian never made more steps toward recovery, she could rejoice that he could find joy in his circumstance.

On her outings, Ann was painstakingly aware that seldom few people viewed Damian like Kevin's children did. What pained her the most was how awkward people could be around him, as if he were from a different planet and they had no idea what to say to him. There were three typical responses from the general public she encountered. The most common was for people to ignore Damian altogether. They might catch a glimpse of him out of the corner of their eye and then determinedly look the other way. She hadn't worked out if they were embarrassed by the sight of him or simply unwilling to acknowledge someone so different than themselves. Then there were the people who did try to say a word or two to Damian, then sheepishly became uncomfortable and started to engage her in a conversation, sometimes about him as if he were no longer there, but most often about something entirely meaningless to pass the time before they could acceptably excuse themselves. The last group of people was either annoyed or flat-out angry about how Damian behaved in public. This was the type of person Ann found herself encountering on one day's town trip.

Target had become her town staple, her lifeline of sorts. It didn't take long to realize the gaping limitations of most public places: the lack of truly accessible bathrooms. What made it even trickier was that Damian was the opposite sex. Most moms solve this when they have little boys by taking their sons with them into the women's bathroom. However, Damian was not "little" in any sense of the word. He was a full-grown man. Also, the nature of his bathroom visits begged for more privacy than was rendered in a public restroom. Target, however, boasted a spacious family bathroom. Town trips with Damian were only possible when she knew she could access a large private bathroom to clean Damian, should an emergency arise.

As she and Damian walked into the familiar box store, the security man greeted them. "Hey, Damian. Glad to see you on this fine day. You're looking good today. Did you get a haircut?" Damian had the status of mini-celebrity; most of the workers recognized him and spoke to him intentionally.

Ann pushed a cart toward the grocery aisles but stopped on the way to browse the card selections. As she stood engrossed in a comical card, a woman passed by them.

"Excuse me, ma'am. This young man with you is tearing clothes off the hangers and throwing them in the aisle. Don't you have any respect for other shoppers?" the middle-aged woman held her nose high and stood with her hand on her hip, pointing at the scene of destruction.

Ann turned to gape at the mess on the ground behind her. Damian started getting agitated and flailing his arms.

"That's just Damian," a young adult in a Target uniform interjected as he walked briskly toward them. Ann recognized him as one of Damian's good friends from high school. "I'll take care of the mess, ma'am. You continue shopping." He turned toward Damian and gave him a firm handshake and a pat on the back. "Damian, man, how are you doing? It's great to see you. I miss having jam sessions with you. Seen any pretty ladies lately?"

Damian murmured a low, "No no no no no no." Damian shook his head up and down and bobbed his body, showing his excitement to see his friend. He spun in a circle away.

Then his friend turned to address Ann. "Is he ever going to get better?"

"We hope so. That's all we can do is hope. He has made small improvements, but we don't know if he will get back to his old self."

"Well, I hope so too," he said and then turned around to get back to work.

As his friend walked away, Damian said in a loud voice, "Fuck you," with a smile pasted on his face. Ann's expression became apologetic.

The friend twirled back around on the spot and started to laugh, "Oh, there's a bit of the old Damian. I love you too, man." He walked away chuckling.

Another passerby loudly whispered, "That young man is very rude."

That set Damian off. Damian always acted out when people whispered about him. He began flailing and kicking. Ann quickly grabbed him around the midsection and dragged him as quickly as she could to the door. The Target trip was over.

The security guard jumped up to help Ann when he saw her struggling with Damian. "Going so soon?" he asked.

"Someone was rude to him again. He hates that. I've got to get him home," Ann said between heavy breaths. He helped her all the way out to the car.

When she came home and told Daphne about it, Daphne shared her own story. "I took him to a restaurant last week. He started getting loud and vocal. I saw a woman stare at us with these laser eyes, like communicating, 'You shouldn't be here.' Then she went over to talk to the manager. I felt embarrassed, so I tried to gather our belongings to leave. But then the manager came over and put his hand on my shoulder, telling me not to worry about it. Then I saw him ask the snarky woman to leave. I have never been happier in my life. Damian and I stayed and enjoyed our meal together leisurely." Daphne paused, laughing at the replay in her mind. "But then on the way out Damian grabbed someone's soda off their table. It's always an adventure with Damian in public."

Ann laughed heartily with Daphne and then recounted another Damian story. "I agree it's never simple. Like last week. I brought Damian home from an especially difficult day in town. He kept throwing things at me while I was driving and laughing. He knew exactly what he was doing, that little stinker. I finally got home and had to shut him in his room. I said, 'God, thank you for this door. This door is my safety net. He is safe in there. I'm safe out here. I'm not going to hit him if I'm out here. And he's not going to hit me if I'm not in the room.'"

Ann spoke with a twinge of guilt in her expression. "But then at the end of the day when I went in to tuck him into bed, he helped me get him into his pajamas. He hugged me while I pulled his shirt over his head. Then he got into bed and pulled the covers up. I said, 'Good night, Damian.' And he said, 'Na na na na na na.' It was so sweet. That keeps me going."

The one place Damian was fully welcomed was at the little Baptist church. The pastor there welcomed people of all abilities, which is not the case in every church. Another man with autism also attended the church service and always sat in the front, sometimes having loud outbursts during the service. Damian fit right in. No one minded if he became verbal and loud during worship or the sermon. The people there loved Damian for who he was, as they had never known him before the injury. They talked to Damian lovingly and gave him an identity separate from his parents. He flourished in the focused attention. Ann praised God that He had led them to a place where they could bring Damian with them confidently and not be made to feel uncomfortable. These people truly had the love of God in them.

And the church had brought her to Daphne. Her list of things to be thankful for continually grew.

DAPHNE NEVER IMAGINED WHEN SHE SAID YES TO this job what it would lead to. She admired how Ann and Lincoln desired Damian to not just get by but truly enjoy living. They incorporated him into family life. Their love for him radiated into the way they cared for him and kept a peaceful home. One day, they said they wanted him to have adventure in his life, so they bought a dune buggy.

Damian lit up at the prospect of going on a thrill ride. Daphne told him, "Okay, Damian, if you poop, then we can go for a ride." Damian didn't communicate when he needed to poop, but he had developed a bit of a schedule, usually pooping in the morning after breakfast and then not again for at least four hours. After sitting on the toilet until the morning bowel movement passed, Damian ran to the dune buggy, designed for speed and fun.

Damian nimbly perched himself in the passenger seat, waiting to be buckled up, and said, "No no no no no no, yeah, no." He bobbed up and down, waiting for Daphne to get in.

Daphne zoomed around every inch of the hillside with Damian by her side in the dune buggy, enjoying the wind in her hair. She packed a lunch for the two of them, and they enjoyed it on the beach at the lake. If someone had told her this was what she would be doing when she sat in jail, she would have laughed at them and said a string of cuss words. Her husband, Chris, came up often as well to zoom

Damian around the property. They would also take Damian to the park together for a change of pace.

The one part of her job she could have done without was the endless amounts of poop. Sometimes she would pray, *Not on my shift.* It became increasingly more difficult to smell it when she got pregnant, just a few short months after being married. And it wasn't the mess she was bothered by so much as seeing Damian in pain. Often, Damian would be doubled over, whimpering in obvious pain caused by his Crohn's disease. She felt terrible, not being able to help ease the pain in any way. As time went on, she saw Damian's fits of anger grow into more moments of joy, but a sense of sadness and pain still loomed.

She often wondered about Damian's life before his accident. The whole story made her sad, losing out on his life at such a young age. His parents gave him the best life they could manage, but it was not the life he was expecting. She thought again about how she could have missed out on so much if God hadn't intervened in her own life. God stopped her before she completely wrecked herself and gave her a life better than she could have imagined, a life with Chris and a boy on the way.

She felt her love for Damian grow daily. He became like her best friend. She could confide in him because he couldn't share it with anyone else. She joked with him and laughed with him. She truly enjoyed her new life.

If Daphne could have summed up her time with Damian with one word it would be love. The home was filled with an overwhelming, all-encompassing, generous love. Day by day, she felt the love changing her. Ann and Lincoln were unlike anyone else she had ever met. They didn't often mention their faith in God, but they silently lived it out in profound ways. What surprised her most was how much they loved her, a complete outsider. They welcomed her and her husband into their family. When she got pregnant, they loved her son before he was born. She felt herself being more loving because of how they treated her. They trusted her to watch Damian in their home for two weeks when they went to Europe to celebrate Nicole's college graduation and Jacob's high school graduation. They never made her feel guilty about her past.

Ann had been reluctant to travel so far away from Damian, but Daphne, and the other caregiver, Rachel, had assured her they could handle it. Thank the Lord, no major incidents happened while they were gone. Daphne was glad to give them the gift of getting away as a small repayment for all the ways they had helped her. And it was nice to earn all the extra overtime as a nest egg for their coming baby expenses.

Daphne gave birth to a son, almost exactly one year after beginning work with Damian. Lincoln kindly offered for her to bring the baby with her to work when her maternity leave ended. When Daphne returned from several months of maternity leave, Damian lit up with joy like she had never experienced. With big arm gestures, hands flapping, and his face full of expression, he gasped, "Oh, oh, oh." The obvious delight showed that he remembered her.

Tears filled Daphne's eyes as she grasped that she had come to make a difference in Damian's life. And he had certainly left his mark on hers.

Damian loves bathing

Damian on trampoline with Kevin's kids

Damian with his first two caretakers in
Ann's home: Rachel and Daphne

Damian

Daphne with Damian in dunebuggy

First time Daphne met Ann and
Nana at rehab program

NINETEEN

LB Visits Home

SPRING 2010

. . . .

"Preach the Gospel at all times; and
if necessary, use words."

—St. Francis of Assisi

. . . .

"HI, ANN," A DEEP VOICE SAID ON THE OTHER END OF
the phone.

Ann almost dropped the phone, recognizing the voice
immediately. She steadied her hand and her voice, then managed a
feeble, "Hi, LB."

Silence met her ears. She waited, unsure what to say next, or why
he might be calling. When it lasted a little too long, she asked, "Did
you want to talk to Damian?"

Hearing Damian's name must have prompted LB to speak. "Well,
yes, Damian is why I am calling. Mario and I want to come visit him.
And the rest of the gang. We haven't seen him in a long time. Can we
come up next Sunday?"

"You are always welcome here, LB," Ann said.

LB didn't say goodbye before hanging up.

Ann hung up the phone, trying not to explode with excitement. LB was coming to her house! He hadn't said much, just that he wanted to come visit Damian. She couldn't believe it. Her son was coming *home* for the first time in ten years. She had imagined this day so many times.

Damian's brain injury had happened a little over two years ago. They had seen LB at the hospital and the meeting, of course, but he had mostly ignored them, refusing to even make eye contact. But now he was coming to her home.

Her excitement then turned to questions. Why had he stayed away so long? What exactly did he blame them for? Was he ready to forgive them? She had never gotten the chance to explain those last words the judge said, that they were not her words. She questioned whether he would believe her anyway. At the time, they had done what they felt was the right thing, chasing the opportunities in front of them to help him. She wanted to apologize for not chasing after him, for not fighting harder to bring him home instead. She never imagined he would cut them out of his life completely.

Ann had fallen in love the minute he came into her home as a tiny four-and-a-half-year-old. She loved his stutter, his cute and flattering ways, even if they were manipulative, and his sweet boyish attitude. He had always been her son and always would be.

She then became determined to put aside all her questions. After all, when the prodigal son returned home, the father rejoiced. And she felt like rejoicing. She wouldn't push him; she would just let him be and see what came of it. That's what Damian had encouraged her to do before his injury. She felt love washing over her, forgiving the past and opening herself to the future. God nudged her to forgive without question, letting go of the past entirely—wiping the slate clean and moving forward into what He had prepared.

When the Navarro family arrived, Ann walked outside to greet everyone. She walked expectantly toward the car, hoping for a chance to hug LB. Mario got out of the car first and walked toward Ann, giving her a hug and thanking her for letting them come. LB slowly emerged but deliberately did not look in her direction. He leaned on the car in a detached stance. He had sunglasses on, blocking Ann's view of his eyes. She resisted every urge pulsing through her body to throw her arms around him and welcome him home. He clearly wasn't ready for that yet.

Larry and Milo exited the car with cigarettes in hand, forming a circle around LB, almost like his personal bodyguards. Connie remained in the car, looking agitated.

"You're all welcome to come join us out back," Ann announced. "Damian and Lincoln are on the deck. Damian will be so glad to see you all."

Mario followed Ann eagerly, but the rest remained where they were. Ann glanced back, confused, and a smarting tear threatening to plunge down her cheek. She had so hoped it would be different, that LB would say but one word to her, even look at her. But he stood rigid and unrelenting as she turned the corner.

Mario sat in the rocking chair next to his brother. "Hi, Damian. Man, am I glad to see you."

"Yeah yeah no buddy no no no," Damian said, showing obvious signs of recognizing his brother.

Ann stood pacing the deck, craning her neck around the corner to try to see the others still standing in the driveway. "Hey, Mario . . ." She trailed off as she saw Connie get out of the car and walk over to the big wide oak tree. She lay down under the tree and started petting Jackie, the drooling cat.

"Yes, Ann?" Mario answered, cocking his head sideways in question.

"Is Connie okay?" Ann asked. "She's just lying under a tree."

"She's fine. I mean, she's just being herself. This is what she's like when she's high; she's crazy. Well, she's crazy when she's not high too, so yeah, she's pretty much crazy all the time," Mario said.

"They're all fine, Ann. Just come sit down," Lincoln soothed.

"Okay," Ann said reluctantly, choosing another rocking chair next to Lincoln, facing Mario. Lincoln seemed unbothered by the fact that Connie was high at their home, but Ann was a bit concerned about what Connie might be capable of while high. She made an effort to refocus her attention on Mario and forget about the others.

Mario straightened his back, looked over at Damian, and then at Ann and Lincoln. "I thank God every day He lets Damian live."

Lifting her eyebrows in shock, Ann said, "I've never heard you talk about God. Ever."

Could this even be the same Mario I've known almost his whole life?

Mario's aunt had taken him in when the other three boys were adopted out. Mario was two years older than Damian, and he too was well acquainted with hospitals; he had childhood leukemia and had brushed with death twice. His aunt took care of him, making sure he received all his treatments—but from the way he had talked about her and her Catholic faith, Ann thought he was ungrateful. *Wow, I really used to judge people harshly. I don't see a bone of ungratefulness in him.* He emancipated when he was seventeen to go live with his birth parents, Larry and Connie, who were in and out of homelessness, a choice she definitely did not understand. But then again, you never know about a person until you ask. Ann resolved to get better at asking more questions and withholding judgment.

"Well, it was something important to Damian. Before his injury, Damian was always talking to us about, 'You guys are going to go to hell if you don't believe in Jesus. So you need to believe in Jesus,'" Mario said, rocking back and forth in his chair. "I never prayed for my brother. I never prayed at all, but I find myself praying more now. Damian was real faithful. I know he had faith because he told me."

"You're right, Mario, Damian was faithful," Lincoln said. "You know, I had several conversations with him about how much he wanted you to know Jesus like he did. If he could understand what you're saying right now, he would be jumping up with glee."

Tears streamed down Mario's cheeks. "I prayed before I came here to help me not feel so sad about Damian. I used to be so angry. I was angry that God let this happen to Damian. But now, I want to go to church to let Jesus know I'm thankful He saved my brother. Even if he's in this condition, I still have a brother."

"That's beautiful, Mario," Ann said.

"We will be coming up every other week," Mario informed them. "I want to stay involved in Damian's life. I still believe he's going to get better and be Damian again. I want him to know we're here for him."

"He will love the company," Ann said, in complete awe of Mario's transformation.

The others never made it to the porch. Ann let Damian out of his chair to walk over to where the others still stood near the car. She saw LB greet Damian and half a smile flicker over his face before the unaffected grimace reappeared. She tried to imagine how hard it must be for him to see his brother like that. Maybe that's why he had stayed away so long. He must be grieving the loss of his best friend.

Ann walked near enough to say, "I hope you'll come in next time. I'm glad you all came up."

They all got in the car and left.

BUT THEY DID COME BACK AGAIN TWO WEEKS LATER. By the fourth visit, Ann set up dinner during their visit, trying to lure everyone into the house or at least onto the deck. Ann desperately wanted a chance to talk to LB. So far he hadn't even acknowledged their existence. She knew it would have to be her to bridge the gap. This next visit she was determined to say, "Hi," at the very least.

To Ann's delight, Larry, who wore his hat backward, entered the house first, and the others followed him to the living room. He chose the seat on the couch closest to Damian's chair. "Damian, why the hell did you let this happen to you?" Larry said to him. Then he pulled a beer out of the small bag he had been carrying. "Here, Damian, I think you need this more than I do," he said, extending the beer toward Damian.

"What are you doing, Dad?" Mario cried from across the room. "You can't bring him a beer. If you're going to be like this, I can't bring you anymore."

"Well, I just don't know if these people are treating my son right," Larry said.

"C'mon, Dad, be respectful. You know they are doing everything they can for Damian," Mario cried, then stormed out of the room, obviously upset at his dad.

Ann took the opportunity to try to say something to LB. "Hi, LB."

LB looked up quickly at Ann, a short glance, and then continued to stare at the floor. A low grunted, "Hey," was all that came out.

Lincoln filled the silence next. "You know, Larry, we haven't given him beer yet, but I believe he did enjoy a good beer in his pre-injury life. He might like it. I don't think you're too far off. Damian is surrounded by women all day, so I try to occasionally create an environment where it's just the two of us guys for 'dude time.' I like to do some things for him reminiscent of his former life like playing kickback music instead of Christian music all day long. I started giving him his goatee too, instead of clean-shaving him. So I think you had the right heart, wanting to share a beer with him."

In the corner, Larry puffed up with pride. He nudged LB and said, "See, I have good ideas. So you think he can try it?"

Ann interjected, "Let me go check his medications before we take any chances."

She walked to the kitchen with Mario following her. As Mario was passing the hallway bathroom on the way to the kitchen, Connie opened the door.

Ann read the labels on Damian's pills that clearly instructed not to mix them with alcohol. That settled the beer issue easily enough.

"Really, Connie?" Ann suddenly heard Mario say. "You had to go and shoot up in the bathroom? You can't do that. That's it, we're leaving."

Mario marched Connie straight past the kitchen out the back door to the car. Ann watched him stride back to the living room where everyone was spending time with Damian before dinner and announce, "We're leaving. Everyone to the car."

"You're leaving before dinner?" Ann called from the kitchen as she pulled baked lemon chicken out of the oven. She emerged in the opening of the living room.

"I'm sorry, Ann." Mario faced her. "I don't want to leave. But I can't let Connie do drugs at your house. She has a bad addiction. I thought it would work to bring her up here. She won't be back. I hope we can stay for dinner next time."

After everyone left, Ann said to Lincoln, "LB grunted at me. It's a start. Do you think he would bring our grandson?"

"All you can do is ask," Lincoln told her. "Let's not push him. He will come around in his own time if he wants to. God has to break down the giant wall that LB built against us."

"I just love him. He's our son." Ann prayed, "Jesus, please give us a relationship with LB."

TWO WEEKS LATER, THE NAVARROS SHOWED UP without Connie. Mario reminded Larry on the way in to be respectful.

They shared dinner together, and Mario wanted to help feed Damian. It seemed a miraculous transformation had taken place in Mario. His hard shell had melted away; he was soft and compassionate with Damian.

"So how much money do you make off Damian from the state?" Larry asked while they were eating.

"Larry," Mario warned, his voice remaining calm. "I thought we talked about this. That's not a respectful question."

Lincoln laughed merrily. "It's fine, Mario. We are always open about our finances. We do receive funding for Damian from the state, but it's hardly enough to cover his care. We have two full-time caregivers that we pay out of our own pocket, and then we are able to reimburse ourselves maybe up to half of what their wages cost us with the money we receive from the state. I did hear they might be reforming the laws about it, though, so maybe soon we will get a fairer sum to help us with Damian's care. As for now, it costs us quite a bit, but the cost is worth it to keep us all sane around here." At that, Lincoln looked lovingly in Ann's direction.

Mario listened with a cocked head while feeding a forkful of spinach to Damian. "So how are things going with Damian? Anything new he is trying?"

Ann responded, "We just got this new communication device. It has picture symbols on buttons that correspond to what he might want to say. We just started testing it out; we have to get all the right symbols in there to see if it will work. We're hopeful that he might be able to understand basic communication at first, like telling us if he's hungry or thirsty, or needs to use the restroom. But if he gets the hang of it, he could tell us so much more. We're eager to try it out fully once we finish setting it up. Then we have to be super responsive if he presses a button so he gets the idea that pressing the cup gets him a cup of water. That's the idea."

Lincoln added, "We just finished reading this book called *Ghost Boy* about a man who was trapped inside his own body, fully aware, but unable to communicate for several years. Finally, someone noticed and took the time to help him communicate. He ended up with a very happy life after that. Who knows how much of the old Damian is in there, or how aware he is, until we at least try to access him? The parts of the brain that were injured were the front and side, which cause him to be impulsive, unable to communicate, and have no ability to plan. But the back of the brain that holds all his memories is possibly intact. So he could potentially remember his childhood. We know he remembers people. It might totally fail, but at least we try."

Mario smiled wide. "Well, I hope it works." Then he winked at Damian. "I know you're in there, little brother. Give it your best shot."

Damian reached for more food off his plate. Before Mario could stop him, he stuck an entire roll into his mouth.

"Damian, dude, you gotta slow down." Mario chuckled.

At the end of the evening, Ann peeped over at LB, who was scanning the horizon out the window. She took the chance she had been waiting for. "It would be neat if you could bring Raphael with you sometime."

"Yeah," LB said without looking at her, and then he turned to walk away.

Ann's heart leaped. *He said, "Yeah."*

TWO WEEKS LATER, THREE-YEAR-OLD RAPHAEL BOUNDED up the sidewalk leading to the house. Overjoyed, Ann gathered all the boy toys she had and scattered them on the floor in the living room. She plopped herself next to Raphael on the floor. They built train tracks, they vroomed cars, they bounced the ball, and they read books. Then Ann said, "Raphael, do you want to go jump on the trampoline?"

"Yes," Raphael said, nodding his head up and down, eyes wide with joy.

Ann jumped on the trampoline with Raphael, holding his sweet little hands in hers. They bounced and laughed and bounced and laughed until they both fell down, still laughing.

Raphael looked up at her with a big smile on his face. "What your name?" he asked in his sweet three-year-old voice.

"You can ask your dad what to call me. I know you have quite a few grandmas in your life, don't you?" Ann asked.

Raphael nodded his head.

"You can just call me Ann. Or Grandma Ann. You and your dad can decide. Whatever you want to call me is fine with me."

LB came out of the house, calling to Raphael, "Hey, bud, it's time to go."

"Daddy, can we come back?" Raphael asked.

"Yeah, bud, I'll bring you back," LB said, scooping him up into his arms.

Ann remained calm on the outside but was doing cartwheels on the inside. *Yes, yes, yes, yes! I get to have a relationship with my grandson. God help me, my son has returned.*

"I'll see you next time," Ann called out to Raphael, waving at him. "We can make bubbles."

Ann, Raphael & Damian at the park

Ann with Damian 2010

Milo visits Damian at Ann and Lincoln's home

Damian with brothers—Mario, LB, and Milo—and birth father Larry in jumphouse

TWENTY

Heart Surgery

WINTER 2011

. . . .

"The world as we have created it is a product
of our thinking. It cannot be changed
without changing our thinking."

—Albert Einstein

. . . .

LB WOKE UP NEXT TO BROOKE, DETERMINED THIS
would be his last time waking up next to her. He didn't love her.
Why should he stay with her? For the longest time, he had stayed
because of Raphael. But Raphael was already three, and nothing had
changed in their relationship. Plus he had a new opportunity at work
to become the foreman; he was making a name for himself. LB was
sure he could afford a down payment on a house now. Then he could
get into house flipping. Though he would love to have Raphael full-
time, he knew she would fight for him. He hated that she would use
Raphael to spite him, but he couldn't think about Raphael too much,
or else he couldn't go through with what he had to do.

Brooke's eyes fluttered open as he studied her. Should he break up with her now? Better to do it before he lost his nerve or she dropped some other big news.

"Brooke, I don't think it's working between us," LB said emotionlessly.

Blinking her eyes awake, Brooke abruptly sat up. "What do you mean it's not working?"

"Just what I said. I'm ready to move on. You know we haven't had a spark in a long time. We're both just in the relationship for Raphael," LB explained.

"What are you talking about? You can't just leave me. We've been together for five years. I gave you a child. You think you can just walk away?" Brooke screamed at him, tears streaming down her face. "Is there another girl?"

"No, there's no one else. I just can't see myself in this relationship long term," LB said.

Then he got out of bed before she could say another word. He walked to the bathroom, quickly shaved, and brushed his teeth. He packed his belongings in the bathroom, then walked out to the kitchen to make his protein shake for breakfast. Returning to the bedroom, he packed whatever belongings he could fit in his overnight bag. He would return for the rest when he figured out where he was going.

Brooke had rolled back over in bed, pulling the covers over her head. Now that she heard him in the room, she sat up again. "You'll regret this, LB Young. You're wrong about this, and you're wrong about your parents too. They love you. I love you. But you won't let anybody in. I'm sorry for you. You'll end up all alone."

LB left the room without looking back. He would go crash on Mario's couch until things settled down and he found a place of his own. That sounded like freedom. As he skipped down the steps, he had a passing thought, *Is something wrong with me that I don't feel any sadness leaving the girl I've been with for more than five years?* He pushed the thought aside. It was time to move on.

AND HE DID MOVE ON. IN THE NEXT SEVERAL months, he moved on to the next girl, Katie, who found him too shallow. But he found girl after girl who entertained him for a while before he set them aside, all of them enamored with Raphael. Raphael spent half the week with him and half the week with his mom. He stayed busy with work and softball teams; he played four nights a week. He bought his first house and worked constantly on fixing it up.

LB also continued visiting Damian every other week. He had been going up to Ann and Lincoln's twice a month for over a year now. LB hated to see Damian in the state he was in. He kept hoping Damian would have a breakthrough and become his best friend again, just like the old Damian. He always thought the brain injury would be temporary. Or that one of these computers would work for Damian to be able to communicate. Ann and Lincoln were always trying something out—speech therapy or a new technology—but it seemed nothing stuck or worked.

As he drove up this time, he felt the familiar inner turmoil. Brooke's words echoed in his head, "You're wrong about your parents." Since the first time he saw them in the hospital, the audacious feeling that he was wrong had grown and taken on legs of its own. He couldn't ignore the old thoughts about them, alongside this new thought about how much they loved Damian. It baffled him. How could both be true? How could they be the terrible people who sent their son, himself, away—yet also demonstrate the most selfless form of love, giving up their lives to take care of his brother? They had always liked Damian more—he had behaved himself—would they have done the same thing if it had been him? They fought hard to bring Damian out of an institution but never went to bat for him.

Yet it became increasingly difficult to not like the people who kept showing up for his brother whom he loved so much. No one could doubt their love for Damian; showing up at the hospital constantly, bringing him home, finding a home that could help him, then bringing him home again. LB observed how much work it was to take care of Damian. And at their age, they should be enjoying their empty nest, going on trips, having fun. But there they were, happy to be stuck at home with Damian, happy to sacrifice everything. How did they do it?

LB wiped his sweaty palms on his pants. As he thought more and more about Ann and Lincoln's love for Damian, he felt his ten-foot-wall crashing down. He had scrupulously guarded himself from these people who were the "absolute worst," people he swore to never talk to again. And yet he couldn't deny their love in action, overwhelming love, as they wiped Damian's poopy bottom and sat with him through all his yelling manic episodes. Then seeing Ann take interest in Raphael and get down to his level to play with him reminded LB of how she had done the same with him when he was a young boy. She would climb under the table with him, listen to him endlessly, and try to make him laugh when he felt sad. Ann went the extra mile to make Raphael feel welcomed every time, and that brought LB a fleeting smile.

The two opposing convictions in his heart collided. A tear crept down his face. How could he have been wrong for so long? Remorse flooded his heart. If they loved Damian enough to take care of him into his thirties, did they love him like that too? Maybe, just maybe, the reason he had always felt so distant was partly on him. It had been his choice to never call them Mom and Dad, even though they adopted him at such a young age. It had been his choice to steal, to act out. It had been his choice to distance himself from them in adulthood. Sure, they made mistakes—but hadn't he, as well?

Confusion flooded his brain. Then he drove past the church the family attended while he was growing up. That was it. That was how they could do it. They could love Damian because of God.

LB sent up a prayer for the first time in years. *God, if you're out there, show me the way. I don't know how to move forward. I've been wrong for such a long time. Show me what they are genuinely like when I see them today.*

WHEN LB ARRIVED AT THEIR HOUSE, HE HAD NEW eyes, newfound wonder, as though he were truly seeing for the first time.

"Damian, am I ever glad to see you, buddy," LB said, giving his brother a big hug before he walked into the house.

Ann watched the scene through the window from the kitchen where she was washing a baking tray. "Wow, that's the most animated I've ever seen LB with his brother. He must be in an especially good mood today," she said to Nana, who sat on a stool chatting with her.

LB opened the door and stepped into the kitchen. "Hey, Mom," he said, coming over to embrace her in a side hug as she chopped vegetables.

Ann almost dropped the knife in her hand. She glanced at her mom with a puzzled look on her face.

LB pulled away. "Would you want to come down and watch one of my softball games? Raphael's been asking to see you."

Ann didn't respond, frozen in place for a moment.

"Would you want to come, Mom?" LB asked again.

"We would love to. That would be fun," Ann said, finding her voice again and holding LB's gaze. "We could take Damian on an outing."

"Great. I'd really like that," he said.

"Can you go call Lincoln and Damian in for dinner? I think we're ready." As he left the kitchen, Ann muttered under her breath to Nana, "Did you hear him call me Mom? He said it twice."

"I heard it, honey," Nana said.

LINCOLN, ANN, LB, DAMIAN, AND NANA SAT DOWN for dinner and prayed.

"Where are Mario and Larry today?" Ann asked.

"They couldn't make it," LB said. "Hey, Dad, I was wondering what you think about the housing market right now. I'm thinking of getting another house to flip."

Lincoln paused a minute before answering, cocking his head to the side as if he were confused. Then he talked about the ins and outs of housing, a thorough and long explanation in his usual fashion. LB watched him feed Damian forkfuls of food as he talked seamlessly. Damian would take the fork, put the food into his mouth, and give the fork back to Lincoln. Ann wiped a bit of whipped cream off the edge of Damian's mouth. They worked together as a team caring for Damian, pouring their love out for him in every act of service. After dinner, Ann got up to get Damian his evening pills.

LB licked the last of the peanut butter pie off his plate and said he had to get home for his early day in the morning. He had too many emotions welling up to stay a minute longer.

"We'll see you next week," Ann told him. "Drive home safe, son."

"Bye, Mom."

Ann stood waving at him with a dumbfounded look as he drove away. The words that had taken LB almost a lifetime to say felt more natural than he expected. Why had he waited so long?

A FEW WEEKS LATER, ANN FOUND HERSELF ON THE way to LB's softball game, talking to God about her heart's desires. She marveled at the fact that LB had called her Mom at his last visit, something she had given up entirely on him ever saying. She wondered at the remarkable heart transformations that must be taking place that he still wasn't ready to talk about. She praised God for bringing her son home. It wasn't exactly like she imagined, where she threw her arms out and welcomed him in a long embrace and killed the fattened calf to celebrate with a party. It seemed to unravel slowly. Over time, his wall was crumbling, perhaps as he watched them love Damian and realized that they had always loved him too.

She couldn't be sure, but what she was sure of was that the Bible worked. She had chosen to welcome him with open arms and forgive and forget the past. And now he was inviting them into his life. Knowing that she was going to see him and Raphael brought a warmth to the deep and broken crevice in her heart, beginning to mend that dark spot. She decided to come alone to the first game so she could pay attention to Raphael as well as the game and scout out if Damian would do okay at the ballpark.

Filled with gratitude and praise, Ann poured out her heart to God as she drove.

God, I want to serve you again. Other people keep telling me Damian is my ministry, but I want more. I'm missing loving your people just for the sake of loving them. Your love in my heart is overflowing again. I have space to serve in a small capacity, but where?

"I'm not sure you're going to like what I have for you."

Try me.

"I want you to call up your friend, Wendy. She feeds her homeless friends weekly."

No way. Forget I asked.

Silence.

"Remember your dad?"

Forget I asked.

Ann arrived at the softball game and put her conversation with God out of her mind entirely. She walked over to LB and Raphael and bent down to give Raphael a big grandma hug. Then she straightened and brought LB in for a hug.

"Thank you for inviting me," Ann said. "I've been missing playing softball with my girls. Maybe I should get the league up and going again."

"My dad is good," Raphael said, smiling up at LB.

"Well, I can't wait to see. Should we go sit over here, Raphael? What do you want from the snack shack?" Ann asked.

"Hot dog!" Raphael jumped up and down.

LB smiled and walked toward the dugout with a wave.

Ann and Raphael loaded up at the snack shack and found a spot on the bleachers. They played make believe, then Raphael told Ann his best jokes and they laughed heartily.

LB came up to bat and hit a ground ball into the outfield; he rounded toward second base, sliding in to safety. A fly ball was caught by the third baseman. Then the next batter hit a home run. LB trotted easily into home, and Ann and Raphael stood cheering and clapping, whooping and hollering.

The time passed quickly, and the game was over before Ann knew it. She hugged LB and congratulated him on the win.

"I'll definitely bring Damian next time. I wanted to make sure the setup would work for him. He will love getting to see his brother play ball," Ann said.

"Yeah, I'd like that too." LB bent to give Raphael a hug, then looked into his eyes. "Did you like the game, bud?"

"You were awesome," Raphael said.

Goodbyes were exchanged, and Ann headed home, her heart filled with joy.

A WEEK LATER, ANN RECEIVED A PHONE CALL FROM her friend, Wendy.

"Hi, Ann. I know this may sound strange, but God put it on my heart to call you to ask if you want to come help me feed people at the park on Friday? I've been taking my lunch on my lunch break and sharing it with a few people at a picnic table, but more people have found out about it, so I need to bring more food."

"No, I don't think I'm available," Ann replied, looking at her calendar that was mostly blank outside of Damian's occasional doctor's visits. She couldn't believe what she was hearing. But she was too stubborn to give in easily.

"I understand. I just thought God told me to reach out to you. I could use another dish to go with mine. I had another friend helping me the last few weeks, but she is out sick this week."

"Okay, I'll see what I can do. But only this week. Don't count on me becoming a regular."

She hung up the phone and sighed to herself. "You must be laughing up there, God. You know this is the absolute last thing I want to do."

ON FRIDAY, ANN WALKED TIMIDLY ACROSS THE GRASS clutching her oversized lasagna to where Wendy sat at a picnic table talking to a woman with matted hair and torn, ragged clothes. A few others sat at the table as well.

"Ann, I want you to meet Madonna," Wendy greeted her, taking her dish from her and setting it on the table.

Ann's hands were frozen in midair, grasping for something new to clutch, a new barrier between her and this *different* kind of person.

Madonna wrapped her arms around Ann as Ann stood rigid. "Hi, Ann. It's so nice of you to be here. You have no idea what it means to know we get a hot meal once a week. If you're friends with Wendy, then you're friends with me. I didn't think there were any good people until I met Wendy. She just brought her lunch and started talking to me. And then the next week, she brought me lunch. I used to be so afraid to talk to anyone. That's how I got kicked out of my apartment. I was just too afraid to go out and find a job. My husband left me. My kids won't talk to me. But then I found my way in the jungle. That's my home now. They treat me better than society has. They help me when I need it." Madonna rattled on, not waiting for a response, spilling out her whole story.

Ann found herself listening to Madonna's heart-wrenching tale with great interest.

"And this is Ben. He's like my son. His parents just kicked him out when he was eighteen. Set his belongings on the front porch and told him to go find his own way. But he couldn't find a steady job that paid enough to rent an apartment by himself, so he ended up in the jungle with us. We took him in, under our wings, like a lost puppy. We taught him how to survive with us."

Ann could hardly believe what she was hearing. This was not at all how she pictured a homeless person. Before she could help it, her mouth opened. "It sounds like you certainly take care of one another down there. Do you ever miss anything about your old life?"

"Oh yeah, the only thing I miss is talking to my daughter. I just wish I could have a relationship with her. She doesn't want anything to do with me. She thinks I'm trash. She hates me for not wanting to make my life better. But I don't mind the rest. Sure, when it rains, it's not that great living in a tent. But I do love the outdoors. I feel closer to God in nature anyway," Madonna said.

"You know about God?" Ann's amazement grew.

"Yeah, doesn't everybody?"

"I don't think so."

"Everyone I know talks about Him. They just don't always live like they know Him."

Stunned, Ann sat down. She was hooked now. This woman was no different than her, really. Sure, her clothes were dirty, she hadn't showered in who knew how long, but just like Ann, she longed for a relationship with her child, to be known and accepted, and even helped others when she could.

Ann had it wrong all along. These two people in front of her weren't homeless because they could have worked their way out of it. Society hadn't treated them kindly, and Madonna's fear kept her there. And she wasn't even sad about it. In fact, it looked like she was thriving and giving of herself.

Ann compared Madonna's story to her own life. Could she have been homeless if she didn't have the connections she did? If they hadn't been able to afford all of Damian's medical bills, they could have easily ended up in a similar situation. She felt her heart opening and changing as she sat there with her perceptions challenged.

She had let the conversations carry on around her, and now everyone was standing up to go. Wendy had to return to work from her lunch break. Ann stood up and gave Madonna a hug. "I enjoyed meeting you, Madonna. I'll be back here next week."

"Really?" Wendy eyed Ann with a look of astonishment. "I thought you said you would only come once. What changed your mind so quickly?"

"I suppose God did. And hearing Madonna's story today . . ." Ann wrung her hands, looking for the right words. "I'm amazed to meet you. I've been so wrong my whole life. I'm making chicken pot pie next week."

"I'll tell my friends. Make enough for twenty."

As Ann got into her car, she felt the Holy Spirit laughing at her. She had tried to tell God no, but there she was, ecstatic to come next week to meet more homeless friends.

Ann chuckled to herself, thinking about her dad up in heaven, how he must be smiling down. He must have concocted some plan with God to get her into this.

The next week, Ann met more friends and she felt as though her heart had expanded tenfold. She met more people with more stories and fell in love with them. They made her laugh, they taught her about God, and they challenged her ideas. They were quickly becoming her friends. Who could have imagined?

She became an advocate for her homeless friends. She told everyone who would listen about her radically changed views—how her heart had suddenly expanded to love people she formerly thought unlovable. She invited more friends to join. Every Friday, rain or shine, the hungry homeless could count on Ann showing up with a full-fledged hot meal, including dessert.

TWO MONTHS AFTER BEGINNING HER NEWFOUND delightful work, Dawn, Damian's caregiver for Friday, called out sick. Instead of canceling or feeling discouraged, Ann decided to take Damian with her.

At the park, Damian bounded out of the car, joy exuding from his every movement. "Yeah yeah yeah yeah yeah." He smiled and twirled his body.

Brian, another homeless friend, walked up to Damian and embraced him in a strong hug. "You must be Ann's son that I heard about. I'm so glad you're here."

Damian broke free with a jump, exclaiming another string of "Yeah."

More of her new friends came up to Damian, embracing him, and talking to him as though he were perfectly normal.

Damian reveled in their attention. Ann smiled to herself as she prepared the table of food to share. She asked Brian to pray for the meal before they served it.

After a short prayer, Brian got his guitar out and started to play a worship song while everyone was served chicken enchiladas with rice and beans. Damian rushed the table to grab a bite. Ann fended him off and made him a plate, then sat on the ground with him in a circle of friends.

"Ann, why didn't you bring your son until now?" one of them asked her.

"I wanted to be able to focus on you. Plus he's very good at stealing food that's not his."

The circle of friends laughed. "You've got to bring him from now on."

"You know, I think I will. I think I'll bring my mom too."

Ann smiled, looking around the circle. Here again, she met the God who sees her. He saw her need to get outside the four walls of her home and be used in service to Him. Only He could have changed her hardened heart toward the homeless, and even her own son, whom she had once judged so harshly. God's plans were always better, always more mysteriously wonderful, than her own. God gave her a place to give of herself and her resources freely, to people who received it gladly. And the cherry on top—Damian fit in perfectly. She could do ministry and love her son at the same time. In fact, she wouldn't be there at all if not for Damian. But she had the feeling that this ministry would be the most fulfilling assignment God had given her yet.

TWENTY-ONE

ER Visit

SUMMER 2012

. . . .

*"Isn't it funny how day by day nothing changes,
but when you look back, everything is different."*

—C.S. Lewis, *Prince Caspian*

. . . .

"I NEED YOU TO MEET ME AT THE ER. SOMETHING IS wrong with Damian."

Dawn hung up with Lincoln, regretting that she had to call him not even twelve hours into their vacation to the coast. Lincoln said he would be there as quickly as he could. That man's patience amazed her. He had so much love for Damian. Since the day she started working for the family, at least two years ago now, she had felt the strongest presence of peace residing in their home.

Dawn had replaced Daphne as one of Damian's caregivers when Daphne chose to stay at home after her second child was born. That morning when she arrived at 7:00 a.m. to take over for the other caregiver, Damian looked ashy white and was crawling naked in the kitchen. When Dawn questioned her about it, she simply told her that

Damian was acting funny. Dawn had immediately jumped to action. As the thermometer showed a 103-degree fever, she had gotten him dressed and announced they had to get him to the emergency room.

She decided to bypass the local hospital and take him to UC Davis, remembering that's what Lincoln had suggested. The doctors there knew Damian, which always helped. But she hadn't expected to get so many questions. They kept asking Damian the questions, not realizing he couldn't answer for himself. She hadn't thought about it, that she wasn't family to Damian so they might not let her admit him. They kept questioning her relation to him and why she was with him. She didn't have any paperwork with her to prove she was his caregiver. It was all a lot of rubbish. But Damian needed her, so she was there. Hopefully Lincoln could get there soon to sort it out.

Damian had become her best friend, listening endlessly to her. He smiled at her when she told him her joys in life. He cupped her face in his hands and said, "Dawn," when she told him something sad. She would say, "Oh, I screwed up yesterday," and he would say, "No, Dawn." He was truly kind and caring. And he couldn't let any of her secrets out, so she told them all to him.

She told him about how desperately sad she was to be barren. She wanted nothing more in the world than to have children of her own. But after years of trying, she and her husband decided to adopt two children. They were still settling into life with a seven-year-old girl and a four-year-old boy after a few rough months. Hearing Ann's story of adopting the boys inspired her to make the final call, and being with Damian made her feel brave enough to do it. She saw how he courageously faced life, no matter what it threw at him, including random sickness—like the current situation.

Dawn sat in the waiting room, praying that Damian was getting the care he needed. They wouldn't talk to her about anything, but at least they finally admitted him.

Before she started working with Damian, she had mostly fallen asleep to the existence of God, but now she was constantly reminded of God's inner workings. She felt God's presence strongly with Damian. Damian's story was a true God story.

Only God could save a man from the clutches of death over and over. She could swear Damian was a cat with nine lives—or maybe even fifteen or twenty. God had even saved him from himself. Rather than being stuck in all that anger and frustration, God's hand gave Damian joy.

The thing about Damian's joy was that it had no filter. Every emotion he experienced was shown on his sleeve. When he was excited, he was elated, beaming in joy. When he was upset, he flailed his arms and entire body to show his frustration. He had no walls to hide behind. If he ate good food, he would drool over it because it was so good. And her favorite, when he went for a ride in the dune buggy, he had his arms over his head, fists pumping, yelling, "Yeah, yeah, yeah." She would say, "Hang on. We're going to go faster," and he would die laughing. He experienced pure, raw, beautiful joy in its truest form, completely uninhibited. And when he was beaming, she couldn't help but smile.

Dawn laughed aloud as she remembered dancing with him on the deck last month. She put music on, and they danced around together. He enjoyed life to the fullest capacity that he could. She could tell he wanted so badly to be able to carry on a conversation. She had learned to be his voice.

It had taken time, of course, like anything, for him to trust her. He used to be so violent to her, pinching her, hitting, fighting her on everything. But slowly he started to trust her, and now she couldn't imagine being anywhere else. He truly had become her best friend. She loved her adventures around the lake with him, paddle boating and cheering him on as he dared to plunge into the deep water to swim. So quickly he went from thriving to deathly sick.

The whole family had gone away to a house in Fort Bragg for a week, including LB, their son, who was now integrated into family life with them. Lincoln had snapped a photo yesterday and sent it to her of the four generations on a swing all spaced twenty-five years apart. Patty, the grandma (or Nana), was seventy-five; Ann was fifty; Nicole was twenty-five; and her sweet newborn, Olivia, was nearing one. It was the sweetest photo. Dawn desperately wished she could have let them enjoy their time on the coast. They deserved to have time away. They loved so many people so well.

Finally, Lincoln and Ann approached her, looking weary from the journey. She quickly calculated in her mind—it must have been at least a three- or four-hour drive for them. She rushed over to greet them. "I'm so glad you could make it. I'm sorry about this. He went septic so suddenly, there were no signs of it yesterday, and then suddenly when I got there this morning, I could tell something was so wrong."

"It can happen quickly, especially because he can't tell us if he does have any pain. It's happened two times before. Thank you, Dawn. You have done well to bring him here," Lincoln said, extending his arms to wrap her in an understanding hug. Ann joined the hug and sandwiched Dawn in the middle. Dawn felt bolstered by the warmness of the expression.

Tears started streaming down her face. "I was just so worried for him. I can't stop praying for him and being thankful for him. He has changed my life so much, you know. He is my hero. I don't think this is the end for him. He is such a warrior. He will fight this battle too."

"Thank you for being there for him, really Dawn," Ann said, starting to tear up herself. "We appreciate everything you do for him. I know how much you love him. You can go home and get some rest now. We can take it from here. Thank you again for letting us get away. It was short, but we still made memories. Even a quick trip to the coast is refreshing for the soul."

Dawn patted Ann's back. "I just wish it could have been longer. You've been looking forward to this for so long, an opportunity to escape and relax. You're never truly off duty, are you?"

"No, but I've learned to be thankful anyway, in all circumstances. God usually has a way of thwarting all my plans, but I know He has His reasons for it. I'm just praying Damian makes it out of this scrape all right. I know God's not done with him yet."

"I agree entirely," Dawn told her. "That guy should have been gone a long time ago, but God has a purpose for him. That's why he's still here. I believe his most important purpose is yet to come, as is true for all of us who have breath. I know in the end everything you go through is for God's glory. Damian's glory moment is going to be amazing."

Lincoln had busied himself checking in with the nurses at the station. He motioned for Ann to come over so they could go in. "Do you want to come see him with us, Dawn?"

Dawn found herself nodding her head. She wanted to check on him, before she left, now that she could. When they walked into his room, they found him sleeping peacefully. She said a quick prayer of thanks to God and left to go home.

A few days later, Ann called to tell her Damian had miraculously pulled through another sepsis. His body accepted the medications and was stable again. He would spend two weeks being monitored at the hospital and then she could come back to work. Dawn decided to use the time off to take her kids on fun outings; she would start with the aquarium, since her daughter had been excited about ocean animals the last few months. Maybe they could even sneak away to the coast themselves.

Dawn & Damian go for a drive
in the Jeep, Damian's favorite

Damian waits in the
jeep for someone to give
him a ride

Lincoln & Damian in
his stick eating phase

Dawn & Damian go for a
paddleboat ride at the lake

Damian enjoys swinging on the porch immensely

Lincoln & Damian enjoying
a peaceful moment

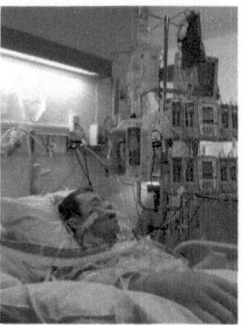

Damian at the hospital
in septic shock

Damian lights up with joy on a boat ride

TWENTY-TWO

The Epiphany

FEBRUARY 3, 2013

. . . .

"To fall in love with God is the greatest romance;
to seek him, the greatest adventure; to find
him, the greatest human achievement."

—St. Augustine of Hippo

. . . .

ON HIS THIRTIETH BIRTHDAY, LB WOKE UP ALONE. HE could not make sense of it. Why couldn't he find the right one? Not every woman out there was terrible. Why did none of his relationships work? It certainly was not for a lack of trying; he had been through too many relationships to count.

Most of his friends were married by now. They had found someone to spend their lives with. LB thought that his accomplishments could make him happy—he had bought a home and renovated it, he had worked ten years at his job, and was the foreman of his company. He felt proud of himself, but the obvious gaping hole was a substantial relationship.

At age thirty, he should have at least had a broken heart by now. Yet, as he thought about it, he had broken up with every single one of his girlfriends easily, with no tears, and moved on. And that's when the epiphany struck.

Maybe *he* was the problem. Maybe he was the one who could have done things better. Why was it so easy for him to walk away from relationships? Especially after spending a considerable amount of time with a girl. Why was he so distant? Was he capable of truly connecting with and loving another person?

It was LB's lack of bonding that his counselor tried to tell him about so many years ago. He could see it all clearly now. He never grew the ability to bond with anybody. That's why he could so easily cut people out of his life.

Early memories started flooding his brain. Memories before he met Ann and Lincoln. He had been in eight homes in less than a year. A grandma figure flashed through his mind; she had beat all the children in her home, leaving him cowering in the corner. Glimpses of men and women promising to be his mom and dad and be the most important person in his life skimmed through his mind. They promised he was safe and they would love him forever. Then something went wrong, and they were torn out of his life. It happened again and again at a time when he was so young and vulnerable. They robbed him of his ability to care about people. He saw now that he never allowed himself to get too close to anybody to protect himself from feeling that searing pain again. It served as his protective armor. But how would he ever move past it? How would he ever get married? How would he find love and genuinely feel good about it if he could not bond?

In every relationship, it was easy for LB to throw in the towel when things got tough. Would he find someone worth fighting for through the hardships, where the love is worth enduring the hard things? Now that his eyes opened to the pattern, he wondered if he was broken or if he could somehow grow the ability to bond, to love someone unendingly. He thought of Mom and Dad with Damian, caring for him for six years. How could he love someone that much?

Raphael popped into his mind. He did love Raphael, his son, and would do anything for him. That gave LB the spark of hope that he needed. If he had the ability to love his son and bond with him, perhaps he could break the barrier and learn to love others in a deeper capacity.

He made himself breakfast and then called Mom and Dad. They were the only people he wanted to spend his birthday with. He wouldn't even tell them it was his birthday.

On his drive up, he saw a blue van pulled over on the side of the road with its hazard lights blinking. LB slowed his car down and pulled off behind it, clicked his hazard lights, and approached the passenger window.

"Can I help you out? I saw your hazards," LB said, noticing the three children in the back of the young woman's car. He scrutinized the car to check for any problems. "Oh, I see you have a flat tire up here. I have tools in my car. Would you like help fixing it?"

"Thank you for stopping. I was trying to get a hold of my husband, but I haven't reached him yet. I have no idea how to fix it," the woman said as a baby began to cry in the background.

LB rolled up his sleeves and quickly got to work. He jacked the car up, removed all the lug nuts, and had the spare tire on in less than ten minutes.

"Ma'am, I wouldn't drive too far on that spare. It's considerably smaller than the rest of your tires. There's a tire shop not too far from here that I sometimes use. Take the third exit, and go down three lights onto Douglas. You can't miss it."

"Thank you, sir. I don't even know how to thank you properly. So many people drove past us," she said, offering a handshake.

"I just figure people deserved to be helped when they're in need," LB said as he shook her hand. "Must be the way I was raised. Have a good day, ma'am."

LB smiled to himself as he got back into the driver seat. It always felt good to help others. He kept his car stocked with a medical bag and jumper cables for that reason. Mom and Dad always helped people just because they loved them, not to get any credit or promote themselves. They always gave to anyone and everyone. How could he have been so blind for so long?

As LB pulled up, the neighbor kids were outside playing basketball with Damian. He quickly parked and walked over to the scene, amazed.

"Damian! Man, am I glad to see you."

"Yeah yeah yeah buddy yeah buddy yeah!" Damian's joy and excitement poured from him. He spun in circles, stood on his tiptoes, and bounced his body up and down animatedly.

"Watch what he can do," one of the kids playing with him said. He bounce-passed the ball to Damian. Damian caught the ball and started dribbling with his right hand. He dribbled the ball around LB, without even looking at the ball, like it was second nature to him. Then the ball hit Damian's foot and rolled away into the dead yellow grass.

"Damian, you can dribble a basketball? Where did that come from?" LB said enthusiastically, amazed at this new development. "Can I try?"

"Of course," the boy said, running back with the ball and passing it to LB.

LB bounced the ball to Damian, who caught the pass and began to dribble again, all around the pavement. Damian crouched down low and dribbled fast, then stood and walked casually, dribbling the ball seamlessly.

Kevin, the kids' parent, walked out the back door of the house. "Da-mi-an-o! Look at you, man—you've got it now. You could go pro. You can do new things every time we come up here." He walked over to Damian and patted him on the back. He greeted LB with a head nod. Then he gave Damian a strong manly hug. "We'll come see you again in a few days, Damian. All right, kids, time to go. See you later, LB."

LB could sense that Kevin truly loved Damian. He lit up every time he saw Damian and always talked directly to him when other people shied around Damian, unsure of what to say or how to respond. Even LB didn't always know what to say around Damian.

Parched from the bit of balling with Damian, LB walked inside the house to refresh himself. The refrigerator was stocked with his favorite root beer. Ann stood inside, busying herself in the kitchen with meal prep, ready to greet anyone who walked in her door.

LB popped open a Mug root beer and sat in one of the barstool seats, opposite where Ann cooked. LB marveled at Damian's new skills, which set Ann into "recounting Damian stories" mode.

"Yes, he's been dribbling the ball for about a week now. Kevin's kids are so great to play with him. They keep him playful and childlike. Damian's been doing all kinds of things lately. He walked down into the campground last week. We found him just sitting in someone's campsite helping himself to their food. We have to keep a GPS on his shoe now. And last week, he said a full sentence," Ann prattled on.

"He said what?" LB asked, shocked.

"He said a full sentence! The nurse was about to poke him with a needle, and he said, 'Don't tell me it won't hurt.' We all looked at each other, shocked. It just came out of him. And then he went back to saying, 'No no no no.' So I think it was just a fluke. Sometimes words just flow out of him, but then he can't repeat it." While she talked, Ann whirled around the kitchen making peanut butter brownies. The smell wafted to LB, and he was brought back to his childhood. "I know his brain must be processing more than he can communicate, but it's so sporadic when he has breakthroughs like that. It did give us a renewed spark to continue work on his speech therapy. It's easy to let that slide down on the priorities list, but we're back to doing daily exercises with him."

"Did the speech computer thing ever work out?" LB asked as he snooped around in the pantry for a snack. *Aha.* He plucked the Doritos off the shelf. *How does she remember all my favorites? Or is it coincidental?*

"Not really. He pushes the buttons, but it doesn't seem to hold any meaning for him. He hasn't shown that he is truly comprehending the concepts. It was a good try, but we may just have to accept that Damian may not be able to communicate with us in the way we would hope he would. But then again, every once in a while he does these little glimpses of hope. I think we just have to love Damian for who he is today."

LB nodded his head in agreement and then walked out with his bag of chips to the spacious deck with sweeping views of the valley. The wide deck with varied leisure furniture was his favorite part of their home. Lincoln sat facing the valley, and Damian was sprawled out on a green-and-white-striped hammock. LB walked over and nestled himself onto the hammock with Damian. Damian reached for the bag of chips, so LB shared it with him.

LB and Damian swayed on the hammock together, sharing chips and laughing while LB reminisced about old funny stories. Damian glowed with joy, elated to have his brother's full attention. LB felt he could accept that this was the new Damian. He might be trying to eat his shirt half the time, but that was okay; he still loved him. He felt he would always wish for his best friend to be back, his best friend who had a future ahead of him, but also felt grateful he was reunited with his parents as a direct result of Damian's injury.

As their laughter settled, LB wondered aloud to Lincoln, "Why do bad things happen to people who are so nice? There are a lot of jerks out there. Why couldn't it have happened to them?"

Lincoln rocked in his swinging chair and looked at LB with his piercing, compassionate blue eyes. "You know I spend a lot of time thinking about that myself." He trailed off for a minute and then continued. "The verse I've clung to all these years is Romans 8:28. It says that 'All things work together for the good of those who love God, who are called according to his purpose.' I know without a shadow of a doubt that I love God with all my heart and am doing my best to take part in what he has called me to do. I can say the same is true of Ann and of Damian. So, if I believe God to be true to His word, then no other outcome is possible. God will somehow, someway use even Damian's injury for good. God is going to make something beautiful out of it. We just have to trust Him to be God and be watchful for what it is along the way."

LB folded his arms as he stopped rocking the hammock with his foot. He squared up so he could see the contours in Lincoln's face. "You really believe that? I mean I was thinking on my way here that the only reason I'm reunited with you and Mom is because of Damian. You think God had a role to play?" LB's eyes rested on Lincoln's Timex watch, noticing how much it was like its owner—timeless, trustworthy, no frills, reliable.

It was as if LB had unlocked a door Lincoln had long been waiting to open with that question. "Yes. Yes, I do believe it. I believe God's Word to be absolute truth. And then I think about what Damian was agonizing over right before his injury—it was *you*. He genuinely wanted you to return to the family and return to God. I truly believe Damian wholeheartedly trusted his life to God, no matter what happened. Even if it led him to this wilderness place where he no longer controlled his life. If Damian was in a place of full surrender, giving his life to God to use as He would, I have to believe that God took him up on the offer to go all in and said, 'You know, this injury is the only way I'm going to shatter the darkness with hope for LB.' Which leads me to believe either God had this plan all along to pursue *you* and change the course of *your* life or He used this situation in the way that only He can to change the course of your life. Our God is pursuing you with his relentless, never-giving-up love. And along the way, anyone else who meets Damian and sees his joy amid his intense suffering will be able to see God's glory in it."

Lincoln adjusted his focus to the horizon as he spoke with deep meaning in his eyes. "Now, if Damian knew this was what was going to happen when he prayed his prayer of surrender, he may have backed out of it. I'm not sure anyone would willingly sign up to be in Damian's position. Especially when it means Mom and Dad wiping his bum all day, every day. I don't believe God caused his injury, but He has ways of redeeming all things for good. And yes, I do see good. I see changed lives for you and Mario. And countless medical professionals, caregivers, even his old friends, who get to experience God's love and joy through Damian."

"Do you think he will ever get better?"

"Some days, he will do amazing feats like you witnessed today, dribbling a basketball. Then three or four months later, he just stops doing it altogether. In the beginning, he held a fork and could feed himself. Now he can't hold the fork steady enough to pick the food up off his plate. He enjoyed strumming at the guitar for a few months, and now he won't touch it. He will say his name and several words for a few months, and then he just stops. I'm no expert on how the brain works, but for him, it seems to work in stunts, like he's trying to resurface but then gets a mental block and loses the ability or simply forgets the new skills. At this point, he has far surpassed what doctors said he would do. But they also said the bulk of the improvement will happen in the first year or so. We are well past that, so I'm not putting it out of the question, but I'm also choosing to embrace Damian for who he is and not expecting him to be more than who he can be. And I see victory in that, in Damian living life with joy—yes, not as expected, but still good and beautiful."

LB thought about how similar that was to what Ann said, about choosing to accept and love the person in front of you for who they are—the new normal. "I think I'm starting to accept that. But I think I will always miss my goofy best friend. His care is so intensive. What keeps you going day after day?"

"It is a lot. We have great help during the day with him. The thing that keeps me motivated is how would I want to be treated if I were in his shoes, if I was in the prime of my life and suddenly became helpless? Would I want to spend all my days in an institution or an endless boring routine? We want to keep his life as adventurous and abundant as possible as we care for him because that's what I hope someone would do for me. That's why we buy fun toys like the dune buggy and the Jeep."

Not wanting to give in to the emotions welling up in him, LB returned inside. After grabbing another root beer out of the fridge, he jumped onto the counter, just like he had when he was a boy. Ann stood nearby putting the finishing touches on dinner and pulling his favorite brownies out of the oven.

SEEING HER ADULT SON ON THE COUNTER, IN THE exact spot he had sat for years as a growing boy and then teen, nearly brought Ann to joyful tears. Her prodigal son was home. She turned away from him to hide her emotion.

"Happy birthday, by the way. I would have made a cake if you would have called to say you were coming. But I know you don't like making a big deal of your birthday. I hope you'll stay for dinner."

"How can I resist an offer like that," LB said with his cunning smile and twinkling, charming blue eyes.

He seemed changed, different, even open in a new way. She had welcomed him with open arms, choosing not to bring up the past, but she wondered if he wanted to. "We never talked about the past. Did you want to ask us any questions?"

"I used to have so many questions. But not anymore. Let's just leave it in the past where it belongs. No use bringing it up and causing any more trouble than it already has," LB said, drumming his feet on the cupboards below him, looking resolute.

Ann watched him for a moment, not wanting to miss the opportunity while she had it. She respected his desire, knowing she had already forgiven him completely, but wanted to clear the slate altogether. "I used to have questions too. But I don't need to know the answers. I am just so happy you're home. You know I always wanted you here. I'm sorry I didn't fight harder to bring you back. I kept seeing your actions as they affected me at the time. My blurred vision didn't allow me to imagine how hard it must have been for you, LB."

Ann watched a tear slip down LB's face before he turned away. "Thanks, Mom. I'm sorry too."

"We forgave you a long time ago." Ann took a deep breath and busied herself with dinner prep once again.

LB sat a few minutes in silence, and then, in a brisk change of tone, said, "Did I tell you I started going to church again?"

"No, that's great news. Tell me about the church."

LB chuckled before beginning. "Well, it's funny—we actually have been going to two churches. I like the preaching at the bigger church, and Raphael likes the Sunday School at the small church across the street."

"So you go to two churches? If that's not an answer to prayer, I don't know what is." Ann laughed with LB, rejoicing that her son wanted to prioritize his relationship with God.

"Yeah, Raphael really likes it, which I'm glad about. He's been acting out lately at school and home. I don't know how to get through to him."

Ann smiled to herself. "You know what they say, the apple doesn't fall too far from the tree."

LB smiled back. "Hey, I know I wasn't the easiest kid, but I think I turned out okay."

"Yes, thank God you don't stay fourteen forever. I'm proud of you, son, and you're doing a fine job of raising your own son."

LB looked embarrassed at the last comment, so Ann changed the subject. "We're thinking of remodeling the kitchen. What do you think?"

"When you do, will you keep one of these tiles for me?" LB requested. "I love my memories of talking to you on this countertop. I don't want it to go away completely."

When they remodeled, they kept one of the tiles as a centerpiece to the backsplash above the stove as a lasting reminder of those sweet countertop talks.

Family portrait Thanksgiving 2015

Mario takes Damian for a
spin in the side by side

LB & Damian sit on barstools in the
kitchen while Ann prepares dinner

LB & Damian in hammock

Damian birthday 2016 with Ann

Nana laughs with Damian

TWENTY-THREE

God's Goodness

SPRING 2015

. . . .

"If you want to get warm, you must stand near the
fire: if you want to be wet, you must get into the water.
If you want joy, power, peace, eternal life, you must
get close to, or even into, the thing that has them."

—C.S. Lewis, Mere Christianity

. . . .

DAMIAN'S DEMEANOR HAD CHANGED IMMENSELY
since first bringing him home. The anger had almost entirely
dissipated, leaving in its wake a calm and continual joy. Ann's prayer
that had seemed entirely impossible when Damian was in a constant
rage was answered abundantly more than expected. Ann rejoiced over
her son's contentment and the restored peace to their home.

With that peace, life cantered into a new normal, allowing for
their home to become the revolving door and welcoming oasis it had
once been before the tragic and fateful day of Damian's injury.

Daphne came up for a visit with her two children, who bounded
through the door, giving Damian a big hug. Damian's eyes got big,
and he nodded his head, saying, "Yeah, yeah, yeah," like a giddy

school boy. He twirled two circles and danced around Daphne, excitedly remembering her. Daphne had left to do a home-based job shortly after her baby girl's birth but had continued to visit Damian every couple of months as she could.

"Damian! We stayed away too long. Your hair is getting long. And you put a little meat on those bones. You look so healthy. I'm glad you remember me. My kids got bigger, didn't they?" Daphne spoke to Damian with focused intent.

"It's wonderful to see you, Daphne," Ann exclaimed. "Tell me all about yourself. Children, do you want to play in the living room? I've got all kinds of toys."

The boy and girl both nodded and followed behind her. She pulled out the wooden train tracks, which received a squeal of happiness.

"I can't believe how good Damian looks," Daphne exclaimed. "I miss him. I miss you. I miss being here in your home. But I have good news. I'll be starting as a kindergarten teacher in the fall."

"That is good news, Daphne. Congratulations!"

"Thank you, Ann. I really have to thank you and Damian for everything, you know. I never would have made it out of rehab if not for you taking a chance on me. You believed in me when no one else but my mom did. And this path has led me to so many opportunities. Working here with Damian, I was so inspired by your faith. My kids are getting the benefit of a transformed mama."

"You can thank God for all that. I just listened to him," Ann said. "I'm continually learning to sacrifice my plan for His plans, which are always better. And my selfish thoughts for His."

Suddenly, Ann realized they had been so focused on talking, Damian had disappeared. She heard a commotion in the kitchen.

"Ann?" a shrill woman's voice called out from the kitchen.

Ann wasn't expecting any other visitors, but she excused herself and hurried to the kitchen. She quickly assessed the situation. Her friend, Stephanie, stood behind the door, using it as a shield for her and her three teen daughters behind her. Damian stood in the kitchen holding a butcher knife in the air, waving it around.

"I see you've been greeted by an ax murderer." Ann chuckled and moved swiftly behind Damian, grabbing the arm holding the knife and gently coaxing his hand within her reach. She grabbed on to Damian's wrist and handed him his water cup with her other hand. The simple distraction allowed her to easily wrest the knife out of his unsuspecting hand.

"Whew, that was exciting," Stephanie said, walking over the threshold now and into the kitchen.

Ann laughed easily. "Yes, something you don't see every day, a wild-eyed man holding a knife. Damian's always good for a laugh and an adrenaline kick."

"We just wanted to stop by to bring you these flowers from our garden," Stephanie said. "We were thinking of you. It looks like you have other company, so we won't stay."

Ann waved her in despite her words. "Come in. You remember Daphne, our former caregiver, right? She will be glad to see you."

The afternoon passed pleasantly in the company of friends, reminding Ann of the miracle it was that Damian was calm enough to entertain all these guests at once.

THAT EVENING, ANN TURNED *JEOPARDY* ON THE TV for Damian while she shaved the stubble on his face. Lincoln sat nearby, reclining on the couch.

"I've been thinking about inviting my friends from the park up to a Bible study at our house." Ann took a break from shaving to look over at her husband in earnest.

Lincoln studied her before answering. "Really? When did you start calling them your friends?"

"From the beginning, I met Madonna, heard her story, and realized she's just like me. They all are. They all have hopes and dreams and hurts and stories about what got them into homelessness. Over the last few years, they have become my friends. I mean that. I love these people. I love how raw and real they are about their life, their struggles, and how they relate to Jesus."

"Have you thought about doing a Bible study at lunch . . . or just after? The logistics of getting homeless people to our house—a twenty-five-minute drive from town—may be tricky."

"We have started doing a little sermon or reading for them while they eat on Fridays. Many times, it's one of the homeless who wants to share. But they don't always have the best theology. I thought it might be nice to get them out of their element, invite them into our home for a meal and dig into studying the Bible. They're hungry for God's word. And it would be nice for them to get to meet you and talk to you. You're better at explaining the difficult parts of the Bible."

"I see you've been thinking hard about this," Lincoln told her. "I'm amazed to see your change of heart. Just a few years ago, you didn't want anything to do with a homeless person, and now you want to bring them into our home? God has grown your compassion. It's beautiful, Ann. Of course we can do it. I'll drive to town to pick them up myself." Lincoln walked over to Ann and wrapped his arms around her waist from behind to envelop her while she put the finishing touches on Damian's shave and haircut.

Ann then turned to embrace him, resting her head in his chest. Damian turned from his show to watch them and broke into a string of "yeah" as though to cheer them on. They circled their arms around Damian to include him into a family hug.

A FEW WEEKS LATER, THE LOGISTICS HAD FALLEN INTO place, and friends had rallied around Ann's idea to start a Bible study. Two friends offered to be part of the pickup team, and another offered to bring dessert.

Ann stood in the kitchen, idly checking on the dinner she was keeping warm until her guests' arrival. When the cars pulled in, she ran outside to greet her friends.

"So you have a massive house," came the first thing out of Brian's mouth. He held his guitar in his left hand. "Why do you hang out with us?"

"It doesn't matter how big my house is. All the better to welcome you in." Ann hadn't thought about how bringing them here might make them feel inferior. She silently prayed they would feel welcome and comfortable. "I'm glad you brought your guitar. I was hoping you would. Damian loves when you play guitar."

"Where is Damian? He's a warrior, you know. Nothing keeps that guy down. I'm just thankful when I see him. God didn't make life easy for any of us, but I don't always have a smile on my face like he does."

"He's inside in the living room in his chair. He will be excited to see you."

Ann greeted her other friends and welcomed everyone inside. The biggest attraction was their Keurig machine. All twelve of them wanted to make their own coffee, a single-serve inside a tiny plastic capsule. The smallest pleasures delighted them—ones that Ann took for granted daily. She cherished the reminder to be thankful for the tiniest comforts within her home.

Around the dinner table, comments about the excellence of the prime rib were murmured after Lincoln's prayer.

Ann kickstarted a conversation. "You know, Robert, you ruined me."

"How's that," Robert muttered between bites, hastily shoveling potatoes into his mouth as though the mounding heap might disappear if he didn't eat fast enough.

"Your shopping cart theory. I can't stop thinking about it every time I go to the store now."

Robert looked up, chewing a large bite of food with his fork held in the air, ready to shovel in the next. "You mean my duty to God."

"Yes, tell Lincoln about it. I just had to return my cart in the pouring rain the other day so I didn't feel guilty."

Swallowing his bite and setting down his fork, Robert began. "It's like this, you see. If I use someone else's stuff, I always got to put it back. If I use a grocery cart, I put it back in the stall. I get so mad at the other people who steal the grocery carts to carry their stuff. If I see someone with one, I tell them they gotta take it back. It's not their property."

"I like my grocery cart, and nothing you say can change my mind," one of the ladies piped up defensively.

"And that's why we have a bad rap. It's the little things that matter to God. It might not matter to you, but it matters to the worker who has to collect the carts. If you don't take care of other people's stuff, it's showing them you don't appreciate them. Everyone deserves some appreciation. At least that's what God told me my duty is," Robert said his words with final authority and got back to eating his dinner.

At that moment, Damian reached over and grabbed a potato off Robert's plate, sitting just within reach. Robert's first instinct was to grab his knife and point it at Damian, prepared to fight for the potato.

"It's okay, Robert. Damian thinks everyone's food is his. Put your knife down. There are so many potatoes we'll never eat them all. Here, have some more." Ann shoveled a spoonful onto his plate and moved Damian's chair closer to her own. "Damian, no stealing food."

Laughter rose up from the table in quite a roar.

"Ann, can I take Damian into the living room?" Brian asked. "I want to play guitar with him."

"Of course." Ann fed Damian his last bite of food and let Brian wheel him into the living room.

Brian handed Damian a guitar, then took his own guitar and started strumming a few chords. He watched as Damian fidgeted with his fingers clumsily on the guitar strings. Damian looked at Brian strumming his guitar. Then he started to pick at the guitar strings one by one.

"Wow, Damian," Ann exclaimed, coming into the room. "That sounds melodious. Brian, do you realize what he's doing? Before you got here, he was just banging his hand on the guitar. This is incredible."

Damian sat with the guitar, plucking string by string in a slow, methodical way. Ann was reminded of so many happy memories of Damian sitting there in the living room playing her favorite songs for her and tinkering away.

Damian continued on as everyone gathered in the living room. Brian led the group in rousing worship. He had a way of getting a crowd to jump and clap, even if they were not jumping and clapping types of people.

Brian played a lively rendition of "The Blood of Jesus," shaking his long hair, tapping his toes, and strumming an upbeat tune. Damian imitated Brian's head bobbing and toe tapping as he picked at the guitar strings. Not a single person in the room could resist the urge to clap along.

When the songs ended for the Bible study to begin, Damian didn't stop playing. Ann wheeled him into Nana's quarters to watch a show with her while they had their discussion.

Lincoln opened the discussion by asking whether anyone had questions about God or the Bible they were hoping to get answered.

"I just don't understand why you would go to all this effort to bring us to your house," one person piped up.

"To show you that God loves you. Unfathomably more than you can imagine. And we love you. And we're not going anywhere. We're here to walk alongside you in life and help you where we can and point you to your creator who loves you," Lincoln said. He then passed out a sheet of paper on which he had printed the first chapter of John.

"I think this is a good place to start. Have any of you ever read the book of John?" Lincoln asked.

A few nods of yes, but mostly noes echoed throughout the room.

"Great, then let's dive in."

After the study, Ann brought Damian back out, and Nana came with them.

"He sat like that with the guitar in his hands the entire time. He just kept playing the whole time he was in my room," Nana remarked.

"Wow, something is clicking for him today. Brian needs to come around more often," Ann said, a smile pasted to her face. "I wouldn't believe it if I didn't see it myself."

Brian gave Damian a hug before leaving and thanked Ann for the dinner.

"Thank you for bringing Damian to life with the guitar," Ann told him. "It filled my soul up."

THE FOLLOWING MORNING, ANN SETTLED INTO HER chair in the breakfast nook, a light fare of last night's leftovers on her plate. Dawn, one of Damian's caregivers, walked in the door with a smile on her face.

"Good morning, Ann." Dawn poured herself a cup of coffee.

"Damian's sleeping in this morning," Ann said. "He was pacing last night after our Bible study. He played the guitar for hours. Can you believe it? He finally tucked himself into bed sometime early this morning. He pooped in the middle of the night too."

Dawn chuckled to herself. "I've heard you say before, 'True love doesn't count how many times you wipe poop off someone's behind.' But I'm happy to hear he already pooped on your watch."

"That's right," Ann said, laughing alongside her. "You can either laugh or cry about it all, so we choose to laugh when we can."

"I remember when I first came to the job. I thought for sure I couldn't do it."

"What part was the most overwhelming to you?" Ann asked, finishing the last bite of her breakfast and then sitting back to relish her warm coffee in the aqua mug with a turtle on it.

"The diarrhea. I just didn't think I could do it. Nothing to do with him. It was just the rancid smell, the constant cleaning, the giant mess of it all. I had to pray about it, to be honest. I kept working through it and then, slowly, it became no big deal."

"That's funny. I used to be overwhelmed by the same thing. Like how can one man poop ten times a day? When we brought him home the first time, I couldn't handle it. But then God turned it around on me. He actually saved me with Damian's diarrhea. My perspective on it has changed ever since," Ann said. "Before his injury, I had no idea his Crohn's was so painful and out of control. I used to judge him for not being able to keep a job. You know, I was so frustrated with him because I thought he was being lazy. Then I experienced firsthand how intense his diarrhea is. I had to repent for my former judgments and allow God to grow compassion and love in my heart."

"You know, you should write a book about your experience," Dawn told her.

"People keep telling me that, but I'm not a writer. But if I ever did get someone to help me, I would call it, *God Gave Me Diarrhea.*"

Dawn laughed heartily. "That's quite a title."

"It's totally unexpected, but that's when God showed me that He sees me, that my circumstances are important to Him. I was at my breaking point, I had lost all hope, and that's right where He met me. I didn't want Damian to get sick, and I'm sure God didn't either, but He was able to use diarrhea to get us all the help we needed. God gave me diarrhea to deal with, and in the process, he took my callous heart and transformed it."

Ann continued, "You know, I learned something else too. There's not actually a verse in the Bible that says, 'God won't give you more than you can handle.' People say that all the time, but I don't believe it anymore. I learned from experience and have seen it over and over again that God *does* give you more than you can handle. He brings you to that breaking point on purpose, so that you have to look up, and He is the only one who can step in for you."

"That's beautiful," Dawn said.

"God wants to draw us into a place of fully trusting Him and needing Him. It's not easy to live a life in full submission to Him. But that's what He desires. So sometimes, if we get to the end of ourselves, it's not such a bad thing."

"You've had to sacrifice a lot for Damian. Is it still hard for you?" Dawn asked.

"I can tell you I never thought I'd be doing this. I never thought I had the patience to be a caregiver. Heck, like I was saying, I didn't even really like Damian at the time he got his injury, so I had to swallow my pride and let God open my eyes to love him. God has changed me in the course of this process—this refining circumstance has led me to a place of compassion for people I thought should help themselves. And I've learned to accept help in the process too."

"There have been so many times I've wanted to give up. One time, I thought, maybe if I tell God, 'I want to do it,' maybe He will not make me do it anymore. And I don't know what happened. There was a turning point where I said, 'This is what I'm going to do. I'm going to accept it, I'm going to live with it, and even enjoy it.'"

Ann paused for a moment to reflect.

"There are times I wish we could take vacations that just aren't possible with Damian. We decided we can't go more than a half day's travel away anymore because his health is so unpredictable. I do miss being able to use all my glass and crystal Christmas decorations. Of course, this isn't how I imagined my life at this age. But it isn't how Damian imagined his life either. I'm sure he gets tired of having his bottom wiped all day by his mother. I'm sure he would much rather be able to communicate his needs with us, have a normal life, even have a girlfriend. Yes, God has a way of wrecking our plans, but I believe without a shadow of a doubt that He has a reason for it."

"Your Christmas decorations you do have amaze me," Dawn told her. "I remember, to prevent Damian from picking them all up and eating them, you glued down your entire village set!"

"Yes, I had to find a way to keep my village out." Ann nodded. "Christmas is my happy place, so I was determined to find a way to Damian-proof my favorite decorations. But as we give up more of our favorite things, it's caused Lincoln and I to start asking different questions, to reframe our perspectives. What does God want *for* us in this situation? What does God want *from* us? How do I love Damian well and lead an abundant life at the same time? Instead of, how does this affect me; how would I hope to be cared for?"

"He truly is surrounded in love in this home," Dawn affirmed. "It's beautiful the way you love him. I know what you all hoped and prayed for is for him to have a full recovery. Even though that's not likely at this point, I think it's beautiful how his personality shines through. I love so many things about him. I love how funny he is; he does goofy things to make you laugh. I love his beautiful smile and his kind heart. He is so gentle. When I'm talking to him, he will touch my face. And he's so good with my kids. We have hilarious moments with him. My daughter always laughs about the day Damian ate an entire pizza when we were at the park and then stole a piece of hers out of her hand."

"That's Damian all right." Ann chuckled. "He's a bottomless pit. And still super skinny. He thinks all food is his food."

"But do you know what I've loved about having my children around Damian?" Dawn went on. "I love that they love him so much. They have learned to understand that people with disabilities are beautiful creations of God, and not to be afraid of that person. My daughter told me the other day she ate lunch with the person who was sitting alone. We talk about how you love and embrace all people, regardless of their ability or status. I've seen my kids be compassionate and kind because of Damian. And I know I've become more patient because of Damian. And most importantly, Damian has taught me to accept everything in life. If I think I'm having a crappy day, then I look at Damian, and I think, *Dawn, your day was easy.* He fights through every single day and still laughs and still is pushing harder and pushing forward."

"I can relate to that," Ann said.

A loud thump interrupted them. "There he is, the man of the hour. Damian the Brave is awake. I'll go get him," Dawn said. She set down her half-full coffee cup and scurried off down the hallway toward Damian's room.

Ann could hear Dawn chatting in an upbeat voice to Damian as she got him up and started his morning routine. Within ten minutes, she had Damian dressed for the day, ready to take his morning pills and eat breakfast.

Dawn returned to the kitchen with Damian following her, spinning down the hallway. He chattered away with a smile on his face.

"Good morning, Damian," Ann said.

"Yeah yeah yeah yeah yeah," Damian chanted. Joy burst through his expression. Ann was reminded of so many angry mornings or times Damian only said, "No." She silently thanked God for the beauty of his joy clearly displayed on his face.

Sausage sizzled on the stove as Dawn cracked three eggs into another pan to make Damian's hearty breakfast. She skillfully swatted Damian's hand away as he tried to reach for the hot pan. "No, Damian, hot. I don't want you to burn yourself."

"She don't know," Damian said, as though it was one word, but clear enough for the two of them to understand.

Ann and Dawn both looked at Damian and started laughing. "Did you just say 'She don't know?'" Ann asked through her giggles. "You never know what's going to come out of his mouth."

Damian just twirled around and didn't offer any more.

"How do you know what I don't know?" Dawn asked, also giggling. Then she addressed Ann again as she sat Damian down to eat his breakfast. "You know, I've been inspired by you to start listening to God's voice in my life. I started volunteering at a soup kitchen to feed the homeless with my kids because of you. I love how you show up every single week for the homeless at the park, rain or shine. How did you get to a place you wanted to invite them into your home?"

"God had to majorly change my heart on that one too," Ann answered. "But you should have seen them all here last night. They were eager to learn about the word, and we had a rousing worship time. It really brought Damian to life; they all are so kind to him. It makes me feel good too knowing that I'm following in my dad's footsteps. He never talked to us about it, but we learned at his funeral that he was secretly helping all kinds of homeless people."

Ann paused, then continued, "A lot of people think they know what they would like to do for God, but most of us don't have a clue what He wants us to do for Him. We have to pray about it and then wait for God's urgency on our hearts before jumping in. I know I jumped into youth ministry again and again because that's what I knew. But God had a greater plan."

Before Dawn could reply, Ann heard the phone ringing. She crossed the kitchen to answer it.

"Hi, Mom, it's LB."

"Hi, LB, what's up?"

"I'm getting baptized on Sunday," LB said.

Ann grabbed on to the nearest chair to steady herself. Her other hand came to her chest, and she felt tears forming. Could it be true? "Like this Sunday? In four days, Sunday?"

"Yes, this coming Sunday."

"You know we'll be there. We couldn't miss it," Ann said.

Unable to believe her ears, Ann hung up the phone. "Speaking of God's handiwork, you'll never guess what that was about."

"Who was it?" Dawn asked. She was following Damian, who was walking in circles around the lower story of the house.

"LB is getting baptized. This weekend." Ann had to focus to get the words out, it seemed so unlikely.

"The son you've been praying for? I know he's come back to the family, but now he wants to follow God?"

"Yes, he told me a while back that he started going to church, actually to two churches because LB likes one and Raphael likes the smaller church across the street. He said the churches are combining to do a big baptism day. God has answered my prayers far and above my expectations."

"That's incredible," Dawn said, tears forming in the corners of her eyes.

"When he was an obnoxious fourteen-year-old boy, it was hard to see past his actions that made me so angry every day. But thank God they don't stay fourteen forever. They do grow up. And then you have no control over whether they speak to you or not. All I know is that we prayed for ten long years that we would have another opportunity to talk to him, just to know how he's doing." Ann's own tears multiplied. "I never imagined having a relationship with him. Or him ever choosing to call me Mom—that itself is a little miracle. The fact we get to have him back as a son is God's work in his heart and our hearts. And his baptism is further proof of God breaking down every barrier for him."

"God is good," Dawn said as she cleared Damian's breakfast and finished the last of the dishes. "I think I'll take Damian for a ride in the Jeep. Damian, do you want to go for a ride?"

Damian's demeanor lit up at those words. He bounced up and down and said, "Yeah yeah yeah yeah yeah." He opened the back door and ran out to the white Jeep they had recently purchased for a fun way to transport Damian. He opened the door and climbed into the passenger seat, waiting for Dawn.

"See you later, Ann. Enjoy the rest of your morning," Dawn called out on her way out the door. "I think I might pick my kids up and take them all down to Six Flags for a fun afternoon of people watching. That annual pass has been the best thing for all of us. Damian absolutely loves going down there."

ON SUNDAY, WHEN THEY GOT TO THE COMMUNITY pool where the baptism would take place, people were milling around everywhere. It was a family fun day. There were giant inflatables set up in an obstacle course at the deep end of the pool. There were three kid pools and the giant main pool; it was a huge rec center.

While Ann stood taking in the scene, a woman approached her. "Are you LB's family?"

"Yes, we are."

"I just love having Raphael in my Sunday School class. He asks such good questions, and he always remembers his Bible verses. I'm so proud of him. I know his home life isn't the easiest, but LB is doing a great job," she said.

"That blesses my heart for you to say that. Thank you," Ann replied.

When it was time for the baptism, the pastor called everyone down to the shallow end of the pool. Fifteen people across the age spectrum had signed up to be baptized, from elderly to age seven.

LB stepped up to get baptized.

"Allow the family to come forward," the associate pastor said, who had taken on a mentoring role with LB.

Ann wheeled Damian to the front so he could witness the answers to his prayers for himself. Lincoln stood beside her. The rest of their children and grandchildren also crowded around to support LB.

"Do you believe Jesus Christ died for your sins?" the pastor asked.

"Yes."

"Do you want to live solely for him?"

"Yes."

The pastor grabbed LB's nose and dunked him under water, saying, "You have died to your old self and raised to life with Christ."

Tears streamed down Ann's face. To imagine that, years before, Damian had yearned for this day. She remembered Damian sitting at the table talking about how badly he wanted his brothers to know Jesus. She knew the angels were dancing in heaven as Damian got the honor of witnessing the fruits of his prayer. A tiny seed prayer that seemed so hopeless was now answered in his watch. His brother, LB, stood in front of hundreds of people proclaiming his belief in Christ and desiring to live for Him, reunited with his entire family.

Ann believed in her heart if Damian knew that this much good would come from his injury, he would praise God for it all. And she praised God too, for all the known and unknown ways He had been working all along. Her God, who restored both her sons back from death to life, who blossomed her heart to new capacities of love, who sees her and redeems all things, even diarrhea.

Epilogue

LB's Wedding

MAY 21, 2022

LAUGHTER AND JOY FILLED THE WARM SPRING afternoon as children raced over the luscious green lawn. Anticipation grew as guests gathered, waiting for the signal to walk down the whimsical wooded path to the ceremony.

At last, it was time. The groom stood tall and confident, ready to marry the one his soul loved. A tear streaked his face as he watched his bride walk toward him on this long-awaited day.

The backdrop behind the couple was the breathtaking valley view, stretching to the horizon. Lincoln stood as the officiant and said, "LB, I am honored to be here today to witness this joyous occasion. Watching you as your father, I did not know if this day would ever come. My heart is filled to the brim with joy to see what was once young and self-serving love has matured to wholehearted, self-sacrificing love. You found each other as young adults and then rekindled that love when the time was ripe. I cannot imagine a better match for you than Katie. Your hearts have expanded to be able to love one another through thick and thin, unconditionally. I praise God for making this day possible."

LB pulled Katie in for a passionate kiss, and the hillside crowd cheered loudly.

Stringed lights illuminated the tables and dance floor built on top of the grassy lawn in front of Ann and Lincoln's house. The "Y.M.C.A." came on, and everyone flooded the dance floor. As he made a 'Y' with his arms, LB smiled to the left and right, surrounded by his eight biological siblings. Everyone gathered around Damian in his wheelchair and made him the focal point.

Nine siblings in all posed for a "bio sibling" photo. They had found each other almost ten years ago. Before that, LB only knew he had three brothers from his parents, Larry and Connie: Mario, Milo, and Damian. When Monica found him, the tribe continued to grow. The twins had been adopted by a family in Utah. Sarah and Anjelica lived nearby. And they had one more brother in the foster system who they hoped to contact.

Mario, the oldest brother, stood behind Damian. Out of love for his brother, Mario chose to make caring for Damian his full-time job in November of 2019. Damian continues to live with Mario to this day. He has come through countless near-death experiences, pulling through every time. Mario tenderly cares for Damian, seeing that all his needs are met. God continues to write their story together.

The joy on Damian's face exploded into laughter as his two beautiful sisters, Sarah and Annie, danced beside him. "Ice, Ice Baby" began to play, and Damian's head started to nod. He swayed back and forth, and his face showed he recognized the song. Surrounded by family and good music, life was as good as it got for Damian.

All of them grew up in different homes, but were united by blood. Their love for Damian and one another was obvious. They gathered together for vacations and barbeques as often as possible now that they knew they had each other.

Ann smiled at them, amazed at the beauty God created from two addicts. Ten kids from one family placed in the foster system found each other and reunited as adults. Redemption and hope shined into the darkness. Beauty emerged from ashes. Oh, what a day.

Encouraging Verses
for Caregivers

The following are Bible verses that Ann and Lincoln found encouraging in their journey with Damian. The first three verses spoke loudly to Lincoln about how to proceed after Damian's injury. Deep in his soul, he knew these were absolutes! There was no room for doubt in his mind. Some of the listed verses are also those that encouraged his mother, MJ, in her final days on earth battling cancer. All verses listed are the New Living Translation, unless otherwise noted.

John 14:15–18: "If you love me, obey my commandments. And I will ask the Father, and he will give you another Advocate, who will never leave you. He is the Holy Spirit, who leads into all truth. The world cannot receive him, because it isn't looking for him and doesn't recognize him. But you know him, because he lives with you now and later will be in you. No, I will not abandon you as orphans—I will come to you."

Romans 8:26–28 (NIV): "The Spirit helps us in our weakness. We do not know what we ought to pray for, but the Spirit himself intercedes for us through wordless groans. And he who searches our hearts knows the mind of the Spirit, because the Spirit intercedes for God's people in accordance with the will of God. And we know that in all things God works for the good of those who love him, who have been called according to his purpose."

Deuteronomy 31:6: "So be strong and courageous! Do not be afraid and do not panic before them. For the LORD your God will personally go ahead of you. He will neither fail you nor abandon you."

I Corinthians 2:9: "No eye has seen, no ear has heard, and no mind has imagined what God has prepared for those who love him."

Romans 15:13: "I pray that God, the source of hope, will fill you completely with joy and peace because you trust in him. Then you will overflow with confident hope through the power of the Holy Spirit."

Psalm 68:19: "Praise the Lord; praise God our savior! For each day he carries us in his arms."

Psalm 63:6–7 (NIV): "On my bed I remember you; I think of you through the watches of the night, because you are my help; I sing in the shadow of your wings."

Psalm 48:14: "For that is what God is like. He is our God forever and ever, and he will guide us until we die."

Romans 12:16: "Live in harmony with each other. Don't be too proud to enjoy the company of ordinary people. And don't think you know it all!"

Psalm 54:4: "But God is my helper. The Lord keeps me alive!"

Job 23:10: "But he knows where I am going. And when he tests me, I will come out as pure as gold."

Psalm 145:14: "The LORD helps the fallen and lifts those bent beneath their loads."

Psalm 31:15a (NIV): "My times are in Your hands."

Isaiah 43:1b–2: "Do not be afraid, for I have ransomed you. I have called you by name; you are mine. When you go through deep waters, I will be with you. When you go through rivers of difficulty, you will not drown. When you walk through the fire of oppression, you will not be burned up; the flames will not consume you."

Isaiah 61:1–3: "The Spirit of the Sovereign Lord is upon me, for the Lord has anointed me to bring good news to the poor. He has sent me to comfort the brokenhearted and to proclaim that captives will be released and prisoners will be freed. He has sent me to tell those who mourn that the time of the Lord's favor has come, and with it, the day of God's anger against their enemies. To all who mourn in Israel, he will give a crown of beauty for ashes, a joyous blessing instead of mourning, festive praise instead of despair. In their righteousness, they will be like great oaks that the Lord has planted for his own glory."

A Poem by Rachel

Adversity is to be expected.
All of nature struggles before their beautiful existence,
A seed awakening and finding its path through the soil.
A butterfly's effort to break out of its cocoon strengthens its wings to fly.
A spider's fate is to wait and wait and wait.
A chick struggles to peck out of its shell, and many give up on the struggle.
But the ones who don't give up become mass life givers and producers.

Nature is our greatest instructor.
Beauty springs forth in the midst of adversity,
The vibrant orange of the poppy,
And deep purple of the lupin emerge from the rocks,
On the path, in the midst of the hard places.

And yet this beauty can easily be trampled.
Or stolen by bitter frost.
Withers in the sun's heat.
And forgotten after its beauty wanes in just a few short weeks.
Moments of clarity and beauty are fleeting.
But we must cling to them, remember them, memorialize them
Before they dissipate like the morning fog.

Acknowledgments

Life is best lived by focusing on your goals and dancing through all other distractions.

The writing and publishing of a book is infinitely more involved than one expects. Writing the book itself seemed like a mountain I would never get to the top of. And then when all my ideas were incorporated on the pages of a document, the editing process began. This was where I truly felt the mountain was insurmountable. I had already given all my energy to writing it, and now more was required of me. But getting to the end, I believe all the sacrifices and time spent alone holed up in a room when that was the last place I wanted to be—all of it was worth it.

I have spent countless hours away from my precious children to do what I believed was my calling. Thank you to my husband and both sets of grandparents for pouring into my children while I typed words upon a page. Thank you, my dear, sweet family, for eating noodles for a last-minute dinner and enduring a messy house while I stayed in the flow of writing.

Thank you to my mother and Keith for providing me with a weekend away when I felt like giving up on the project altogether. Thank you to the staff at Meritage Resort and Spa for treating me like royalty and taking care of my every need. From bringing a microwave to my room, to providing me with a delightful and whimsical coffee cup and saying yes to every request. Your kindness and genuine smiles encouraged me to keep being brave and to stay focused on my goals.

Most importantly, I must acknowledge Yogi tea, which truly without this book would not exist. Yogi tea was my most constant and faithful companion in the wee hours of the morning, in the late hours of the night, on the gorgeous afternoons that I wanted to frolic instead of work. Your inspiring messages were always timely, always applicable, and often life-changing. The reason this book made it to completion was this inscription: "Life is best lived by focusing on your goals and dancing through all other distractions." Because of that very tea bag, which I taped to my computer, I put the book as my all-important sole-focus goal and chose to dance through the distractions that begged me to take notice. Thank you, Yogi tea.

I also must acknowledge the very reason and essence of this book. Ann, thank you for wanting to share your story with the world. Thank you for choosing and entrusting me to tell it. Thank you for sitting with me on countless afternoons, retelling me all your stories, sharing your life with me, and choosing to be vulnerable about your times of struggle. Thank you for choosing love and a beautiful way of life. Your story inspires me.

My in-laws are very unique people, truly filled with the love of God and desire to serve him. When I was talking to Kate about them she said something that I had to share. If you meet them, they are not extraordinary in any sense of the word. They are very much like the disciples, in that they are the most ordinary kind of people, but because they walk the walk and talk the talk, that's what makes them extraordinary. Thank you Ann and Lincoln for walking out faith in a way that has impacted more countless lives than you will ever know simply because you are filled with God's love and share it with others.

Thank you also to LB, Laura, Mario, Dawn, and Donna. Thank you for sharing the wonderful workings of God in your lives and Damian's. Thank you for allowing me to ask you hard questions and choosing to answer them frankly. Thank you for teaching me and opening my eyes. And thank you, Damian, for blessing us all with your beautiful smiles, your exuding joy, and your warrior-like way of beating death and clinging to life.

I must also thank my incredible editing team. I almost gave up on ever finding the right editor after my first attempt. But when Qatarina Wanders and her highly qualified team at Wandering Words Media came into my life, I knew I had found the right path. While I cannot say it was easy, Lynn and Christina encouraged me and pushed me to dive deeper and develop my book to be the best it could be. Christina truly "got" my book and helped me find my moment of clarity where everything aligned. I cannot express enough gratitude for that.

Thank you to my fabulous sister, who I call my editor-in-chief. She championed the book alongside me, did the very first read-through of my roughest draft and kindly pointed me toward improvements. She read the book numerous times in various stages, answered all my panicked phone calls, and helped me make decisions every step of the way. I cannot thank you enough for being my dearest friend, my ultimate editor, and the person who knows me the best.

I would be remiss to not thank my team at SelfPublishing. com. Truly, the book would not exist if not for the conference call I happened upon with Aaron Schafer, who said, "A writer has to write," and I was undone in tears. I was also eight months pregnant with my third child and said, "God, you can't possibly be serious." However, it was absolutely God's divine timing, and with a helpful call from Aaron, I got plugged in and started the serious work of becoming an author. Allison was another key player with her "three words a day" theory that got me in front of my manuscript as often as possible. And thank you to Barbara, who gave me new vision on my first call and has never given up on me throughout this process.

Lastly, thank you, my love, Jacob, who never gave up on me, encouraged me in the darkest parts of the night, and believes in my every dream. You are my soulmate and my castle, the love of my life. Thank you for being my cheerleader who wouldn't let me give up.

References

Brown, Brené. *The Gifts of Imperfection*. New York: Random House, 2020.

Chan, Francis. *Crazy love: Overwhelmed by a relentless god*. Colorado Springs, , CO: David C Cook, 2008.

The Chosen: Season 1 , Episode 8. "I Am He." Angel Studios, 2017. Dallas Jenkins https://www.thechosen.tv/en-us.

Ivery, Donna Fado. *Sleep, pray, heal: A path to wholeness and well-being*. Sacramento, CA: Adventures in Healing, 2019.

Lewis, C. S. *Mere Christianity*. United Kingdom: Geoffrey Bles, 1952.

Lewis, C. S. *Prince Caspian: The return to Narnia*. New York: Collier Books, 1977.

Lucado, Max. *Great Day Every Day: Navigating life's challenges with promise and purpose*. Nashville, Tenn: Thomas Nelson, 2012.

Tolkien, J. R. R. *The Fellowship of the Ring*. United Kingdom: Allen & Unwin, 1954.

Weijer C. (2005). A death in the family: reflections on the Terri Schiavo case. CMAJ : Canadian   Medical Association journal = journal de l'Association medicale canadienne, 172(9), 1197–1198. https://doi.org/10.1503/cmaj.050348 (Accessed 2024 Jan 18).

Thank for choosing to purchase and read this book! I hope reading this book brought you joy and a new found gratitude for your own everyday life. If you did enjoy this book and found benefit in reading it, would you consider sharing it in your world by posting to social media or talking about your favorite part with a friend? And to help others discover this story, would you go one step further and post an honest review on Amazon or wherever you bought your copy? Your voice matters!

Artwork by Olivia Bradley

About the Author

Rachel Young adores her role as wife to Jacob and chaos manager of four littles six and under. A lover of life and fun, she attempts to make every moment meaningful with the people in her circle. This is her first book, a project of love she completed with her in-laws, who have shown her generous and abundant agape in action. Rachel enjoys a good laugh, dark chocolate, reading on a hammock, and baking  delectable treats to be enjoyed for tea time at her cabin in the woods of Northern California. Her motto is everyone has a story worth telling. Reach out to her with yours.

Rachel has a bachelor's degree in journalism from Azusa Pacific University and worked as a daily reporter in Pasadena for several years before joining her husband in their venture to continue the family business at a campground in Northern California. Her writing journey began in the fourth grade when her teacher read her adjective-infused story aloud to the superintendent. And a writer has to write.